Personnel Selection
and Placement

Behavioral Science in Industry Series

Edited by Victor H. Vroom
Yale University

☐ = *II*

Personnel Selection and Placement

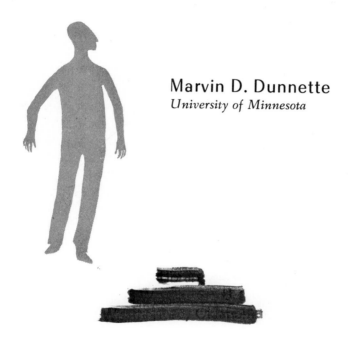

Marvin D. Dunnette
University of Minnesota

Brooks/Cole Publishing Company
Belmont, California

Tavistock Publications, Ltd.
London

Dedicated to the memory of a master teacher

Donald G. Paterson

who instilled his rich appreciation
for human individuality in everyone
who knew him

L.C. Cat. Card No.: 66–24535

Printed in the United States of America

Published simultaneously in Great Britain by Tavistock Publications, Ltd., London

9 10   74

foreword

The heterogeneity of behavioral science in industry makes it impossible for a single author to do justice to the subject's many facets in a single text. Although full-length volumes on particular topics are available for the specialist, these books are often beyond the level of the advanced undergraduate or beginning graduate student, and they typically go into more detail than is justified in a general course. To meet the changing educational needs generated by this complex subject matter, the Behavioral Science in Industry series was conceived.

The concept is simple. Leading authorities have written short books, at a fairly basic level, to present the essentials of particular fields of inquiry. These books are designed to be used in combination, as a basic text for courses in industrial psychology or behavioral science in industry, or singly, as supplementary texts or collateral reading in more specialized courses.

To implement this concept, the editor outlined the general scope of the series, specified a list of titles, and sketched the content of each volume. Leading social scientists nominated authors for each of the proposed books, and, in following up these leads, the editor was extremely fortunate in enlisting the enthusiastic cooperation of the kinds of men who are not only specialists in their subjects, but who can communicate their ideas in highly readable fashion.

The need for such a series is apparent from the marked changes that have occurred in the last two or three decades in the application of the scientific method to the study of human behavior at work. Perhaps the most significant of these changes is the extension of the range of problems subjected to systematic research. The continuing concern of industrial psychology with methods of assessing individual differences for the selection and placement of personnel has been supplemented by intensive research on such diverse topics as leadership and supervision, the design of man-machine systems, consumer preferences, management development, career patterns, and union-management relations.

This expanding focus of industrial psychology has been accompanied by changes in the objectives and strategies of research. Research has become less concerned with techniques for solving particular problems and more concerned with shedding light on the processes that underlie various behavioral phenomena, on the assumption that improvements in technology will be facilitated by a better understanding of these processes. To implement these new objectives, the psychometric and correlational methods of research in personnel selection and placement were adapted to new problems and supplemented by experiments in laboratory and field settings. As a result, the study of behavior in industrial organizations has been undertaken by researchers who have not previously been identified with industrial psychology. Experimental psychologists investigated problems of human factors in equipment design; social psychologists worked on problems of leadership, communication, and social influence; and clinical psychologists applied their diagnostic and therapeutic skills in industrial settings.

The net effect has been a blurring of the boundary lines among these subdisciplines and a growing recognition of the interdependence of "basic" and "applied" research. These changes have also obscured lines of demarcation among disciplines and professions. Psychologists, sociologists, cultural anthropologists, political scientists, and economists, and specialists in such functional managerial fields as production, labor relations, marketing, and accounting have discovered that much of their work is interrelated and that their interests are often mutual. The resultant cross-fertilization has given an interdisciplinary character to much of the new research and has afforded some currency to the interdisciplinary label *behavioral science*.

This series has been planned to reflect these changes in subject matter and research methods and to provide the reader with a valuable summary of the current status of behavioral science in industry.

Victor H. Vroom

preface

This book is about how people differ from each other and how these differences may be measured and taken into account in personnel selection and job placement. My major theme is that wise decisions about people demand knowledge of their individuality and knowledge of how each person's special talents may be most accurately recognized and most wisely utilized. Learning about people systematically and scientifically is the only avenue toward the effective conservation of human talent. Personnel selection and job placement are not ends in themselves; they are followed by possibilities for job redesign, individual counseling and career guidance, the removal or modification of organizational constraints, and the possible use of specialized training procedures. But individual diagnosis must always be the crucial first step, undergirding and directing all subsequent personnel decisions. In this book, we present systematic procedures for gathering evidence about people, jobs, job behaviors, and for studying their interrelations. We believe that these methods are the best means for assuring that the *right* people move into the *right* jobs at the *right* times and under the *right* circumstances. Society's primary goal should be to conserve human talent; the path to this goal is best mapped by making informed and wise personnel decisions at each juncture.

My own best and wisest personnel decision was made when I asked my wife, Jean, to marry me. She is my inspiration for the good times and my salve for the bad. In this sense, the book is as much hers as mine, and I thank her deeply for just being her and for being with me.

Marvin D. Dunnette

acknowledgments

Many persons helped in the preparation of this book, and I am deeply grateful to them for their excellent assistance. Mr. Howard Carlson of General Motors Institute prepared the first draft of Chapter 4. My research assistant, Miss Karen Hakel, prepared the index, and my hard-working and conscientious secretaries, Sheilah Neet, Carmen Doren, and Charlene Sturm typed the many drafts and re-drafts of the manuscript. Finally, the many costs of putting the manuscript into final form were defrayed by a Behavioral Sciences Research Grant from the General Electric Foundation.

contents

Personnel Selection
and Placement

chapter one

Strategies and Problems in Personnel Decisions

The Context of Personnel Selection

Individual and Job Differences

People differ greatly. At the beach on any hot summer day, even the most casual observer is impressed with the amazing array of physical differences among people. But people also differ in a myriad of other less easily discerned qualities, such as intelligence, abilities, skills, motivation, and temperament. Indications of some of these differences can be observed in the ways people behave. Some are friendly, sociable, and outgoing; others shy and withdrawn. Some are forceful, dominant, and leading; others meek, permissive, and following. Some are constantly active, working or playing with great intensity; others are phlegmatic. It has been said that variability is nature's great joke, perpetrated on man to make more difficult his efforts to understand the universe. If this be so, it certainly is no more apparent than at the human level itself, where the joke and its consequences provide the basis for psychology, the science of human behavior.

The differing patterns of human behavior are also clearly evident in the world of work, where men's efforts have been organized and directed toward production of the great variety of goods and services demanded and consumed by society. The variety of these goods and services is vast, including such diverse services as healing the sick, settling legal disputes, washing clothing, providing police and fire protection, and manufacturing such goods as poker chips, baby diapers, automobiles, Scotch tape, typewriters, and nuclear weapons. Thousands of jobs are encompassed by the world of work; the variety of task requirements is vast, and the human qualities necessary to get the work done differ greatly from job to job. With such variability in demand, in jobs, and in workers, programs of personnel selection and placement in industry are essential.

The Ultimate Goal

In an idealized world, our aim would be to place all persons on jobs perfectly suited to them and to society. This aim assumes that each person should use his abilities, temperament, and motivations in the best possible way for him; it also assumes that society will make the best possible use of its total manpower resources. Obviously this aim, though easily stated, is not easily realized. However, psychology in its short history has learned much about measuring and describing human variability and has made significant contributions to industry's efforts to select and place personnel systematically and rationally.

Approaches to Selection and Placement

This book is devoted to the explication of psychology's contributions. To lay the groundwork for what comes later, we need to consider carefully the major questions and assumptions associated with personnel selection and placement. Let us look at the problems of selection and placement in industrial organizations.

First, consider the task of selecting, from a number of applicants, one person to do a particular job. For example, a sales manager desires a new secretary; a production foreman seeks a lathe operator, or a research chemist has a job opening for a laboratory assistant. In each case, the personnel selection process involves choosing one person to fill the job from among a number of applicants. The supervisor presumably has in mind what the job entails and a rough idea of the qualities required for handling the job successfully. The task is to screen as many applicants as necessary to select one whose qualifications fit the job requirements most closely. The need to fill a single specified job illustrates selection in its purest form. Since only one job is open, personnel placement does not enter the picture; only one person will be hired, and no thought will be given to utilizing the skills of the rejected applicants in other ways or on other jobs. This view of selection is admittedly a narrow one, yet many of the important questions inherent in personnel selection are pointed up: What aspects of the job need to be taken into account for determining the human qualities necessary to do the job? How should the job be analyzed and studied? What sorts of behavior constitute successful job performance, and how may job behaviors best be described and measured? What methods should be used to "size up" or measure the human qualities chosen as necessary for the job? What evidence shows adequately the relationships between certain measured human qualities and different job behaviors?

The problems confronting an employment manager of a large firm include all of those mentioned above, but they are even more complex. At any given time, he has personnel requisitions for many job openings, and he must recruit applicants, extend offers to some, and seek to place them on jobs appropriate to the particular qualities each possesses. His view of personnel selection is much broader than that of anyone trying to fill a single job. It is also more realistic and more complicated, incorporating not only selection problems, but also job placement problems.

Faced with this greater complexity, an employment manager may choose from among several different strategies, as illustrated in Table 1-1. The numbers in the table are hypothetical aptitude scores for job applicants; they can be viewed as relative probabilities of success for each applicant on each of five different jobs. For example, applicant B is most likely to be successful on Job V for which his aptitude score is .9; the probability of success for him on any of the other four jobs is less. With these data, what strategies might an employment manager adopt?

First, he might try simply to adopt a pure selection point of view—that is, he would seek to place the most qualified person available on each of the five jobs. This strategy, shown in the first row in the lower table, would yield the highest possible average aptitude rating (.8). However, in our example, as in many actual situations in industry, such a strategy could not be implemented. To do so would require placing both A and G on two jobs each; this obviously is not a practicable solution. If the employment manager were to adopt this strategy, he would need to increase his total supply of applicants in order to fill all five job openings. He could select from this group only applicants A, B, and G, assign them respectively to jobs I, V, and either II or IV, and then recruit further applicants for the remaining two jobs. However, because of the costs of recruiting additional applicants, their lack of availability in tight labor-market conditions, or time pressures to get jobs

TABLE I–I. *Hypothetical aptitude scores for ten applicants to each of five jobs and assignments that would be made under different placement strategies.*

	JOBS				
	I	II	III	IV	V
A	.9	.7	.8	.6	.7
B	.7	.6	.4	.4	.9
C	.4	.5	.7	.5	.5
D	.4	.5	.6	.3	.2
E	.3	.5	.1	.4	.4
F	.3	.3	.5	.4	.4
G	.8	.7	.5	.7	.6
H	.5	.4	.6	.4	.3
I	.4	.5	.2	.1	.1
J	.2	.1	.3	.1	.1

PLACEMENT STRATEGY						APTITUDE RATING AVERAGE
Pure selection (most qualified person on each job)	A (.9)	A or G (.7)	A (.8)	G (.7)	B (.9)	.8
Vocational Guidance (person placed on job for which he is most qualified)	A (.9) G (.8)	E (.5) I (.5)	C (.7) D (.6) F (.5) H (.6) J (.3)		B (.9)	.63
Compromise placement (allocation of available applicants to job openings)	A (.9)	E or I (.5)	C (.7)	G (.7)	B (.9)	.74

filled quickly, it would be rare indeed to find a situation in which all job openings in a firm could be successfully filled by pure selection.

Vocational Guidance

A second strategy open to the employment manager would focus on the best possible job placement for each individual applicant. It might be argued that a firm would profit (via increased employee satisfaction or greater employee self-fulfillment) if each applicant could be placed on the job for which he is most qualified. The results of this strategy are shown in the second row in the lower table. A number of disadvantages and difficulties are immediately apparent. First, job IV would not be filled; none of the applicants is best fitted to do that job. Second, if one were to stick rigidly with this strategy, he would be compelled to hire many more persons than the firm needs; the average aptitude rating would be lowered (to .63) by bringing into the firm some persons who are actually not very well qualified to do *any* of the jobs (for example, applicants I and J). No employment manager could adopt this strategy in its pure form. The strategy is obviously more appropriate for high school and college vocational counselors and for the individual career and job decisions made by applicants prior to their job search.

We have said that an idealized industrial society should place all persons on jobs best suited to them. It is clear now that this is not easily carried out. The two strategies discussed so far are essentially incompatible with one another; pure selection maximizes the over-all effectiveness of employees in the institution, but it is nearly always impossible to use pure selection when classifying or placing persons on available jobs. Even if each firm did have a limitless supply of applicants, the procedure is inherently wasteful; skimming off the cream of the applicant crop leaves many applicants unemployed and thereby underutilized. The guidance point of view is equally untenable because it tends to ignore that only a limited number of jobs are available at any given time and that it *is* necessary from the employing institution's point of view to fill the jobs with individuals who have at least a reasonable chance of success. Thus, the two strategies not only result in different outcomes, but, in their pure forms, they are often unrealistic and always incompatible. Decisions giving the best return to the employing firm (pure selection) will rarely be best for each of the individuals about whom the decisions are made.

A Compromise

The result must nearly always be a compromise strategy as shown in the third row at the bottom of Table 1-1. Here, the employment manager has made the best job placement possible with the resources available. Applicants A and B were placed on Jobs I and V because they "fit" those jobs for both the selection and guidance strategies. G was placed on Job IV because he is the best person for that job *and* because he is almost as well qualified for it as for Job I. C is not the best man for Job III, but he is the best remaining after A has been placed, and he is much better qualified for that job than for any of the others. Finally, either E or I can be placed on Job II; neither is as well qualified as some of the others (A, B, and G) but both "fit" that job better than any of the other jobs, and there is at least an even chance of their being successful on it. Thus, the compromise strategy constitutes an effort to allocate available persons as wisely as possible, using elements of both selection and guidance thinking; the average aptitude rating is .74, not seriously lower than the average (.8) for the pure selection strategy.

The compromise strategy is, of course, the one actually employed by personnel specialists for solving problems of personnel selection and placement. In contrast with the pure selection or pure guidance strategies, there are no rigid rules to follow to assure the optimum allocation of available manpower to the jobs available. Instead, the strategy involves a "cut and try," judgmental approach.

Considerations in Selection and Placement

Several important considerations dictate the range over which an employment manager may exercise his judgment and the relative emphasis he may give to selection and guidance as he seeks an optimal solution to any placement problem.

Number of Applicants Relative to Number of Jobs

At one extreme (for example, in the armed services), it may be necessary to assign a certain number of persons to an equal number of different jobs. This is a pure classification situation and places severe demands on human judgment for making optimal job assignments. Human judgment in such situations has often proved fallible, as anyone will know who has witnessed some of the bizarre job assignments occasionally made in the armed services. Some years back, a news service widely circulated a picture of a young army recruit perched atop a gigantic pile of potatoes with an underutilized look on his face. He was indeed being underutilized for he was a brilliant young mathematician with a Ph.D. Human judgment had erred—probably because the Army's need for potato peelers had greatly exceeded its need for highly trained mathematicians, and the accuracy of classification was adversely affected by the necessity for filling job openings from a limited supply of available recruits.

In contrast, when the number of applicants is large relative to the number of jobs, much greater care in the matching of men and jobs may be exercised. However, the number of applicants varies greatly for different kinds of jobs and at different times (for example, in a period of rapid manpower mobilization, such as during World War II, employment conditions in industry may closely approach pure classification). In order to make intelligent selection and placement decisions, an employment manager must be able to estimate accurately how many applicants he may have for the various positions in his company and what the cost of recruiting additional ones will be.

Institutional and Individual Considerations

For the institution, pure selection maximizes the over-all quality or effectiveness of job performance of employees. It should be clear that an employment manager is primarily an institutional decision maker. For each individual, however, the guidance approach is best, because he desires to choose a vocation or job best for him. It is also desirable from society's standpoint to avoid as much as possible the underutilization of the capabilities of individuals. Decisions involving occupations, educational attainment, and various career choices are most strongly affected by family, friends, teachers, and school counselors; the employment manager, especially in large firms, also can guide persons in making wise job and career decisions, within the limits dictated by the institution. As we saw in discussing various strategies for personnel decisions, the most usual approach involves a careful weighing of the relative importance of institutional and individual considerations.

Relative Cost of Wrong Decisions

In making a selection or placement decision, two kinds of error are possible. First, an individual may be placed on a job on which he later fails; because a positive outcome (success) was predicted and failed to materialize, this kind of error is called a *false positive* error. Second, an individual may not be placed on a job in which he could have been successful; because this involves an inaccurate prediction of a negative outcome (failure), it is called a *false negative* error. The relative cost of making errors of these two types greatly affects personnel decision strategies. Recently, a star college baseball player was reported to have received a bonus of $200,000 for signing a contract with one of the major-league teams. If he proves to be a dud—a false positive—the cost of the selection error will be extremely great. On the other hand, the potential cost (in loss of crowd interest, lessened competitive position, and reduced gate receipts) of losing a player of star quality to another team is also great and could well exceed the $200,000 used to induce him to sign the contract. The persons responsible for recruiting and selecting this player are betting strongly on him to develop into a super star of baseball. Their confidence in the bet and their eagerness to avoid a false negative error is shown by the size of the bonus. Similar selection decisions are made daily in industry, and the amount of time, money, and energy committed to filling any given job varies directly with the importance of the job. The cost of an error in placing a file clerk is much less than the cost of an error in placing a research chemist or a senior executive. Jobs of lesser importance are more likely to be filled quickly, with less explicit attention to the relative cost of errors in placement decisions. Jobs of greater importance are likely to be left open until just the right applicant comes along, since differences in employee effectiveness can have a great impact on the firm's over-all effectiveness. For jobs of great organizational importance it is imperative that the relative costs of false positive errors be carefully weighed against the costs of recruiting and against the potential loss to the firm of false negative errors. It may sometimes be wiser to "try a person out" on a job rather than risk his loss to another firm, but this is not a frequent strategy in industry.

Trainability of Persons and Modifications of the Job-Man Relationship

Training programs in industry are widespread. Their purpose is to modify employees' knowledge, skills, and attitudes in order to equip them to do their jobs better. Personnel selection and job placement is inextricably intertwined with personnel training. At one extreme, if all persons were perfectly modifiable through training, individualized programs of job placement would be quite unnecessary; persons would simply be recruited and trained to do the various jobs in accordance with the broad requirements of the organization. At the other extreme, if persons were unchangeable through training or experience, programs of personnel selection would be the *only* way of assuring a good fit between men and jobs. In fact neither extreme is true, and it becomes necessary to base selection and placement partly on information of what training can achieve and to select persons who will be able to profit from training. Jobs differ in the ease with which persons may be trained to do them. Some jobs require very little training (for example, janitorial services); others require a great deal (for example, operating a spacecraft).

A well-designed training program will usually specify the kinds of personal qualities necessary in a person entering the program. If the allowable personal qualities cover a wide range, the burden for selection and placement is lessened, for training can presumably develop the desired job knowledge, attitudes, and behaviors in groups of heterogeneous persons. In such instances, the employment manager's major concern is to avoid assigning overqualified persons (for example, the potato-peeling Ph.D. cited earlier) to the training program; maximum requirements might be set rather than minimum ones. In contrast, if the personal prerequisites for training are very narrowly specified, the burden for selection and placement is heightened, for the training can then presumably develop the desired job knowledge, attitudes, and behaviors only for certain groups of highly homogeneous persons.

In addition to training, other influences can modify the job-man relationship. For example, in many jobs—such as selling, researching, managing, etc.—the actual means of achieving job objectives remain unspecified—that is, the particular individual placed in a job may actually change the job to fit his own propensities, strengths, weaknesses, and stylized patterns of job behavior. With jobs of this kind, no single pattern of personal qualities or "mold" should be established. The placement specialist must discover the *various* kinds of job behaviors leading to success and the corresponding personal qualities of individuals who may be predicted to follow one or more of these success patterns.

Very large firms have such great diversity of jobs that intrafirm job transfers are possible. Large firms, therefore, are peculiarly well fitted to do effective personnel selection *and* vocational guidance. Initial placement errors can quite often be rectified by arranging for job transfers within the firm. In making an initial placement decision with an applicant, the employment manager should consider the degree of irrevocability of the decision—that is, the probability and potential cost of making a wrong decision.

In summary, if the man is to be changed through training, if the job is to be changed by the man or by other circumstances, or if an error in a job placement decision can be rectified rather easily and without too much cost, these factors should be explicitly in the mind of the placement specialist, and he should take account of them when he makes a selection or placement decision.

Accuracy of Prediction

In a real setting, complete information about the relative odds of success for different people and for different jobs would rarely be available. Getting such data is affected by factors such as the number of persons in a job and available for test validation studies, the relative ease of predicting different job behaviors, and the degree of stability in the man-job relationship. To illustrate, suppose a young female applicant for a job as a receptionist has scored very high on a stenographic proficiency test previously evaluated for the jobs of file clerk, secretary, and receptionist. Suppose further that these studies had shown the test to be moderately predictive of success in the file clerk and secretary jobs but almost entirely nonpredictive for the job of receptionist. The dilemma faced by the employment manager is that the girl would very likely succeed in the two jobs for which she is *not* applying but unfortunately no reliable prediction of her success as a receptionist may be made. A placement decision must be based on incomplete information. A persuasive employment manager might be able to convince the young lady to accept a job as a secretary, or he might see this as an opportunity to hire a receptionist who could also double as a file clerk and secretary (thereby modifying the job). On the other hand, if the job did not allow such a doubling of duties, it would be necessary to base the decision on other probably nonvalidated factors such as pulchritude rating, or on other putative predictors such as social poise, quality of voice, previous job experience, and other nontest measures.

All this emphasizes that selection decisions and job placement strategies must still be made even when information is sketchy and incomplete. When such decisions are necessary, the employment manager should at least be aware of what he does or does not know so that he will be clearly aware of the risks he is taking in making personnel decisions. In particular, he should know how well the various test and nontest measures used in assessing applicants predict success on various jobs.

Intraindividual Variation

Not only do people differ from one another, they also differ greatly within themselves—that is, they possess relatively unique *patterns* of abilities, attitudes, preferences, and personality attributes. Few people are "good" in all things; nor are they uniformly "bad." Some may be equipped to do a wide range of jobs effectively and with satisfaction; others may be poorly adapted for just about all jobs. Most persons, however, possess a relatively few outstanding qualities uniquely fitting them for a relatively narrow range of jobs. The placement specialist must heed intraindividual variation as he assesses applicants for job openings.

Situational and Social Factors

So far in discussing the job-man relationship we have implied that each job has certain characteristics requiring, for effective performance, an accurate match with some person possessing certain qualities. This view is probably too mechanistic, for it tacitly ignores the situational and social circumstances surrounding jobs. The kind of supervisor a man has can affect his job behavior for good or for ill. Similarly, the kinds of co-workers comprising the social environment of a job should dictate in part the kind of person to be placed on that job. The kinds of customers a salesman must call on, the types of students to be taught by a teacher, the economic conditions in a given sales territory, the relative success enjoyed by an individual's predecessor in a job and his particular style of job behavior—factors such as these and many more—should be considered by the job placement specialist or employment manager as he seeks to fill a job. Probably the best way to assure this consideration is to incorporate into the statement of job requirements the situational and social circumstances surrounding the job. Thus, the job analysis should be broadened to include these elements in addition to the description of job duties and responsibilities. Admittedly, this step complicates the identification and assessment of the human qualities desirable in the job incumbent. However, ignoring them simply contributes to the probability of inaccurate placement.

Plan of This Book

In the remainder of the book, we will describe at greater length the basic contributions made by psychology to effective personnel selection and placement and spell out in greater detail the actual steps in selection and placement.

Part I (Chapters 2, 3, 4, and 5) covers psychology's basic contributions to solving selection and placement problems. Chapter 2 presents some elementary statistical tools and discusses psychological measurement; Chapter 3 describes briefly the history and the current status of the measurement of human differences. Chapter 4 discusses job analysis and its methods, and Chapter 5 outlines the development of objective techniques for observing and measuring job behavior.

Part II (Chapters 6, 7, and 8) covers the logical and methodological steps in developing strategies for making personnel decisions. Chapter 6 presents a framework or model to guide research on selection and placement. Chapter 7 deals with the relations between measures of human qualities and job behavior observations; the chapter presents some possible methods for learning more about the meanings of test scores and the behavioral observations on which the meanings are based. Chapter 8 summarizes a number of methods for gathering and coordinating information for making personnel selection and placement decisions; the chapter also evaluates commonly used methods of individual assessment.

Part III (Chapters 9 and 10) shows how specific programs of selection and placement have been developed and summarizes the advantages of carefully developed programs. Chapter 9 presents and critically evaluates selection research studies chosen to illustrate the major principles outlined in previous chapters. Chapter 10 summarizes the book, but more importantly it spells out the significant role played in a free society by programs of selection and placement that recognize individuality and make maximum and humane use of human resources.

part one

Measuring People, Jobs,
and Job Behavior

chapter two

Methods of
Measurement
in Psychology

Whatever exists, exists in some amount and can, therefore, be measured. This is our fundamental assumption when we set out to make sense of the chaos of variation present in the world around us. Through measurement, we assign numbers to observable phenomena according to specified rules and operations. For a science, measurement offers many crucial advantages. For one, it enables more precise communication among scientists and between scientists and nonscientists. The simple act of specifying measurement operations forces us to define explicitly what we wish to talk about, thereby ruling out ambiguities of speculation, loose definition, and distortions of personal perception that contribute so greatly to imprecision in everyday discourse. If the weather bureau had no measurement methods, it could only describe temperature conditions with words such as "very hot," "rather chilly," or "downright cold"—phrases meaning very different things to different persons. Fortunately, meteorologists utilize *measures* of temperature; when the temperature is reported as 102° F., the knowledge imparted is meaningful and explicit, to scientists and nonscientists as well.

Moreover, the precision of discourse possible with measurement enables us to do research, to order and to observe systematically the phenomena in the world around us, and to study the patterns of co-variation and lawful relationships among the things we experience.

Measurement begins with something to be measured; day to day experiences and observations arouse our curiosity, and we seek to learn more about them. From simple curiosity, the scientist moves quickly to making systematic observations. Before long, he defines his observational methods and he labels, numbers, or "measures" the phenomena being described. Then, he sets out to learn all he can about lawful relations between his measure and other observable phenomena.

Measurement in psychology has to do with observing and seeking to make sense out of human behavior. In this chapter, we present some of the major methods and statistics used by psychologists as they have sought to make sense out of human variation.

Scales and Scores

Scales

A first step in making sense out of human variation is simply to identify qualitative differences among people and to categorize persons according to these distinctions. Our only assumption is that persons bearing the same labels have something in common and that they differ in this characteristic from persons bearing different labels. Persons are categorized according to physical features (blonde, brunette, tall, fat, pretty, shapely), according to emotional responses (angry, sad, joyful, fearful, disgusted), according to behavior observations (dumb, smart, outgoing, dominant, childish), and according to society's evaluations (eminent, famous, dangerous, brave, neurotic). Each of these classification scales is called a *nominal scale*. The scale can be labeled with numbers, letters, or any other convenient set of symbols. In personnel selection, nominal scales occur most frequently in the form of biographical categories (such as married or single; male or female) obtained from application blanks or other questionnaires. With such information, it is meaningful to count the numbers of persons who belong to different categories and to inquire whether people in these different categories differ from one another in job behaviors.

Nominal scales cannot be dealt with arithmetically because their labels carry no quantitative information. But for many human characteristics, quantitative data can be developed. Persons can be ordered according to how much they possess of a given trait. When this is done, the scale is called an *ordinal scale*. Numbers are usually assigned to different points on such a scale, and they have the meaning *first, second, third,* and so on. Ordinal scales add the concept "greater than" to the concept "different from" in nominal scales. Ordinal scales are very commonly used in measuring human characteristics. For example, in a beauty contest, the judges usually choose the top few girls and rank them—first, second, third, etc.—in order of over-all beauty. The girl receiving the most first-place votes is the winner. The ordinal scale is usually regarded as having certain mathematical limitations, largely because such a scale gives no information about the relative amount of difference between adjacent points on the scale. In our example, the girl ranked *first* might be far more beautiful than the girl ranked *second*, but the girls ranked *fourth* and *fifth* might be very similar in over-all beauty. Thus, a particular scale unit difference can mean quite different things at different points on an ordinal scale; and because of this, it is usually said that ranks in an ordinal scale should not be added, subtracted, or averaged. Strictly speaking, such arithmetic operations require an *interval scale*—a scale that gives information about the *distances* between adjacent points as well as about their order. The ordinary Fahrenheit temperature scale is an interval scale, defined by the amount of mercury expansion associated with a change in temperature. For example, the mercury movement associated with a five-degree change in the neighborhood of 100° is the same as that associated with a five-degree change at other points on the scale; thus, for describing the behavior of mercury, the intervals between adjacent points are equal and the numbers designating the points may be added, subtracted, or averaged.

Most scales developed for measuring individual differences are treated as interval scales. Although this may not be strictly correct, Ghiselli (34) has summarized a number of compelling arguments in favor of doing so:

> *Behavioral meaning.*   It is often argued that psychological measures cannot be viewed as interval scales because a given score interval (say, ten units) has different behavioral meanings at different levels on the scale. For example, in the ability to learn abstract subject matter, moving from an IQ of 105 to one of 115 may be quite different from moving from 115 to 125. However, this argument is not relevant. The Fahrenheit scale is said to be an interval scale, yet, the "behavior" of water over a temperature increase of ten degrees differs greatly, depending upon the location on the scale over which the change occurs (compare, for example, the range around 32° F. with that around 212° F.). Simply arguing that similar scale intervals have

different behavioral meanings at various scale points is irrelevant to the issue. The definition of scale score meanings in terms of human behavior can only be established by careful research. Hence, behavioral markers must be established for any scale—nominal, ordinal, or interval.

Averaging out. Even if immediately adjacent scale intervals differ somewhat in length—including some units of relatively greater length, some relatively shorter, and so on—it is likely that longer intervals will "average out" so that, for all practical purposes, intervals from different parts of the scale can be treated as equal. This is probably the case in most psychological measures that include a broad sampling of test items of various types placed randomly throughout the test.

Scaling methodology. Methods are available (Paired Comparisons, Confidence Estimation, etc.) for scaling stimuli on the basis of the relative ease of discriminating distances or of making judgments about test items or stimuli. These methods result in true interval scales. In actual use, however, such scales yield results showing little, if any, *practical* difference from results obtained with measures that may not have strictly defined interval properties.

From the above arguments, it seems to make little difference whether or not we *really* have interval scales. In the absence of any important differences, it is probably proper to continue to utilize arithmetic operations *as if* our scales were bona fide interval scores.

Scores

In psychological measurement, numbers are assigned to people according to their responses to sets of standardized stimuli (tests). The stimuli may be tasks, problems, questions, descriptive statements or adjectives, words, symbols, objects, or ambiguous pictures or forms. The direct results of the test responses are called *raw scores*. For example, raw scores on a clerical aptitude test might simply be the number of items perceived correctly. Raw scores have little meaning until they are compared with scores obtained by others. Here are scores obtained on a clerical aptitude test by fifteen young ladies applying for a secretarial job.

	RAW SCORE
Amber	20
Bridgit	23
Cleopatra	17
Deborah	19
Elizabeth	22
Ella	17
Heather	20
Hedy	20
Jean	21
Joanie	19
Marilyn	19
Melody	20
Millicent	21
Rita	22
Sheila	20

One good way of summarizing the set of scores is to order them from highest to lowest as follows:

23	20	19
22	20	19
22	20	19
21	20	17
21	20	17

This yields a rough picture of the range of scores, shows their relative dispersion (amount of spread), and indicates the most common scores in the group. However, with any large number of scores, an ordering such as this, although useful, still involves too much information to group easily. Some sort of summary statistics is desired, and ideally each person's score should be expressed in some single index telling the relative standing of the person in the group.

THE MEAN

The need for summary statistics is best served by the mean and the standard deviation. The *mean* is obtained by adding all the scores and dividing the sum by the number of persons tested. The sum of scores on the clerical test above is 300. Dividing this by 15 gives a mean of 20.0. This is a simple, easy-to-calculate estimate of the score about which the rest of the scores are centered; that is, the mean is an index of the *central tendency* of the distribution.

THE STANDARD DEVIATION

Knowing the mean, one can change the raw scores into *deviation scores;* for example, the deviation score for the raw score of 23 is

23 − 20.0 = +3.0. Deviation scores show the number of units by which each raw score deviates from the mean of the distribution of scores. The deviation scores corresponding to the remainder of the raw scores are:

+3.0	0.0	−1.0
+2.0	0.0	−1.0
+2.0	0.0	−1.0
+1.0	0.0	−3.0
+1.0	0.0	−3.0

Deviation scores are direct measures of the amount of spread or dispersion in a distribution. If the deviation scores are very closely clustered about a value of 0, it is obvious that the scores are tightly clustered about the mean. If deviation scores are large, departing widely from 0, it is equally obvious that the scores are spread out and widely dispersed. The deviation scores form the basis for the most widely used and useful index of dispersion, the *standard deviation*. To calculate the standard deviation, one first calculates the *variance,* which is defined as the mean value of the squared deviation scores. If the above deviation scores are each squared and summed, the result is 40. Dividing this by 15 gives the value 2.67, which is the *variance* of the distribution of scores. Since the variance is based on the *squared deviation* scores, it is useful to calculate its square root. The square root of 2.67 is 1.63, which is the *standard deviation* of the original distribution of scores.

STANDARD SCORE

Now we are ready to express each girl's score as a single index showing her standing in the total distribution. The deviation scores are divided by the value of the standard deviation to yield the *standard score*. In symbols, the expression for the standard score is as follows:

$$Z_x = \frac{X - M_x}{SD_x} \, ,$$

where

Z_x = standard score corresponding to raw score, X,
X = raw score value,
M_x = Mean of scores,
SD_x = Standard Deviation of scores.

For the girls' clerical test scores, the corresponding standard scores are:

Bridgit	+1.84	Amber	0.00	Joanie	−0.61
Elizabeth	+1.23	Heather	0.00	Marilyn	−0.61
Rita	+1.23	Hedy	0.00	Deborah	−0.61
Jean	+0.61	Melody	0.00	Cleopatra	−1.84
Millicent	+0.61	Sheila	0.00	Ella	−1.84

There are two advantages of expressing psychological measures in standard score form. First, the mean and standard deviation, and consequently the standard score, bear known relationships to the normal probability curve. Since it has been shown that many human characteristics (psychological measures included) vary according to a normal distribution, the relations between standard scores and the normal curve are important and very meaningful. The basic form of the relationship is depicted in the figure below showing the approximate number of persons in 1,000 who could be expected to score in various standard score regions on a normally distributed measure.

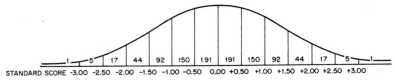

STANDARD SCORE   −3.00 −2.50 −2.00 −1.50 −1.00 −0.50   0.00 +0.50 +1.00 +1.50 +2.00 +2.50 +3.00

The above standard score scale has a mean of 0 and a standard deviation of 1.0. By multiplying each standard score on the above scale by 10 and adding 50, a scale with a mean of 50 and standard deviation of 10 results. This standard score scale is in common use; it is convenient because it has no decimals and no negative numbers. IQ scores are based on a standard score scale having a mean of 100 and standard deviation of 16. There can be any number of standard score scales; the choice of values for the mean and standard deviation is arbitrary. The important point about standard scores is that they bear a known relationship to the normal distribution and that any given standard score conveys information about a person's standing in relation to his peers.

Tables A and B in the Appendix show the percentage of persons who would score at or below each standard score (in increments of .10 and .05) in a normal distribution of scores. The use of Table A can be illustrated by referring once more to the standard scores obtained by our hypothetical group of secretarial applicants. Assuming clerical scores to be normally distributed among the potential population of all similar applicants, Bridgit's score (+1.84), for example, is equivalent to a percentile standing of about 96.8 (referring to Table A opposite the standard score of $+1.85$). This means that fewer than 4 per cent of secretarial applicants could be expected to obtain a score as high as Bridgit's. The scores of the other girls can be interpreted in this same way. Table B is merely the obverse of Table A, showing the standard score equivalents for different percentile scores. If percentile scores are available for a number of persons, Table B can be used to assign them the standard scores they would have in a normal distribution, thereby "normalizing" their scores.

Another important advantage of the standard score is that it provides a single standard comparison for estimating a person's relative standing on several different measures. Knowing that Bridgit's raw score on the clerical aptitude test is 23 and that her raw score on a spelling test is 42 gives us no real knowledge of her relative standing on the two measures. However, if we are then told that her *standard score* on the spelling test is $+2.09$, we know immediately that she is clearly superior in comparison with her peers on both measures and even more outstanding in spelling than in clerical aptitude.

This property of the standard score for showing the relative status of an individual on several different measures is an extremely important one, for it enables us to study and to estimate the degree of relationship among the various measures. This leads directly to a consideration of correlation, to which we now turn.

Correlation

In any selection decision it is crucial to know what areas of job behavior may be related to the psychological measures and other assessment techniques used during selection. One statistic widely used for estimating the relationship between any two measures is the correlation coefficient, r. In order to illustrate what r is and how it may be calculated, let us suppose that a firm hired as secretaries *all* fifteen of the girls for whom clerical test scores were available. Suppose also that after six months we ask each girl's supervisor to "rate" her on a single, but important, element of job behavior. Specifically, we ask each supervisor to indicate on a nine-point scale how well the statement "is extremely accurate in the work she does" fits his secretary. If it is perfectly descriptive of her job behavior, she gets a 9; if it is completely nondescriptive of her job behavior, she gets a 1. Various points in between may be chosen at the supervisor's discretion. The following ratings might be obtained:

	ACCURACY RATING	STANDARD SCORE
Amber	7	+1.15
Bridgit	8	+1.63
Cleopatra	4	−0.29
Deborah	6	+0.67
Elizabeth	7	+1.15
Ella	2	−1.24
Heather	5	+0.19
Hedy	1	−1.72
Jean	6	+0.67
Joanie	3	−0.77
Marilyn	1	−1.72
Melody	6	+0.67
Millicent	5	+0.19
Rita	4	−0.29
Sheila	4	−0.29

Sum of ratings = 69

$$\text{Mean} = \frac{\Sigma X}{N} = \frac{69}{15} = 4.60$$

$$\text{Standard Deviation} = \sqrt{\frac{\Sigma (X - M)^2}{N}} = \sqrt{4.37} = 2.09$$

The usefulness of the standard score for comparing each girl's standing on the clerical test and job behavior rating is obvious. For example, Bridgit has a score of +1.84 on the clerical test and +1.63 on the job behavior rating. For her, the clerical test score is clearly predictive of her later rating on work accuracy. In contrast, Deborah scores −0.61 on the test and +0.67 on the behavior rating. Clearly, the clerical test is less indicative for Deborah than for Bridgit of the later rating on work accuracy.

Scatter Diagrams and the Correlation Coefficient

The total picture of comparisons between the two scores for all fifteen girls is shown in Figure 2–1. This chart is called a *scatter diagram*. Such a chart is useful because it shows at a glance the over-all pattern of relationships between scores on the clerical test and the job behavior ratings. It would be desirable, however, to have a single numerical index to serve as a sort of pooled estimate of the degree of agreement between the two measures for the various girls. The correlation coefficient, *r*, is such an index. It is simply the mean of the products of the two sets of standard scores. Thus:

$$r_{tr} = \frac{\Sigma Z_t Z_r}{N},$$

where

r_{tr} = correlation coefficient between test scores and rating scores,

Z_t = standard score on the test,

Z_r = standard score on the behavior rating,

N = number of persons for whom the two measures are available,

Σ = sum of.

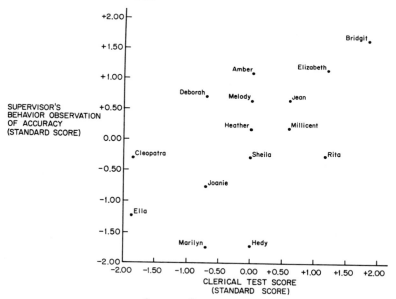

FIGURE 2–1. *Scatter diagram comparing standard scores for fifteen secretarial applicants on a clerical test with their standard scores on supervisors' observations of work accuracy.*

The calculation[1] of r_{tr} for our fifteen girls is shown below:

[1] Since standard scores are calculated from raw scores, means, and standard deviations, it is possible to express the formula for the correlation coefficient in terms of the original raw scores. The formula is:

$$r = \frac{N\Sigma XY - (\Sigma X)(\Sigma Y)}{\sqrt{[N\Sigma X^2 - (\Sigma X)^2][N\Sigma Y^2 - (\Sigma Y)^2]}},$$

where X and Y represent the raw scores. This formula is frequently more convenient for computation.

	Z_t	Z_r	$Z_t Z_r$
Amber	0.00	+1.15	0.00
Bridgit	+1.84	+1.63	+3.00
Cleopatra	−1.84	−0.29	+0.53
Deborah	−0.61	+0.67	−0.41
Elizabeth	+1.23	+1.15	+1.41
Ella	−1.84	−1.24	+2.28
Heather	0.00	+0.19	0.00
Hedy	0.00	−1.72	0.00
Jean	+0.61	+0.67	+0.41
Joanie	−0.61	−0.77	+0.47
Marilyn	−0.61	−1.72	+1.05
Melody	0.00	+0.67	0.00
Millicent	+0.61	+0.19	+0.12
Rita	+1.23	−0.29	−0.36
Sheila	0.00	−0.29	0.00

$$\Sigma Z_t Z_r = +8.50$$

$$r_{tr} = \frac{\Sigma Z_t Z_r}{N} = \frac{+8.50}{15}$$

$$r_{tr} = .57$$

The correlation coefficient varies between −1.00 and +1.00. When the standard scores on one variable are identical in both size and sign to the corresponding standard scores on another variable, r is +1.00. When the standard scores on one variable are identical in size but opposite in sign to the corresponding standard scores on another variable, r is −1.00, and this is called a perfect inverse relationship. When there is no systematic relationship between corresponding pairs of standard scores, r is 0.00 or very close to it, and the relationship is said to be the result of chance.

Limitations of the Correlation Coefficient

There are instances (for example, the relationship between tested reasoning ability and effective job performance on most boring or routine jobs) in which increasing ability might be accompanied first by an increase and later by a decrease in some aspect of job behavior. Consider the hypothetical data below in which the clerical test scores for our secretarial applicants are compared with later job behavior ratings (again on a nine-point scale) based on the statement "shows initiative; goes ahead with work on her own when supervisor is gone or unavailable."

BEHAVIOR RATING

	Z_t	B	Z_B	$Z_t Z_B$
Amber	0.00	5	+0.94	0.00
Bridgit	+1.84	1	−1.52	−2.80
Cleopatra	−1.84	1	−1.52	+2.80
Deborah	−0.61	3	−0.29	+0.18
Elizabeth	+1.23	2	−0.90	−1.11
Ella	−1.84	2	−0.94	+1.66
Heather	0.00	6	+1.55	0.00
Hedy	0.00	5	+0.94	0.00
Jean	+0.61	3	−0.29	−0.18
Joanie	−0.61	4	+0.33	−0.20
Marilyn	−0.61	3	−0.29	+0.18
Melody	0.00	6	+1.55	0.00
Millicent	+0.61	4	+0.33	+0.20
Rita	+1.23	2	−0.90	−1.11
Sheila	0.00	5	+0.94	0.00

$$M_B = \frac{52}{15} = 3.47 \qquad \Sigma Z_t Z_B = -0.38$$
$$SD_B = 1.63 \qquad\qquad r_{tB} = \frac{-0.38}{15} = -.03$$

Figure 2–2 shows the scatter diagram drawn from these data. Girls in the middle range on the clerical test apparently show the most initiative in going ahead with work on their own. Girls scoring at the low and at the high points on the test show less initiative. Scores on the clerical test are clearly related to this aspect of observed job behavior; yet the correlation, r, between the two measures is −.03. The correlation coefficient yields a meaningful index of the relationship between two variables only when increases in one measure are accompanied systematically by increases or decreases in the other measure—that is, when a straight line describes the general trend of the information shown by the scatter diagram plotted between the two variables. In our example the correlation coefficient seriously underestimates the true magnitude of the relationship because a straight line is clearly inappropriate to describe the curvilinear trend of the relationship. The above example shows the importance of plotting a scatter diagram to look at the data gathered in any selection or test validation study. (In Chapter 7

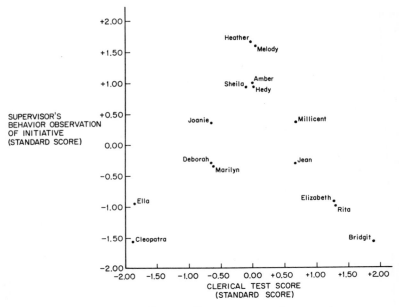

FIGURE 2–2. *Scatter diagram comparing standard scores for fifteen secretarial applicants on a clerical test with their standard scores on supervisors' observations of initiative.*

we will develop another method for looking at data—the use of expectancy charts.)

Because the magnitude of the correlation coefficient depends so much on the form as well as on the degree of relationship between two measures, and because it is nothing more than a sort of pooled estimate of the linear agreement between the two measures for all subjects, it can be argued that calculating a correlation coefficient may cover up a great deal more than it reveals.

In spite of its shortcomings, the correlation coefficient is still one of the most useful and commonly used statistics in psychology. Since it is widely used, let us review some of the problems in its interpretation and use:

> The major problem is not due to any fundamental weakness or inadequacy with the statistic itself. Quite the contrary, *r* is beautiful in its simplicity and in the amount of information it conveys *when based on linear data.* But

r is frequently misused. It is now so easy to calculate (thousands can be electronically computed in seconds) that many investigators seem to be interested in "correlating everything in sight" rather than in looking at the data to study the true nature of the relationships between and among measures. A person conducting selection research will learn much more about his data and the kinds of selection and placement decisions he can make from it by drawing scatter diagrams, developing expectancy charts, and viewing the overlap between distributions (see Chapter 7) than he will by simply calculating any number of *r*'s. After he *really* knows what the data portray, the investigator can calculate *r*'s in order to estimate the magnitude of relationships between predictors and job behavior measures.

Also the correlation coefficient is simply a pooled estimate of the varying amounts of agreement between two measures for the various persons being studied. Refer again to Figure 2–1. Even though a linear trend seems appropriate for the data depicted there, simply calculating *r* (without looking at the scatter diagram) would fail to reveal that some girls (notably Bridgit, Elizabeth, Jean, Heather, Joanie, and Ella) score very similarly on the two measures and that others (Rita, Amber, Deborah, Cleopatra, and Hedy) score very differently on the two measures. The correlation coefficient for the former group would be close to $+1.00$ and for the latter very nearly 0.00. Certainly, it would seem wise to study two such groups further to determine whether or not they might differ consistently in their predictability, and, if so, to seek other measures related to their differential predictability. When investigators do look at their data (via a scatter diagram or expectancy table), it is not unusual to note different degrees of relationship in different portions of the diagram. Very often, a test may be quite accurate in predicting poor job behavior ratings ("failures"), but rather inaccurate in pinpointing good job behavior ratings ("successes"). The scatter diagram in such instances is fan shaped (rather tightly clustered in the lower score ranges and fanning out for the higher scores); calculation of a single *r* for such data is clearly misleading because the value obtained would overestimate the degree of relationship in the upper portion and seriously underestimate the degree of relationship in the lower portion of the diagram. In such instances, it seems much wiser to follow Kahneman and Ghiselli's (53) suggestion to calculate different correlation coefficients for persons at different points in the distribution and thereby obtain more realistic estimates of relative predictability of persons at different score ranges.

Having sounded a rather vigorous note of caution in the use of *r*, we need now to back off a bit and discuss some circumstances in which its use is not only appropriate but, indeed, extremely important and meaningful. The first of these circumstances involves the trait stability or precision of measurement of the behavior being studied.

Trait Stability and Precision of Measurement

If an applicant obtains a standard score of +2.00 on a selection test, we want some assurance that his highly superior standing is not due to luck, error, or chance, but that it reflects a stable individual quality that has been measured with some precision. Traditionally, all measurement error in test development has been encompassed by the term *reliability*. Today, it is recognized that many factors influence and contribute to measurement "error" and that there is no single best way of talking about or estimating test reliability. The somewhat outmoded term "reliability" is being replaced in the testing lexicon by several terms. Thus, instead of considering "reliability," as such, we will present here the major sources of instability and imprecision in individual differences measurement and discuss methods for estimating their magnitude and for controlling or reducing their effects.

Error

Suppose we develop several measures of the same psychological attribute, taking special pains to make the measures as identical as possible. If the measures are then applied to a number of different persons, we should, in the absence of measurement error, expect each person to get exactly the same score on each measure. Any departure from this is due to what we are calling *error*; thus, our discussion is directed toward considering the various reasons why the scores for each person may differ from measure to measure. The various sources of error in psychological measurement are summarized in the following paragraphs.

1. *Errors due to inadequate sampling of content.* Scores may differ from measure to measure because they

sample different aspects of the attribute being measured. In writing examinations to measure course achievement, a teacher tries to include questions from *all* of the course materials—lectures, texts, extra readings, etc. Any differences in the content sampling of a group of achievement tests would result in score differences for those students who had learned some content areas better than others. These differences would be indications of measurement error due to poor sampling of the total content.

2. *Errors due to chance response tendencies.* In the extreme case where a person knew absolutely nothing about a subject, he would have to guess on all the test questions relating to it. On a series of such tests, his scores would differ according to how lucky he was from test to test. The tendency to give random or chance responses may also arise from lack of enthusiasm for the testing situation or from experience inappropriate to the content of the test items. For example, a person faced with the task of responding to a large number of rather personal questions (such as are included in many personality inventories) may react against or resist the task by simply giving random responses. He might react in the same way if he is asked to answer questions that seem meaningless to him (such as answering true or false to the statement "I am more moody than robust"). Obviously, any tendencies toward guessing or random responding will lead to different scores on any series of tests designed to measure some attribute and will, therefore, contribute to measurement error. This kind of error is best reduced by taking special pains to write tests appropriate to the knowledge and background of the examinees and by seeking to motivate examinees to give careful attention to their responses. Many personality tests also include a series of items that act as a sort of "check" on the attentiveness of the examinee during his taking of the test—for example, statements that nearly everyone answers in the same way.

3. *Errors due to changes in the testing environment.* The circumstances surrounding a person's taking a test can significantly affect his responses to it. Physical conditions such as the lighting, temperature, and noise level of the testing room obviously affect someone taking a test. Random distractions such as conversations among bystanders, an attractive member of the opposite sex passing by the window, or an air raid siren may have unknown and unpredictable

effects on the responses obtained from different persons. If the environmental conditions change between administrations of a series of tests designed to measure the same attribute, score differences may be the unwanted and unintended result. Errors due to such changes can be eliminated or greatly reduced by taking great pains to standardize the test situation. The procedures to be followed should be specified in detail, the directions carefully standardized, and the testing environment kept free from all unintended distractive influences.

4. *Errors due to changes in the person taking the test.* Day-to-day, week-to-week, and year-to-year fluctuations in individuals affect the stability of scores obtained on any series of tests designed to measure the same attribute. Changes in mood, physical health, and circumstances encountered just prior to the testing may contribute to inconsistencies in scores from one occasion to another. Moreover, persons may change over time in the amount they show of the attribute, quality, or trait being measured. Often, measures are specifically developed to pinpoint such trait changes. For example, if an experiment were being conducted to study the effects on anxiety of various aversive conditions (such as electric shock or other noxious stimuli), the anxiety measure must be sensitive to real changes in the subjects' levels of anxiety from one experimental condition to another. It is important, therefore, to distinguish between the effects on test scores of random or fortuitous fluctuations (such as mood and physical health) and the effects of actual changes caused by the dynamic nature of the trait being measured. The former effects are legitimately ascribed to measurement error; they can be reduced somewhat by taking pains to avoid giving the tests to persons who are physically ill, emotionally upset, or otherwise not "up to it" on the day of testing. In contrast, the effects due to dynamic trait variation should *not* be ascribed to measurement error; it is important, instead, that the magnitude of such effects be determined and ascribed to real temporal changes in the status of the individuals being tested.

Estimates of Test and Trait Stability

The above listing of different sources of error in individual differences measurement should make apparent the inadequacy of any single estimate of test stability. Actually, many types of estimates are commonly used, incorporating or excluding various of the error sources mentioned above. In studying any test, it is wise to use several of the major types of stability estimates in order to learn as much as possible about the stability and precision of the test and the stability of the trait being measured.

All the estimates in common use compare scores obtained by persons on two or more tests designed to measure the same attribute or on the same test administered at two or more different times. All methods also yield an index that either is or may be interpreted as a correlation coefficient between scores obtained on the different tests or occasions. The use of the correlation coefficient is appropriate for this purpose because the scatter diagrams based on the same test given twice or on two tests designed to measure the same attribute will almost invariably fulfill the assumptions that are crucial in interpreting the magnitude of r.[2] The three kinds of estimates in common use are listed and discussed briefly below.

1. *Retest estimate.* Rather than develop more than one test of the same attribute, the same test can be administered on two different occasions (usually two to four weeks apart) and the scores correlated. Any departure from a correlation of $+1.00$ reflects errors due to uncontrolled changes in the testing environment and changes in the persons tested. However, it does not reflect errors due to the sampling of item content because the items are the same on both testing occasions. It is also doubtful that errors due to chance response tendencies would be reflected in the correlation between the two sets of scores, because memory may play an important part in the second testing. When forced to guess or to choose random responses, subjects will usually try to be consistent with their previous answers, causing the correlation between scores to yield an overestimate of the actual precision of the test. For any given subject, it is difficult to know how important memory might have been in his retest responses; thus, use of the retest method is inadvisable unless memory can definitely be ruled out as a factor affecting the later scores (for example, by separating the two testings by a very long period).

2. *Internal comparison estimates.* If only one test

[2] The reader may wish to consult the statement about test reliability in the American Psychological Association's *Standards for Psychological and Educational Tests* (3).

has been developed, it can still be subdivided to yield two
or more part scores, and these scores can be correlated to
yield estimates of test precision. A very commonly used approach is to obtain two separate scores for each person—one
on the odd-numbered and one on the even-numbered items—
and to correlate these two sets of scores.[3] This estimate, since
it is based on different sets of items, is influenced by content sampling errors and chance response tendencies. However, since both scores are obtained at the same time, the
estimate does *not* include errors due either to changes in the
testing environment or to changes in the individuals tested.
The internal estimates are primarily indices of a test's
measurement precision at a particular time and in a particular place.

There are many other kinds of internal estimates in
addition to the odd-even method. However, they all are
based on various different ways of subdividing a test (for
example, the first half versus the second half). The logical
extreme is to consider each item as a small test in itself and
to compare the consistency of scores (responses) made by
all subjects on all the items. There are several statistical
procedures for making such item comparisons, but they all
reduce essentially to an estimate based on the pooling of
correlations obtained from all possible ways of subdividing
a test. None of these methods has been shown to have any
particular advantage over the odd-even method. In fact, it
can be argued that they reflect, to an unknown degree, any
effects due to systematic changes during the test taking
period. For example, if fatigue or practice effects occur,
they affect early and late responses quite differently. The
odd-even method counterbalances such effects by sampling
items equally from each portion over the entire test period.
Other split-half methods and the item comparison methods

---

[3] The correlation coefficient between scores on the two half tests is an
estimate of the precision of measurement for the half tests. The Spearman-Brown
Correction is used to estimate the value for the whole test. Thus:

$$r_{11} = \frac{2r_{\frac{1}{2}\frac{1}{2}}}{1 + r_{\frac{1}{2}\frac{1}{2}}},$$

where

r_{11} = estimate for total test,
$r_{\frac{1}{2}\frac{1}{2}}$ = correlation between scores on the two half tests.

do not do so and are potentially affected by systematic temporal changes during the test situation.

3. *Equivalent-form estimate.* One of the best ways for estimating the precision of a psychological measure is to develop two or more separate measures of the same attribute. The two measures must sample the same content domain, contain items of equivalent difficulty and discriminability, and yield highly similar distributions of scores when administered to a group of subjects. When these conditions are met, the equivalent forms may be administered to subjects at separate times (two to four weeks apart) and the separate sets of scores correlated. The resulting estimate reflects all four possible sources of error. The only disadvantage of the equivalent-form method is the extra work usually required to develop two or more forms of the same test, but the usefulness of more than one form for carrying out experimental studies, investigating trait stability, "checking" the accuracy of a person's obtained score, etc., offsets the modest amount of extra labor involved.

Summary of Estimates and Error Sources

Table 2–1 summarizes our discussion of different methods of estimating test precision and the sources of measurement error incorporated by each. It should be clear from the table why it is wise to compute and to compare *all* of the various kinds of estimates rather than only one. The odd-even estimate is probably the best indication of the maximum precision for a single testing situation, but it tells us nothing about possible effects due to changes over time. By comparing the odd-even estimate with item-comparison estimates, we gain some knowledge about possible effects due to systematic changes during the testing situation. And by comparing both of these types of estimate with an equivalent-form estimate, we learn about the additional effects of environmental and personal changes over time. If, in addition, we have taken special pains to standardize the testing situation and to standardize or measure the examinee's condition (physically, emotionally, motivationally), we will gain knowledge about the relative stability of the trait being measured. Finally, over a long period (sufficient to rule out the effects of memory), a comparison of retest and equivalent-form estimates will yield information about the magnitude of possible error effects due to the sampling of item content as well as about the long-range stability of the trait being measured. It is clear that much

TABLE 2–1. Three methods for estimating test precision and types of measurement error incorporated by each estimate.

		SOURCES OF MEASUREMENT			Changes in the person	
		Item content sampling	Chance response tendencies	Changes in testing environment	Fortuitous	Trait change
TYPES OF ESTIMATE	Retest method	Not included	Indeterminate because of memory factor	Included	Included	Included
	Internal comparison Odd-even	Included	Included	Not included	Not included	Not included
	Item-comparison and other subdivision schemes	Included (probably more completely than odd-even because all item comparisons are made)	Included	May include effects due to systematic changes during the test (such as practice, fatigue, environmental changes)	Indeterminate	
	Equivalent form	Included	Included	Included	Included	Included

can be learned about both the precision of a test and the stability of the trait it is designed to measure by carrying out a series of studies to estimate the several types of test precision rather than only one.

Effect of Measurement Error on Relationships between Measures

The size of relationships between any two measures may be limited by the precision or stability with which each is measured. This was the concern Charles Spearman (an early psychometrist) had when he developed his Correction for Attenuation—a correction formula that he believed gave the upper limit of what the correlation between two measures would be if each were measured with perfect precision. Today we know that no simple relation exists between the degree of a test's precision or stability and the magnitude of its relationship (expressed as a correlation coefficient) with other measures. The matter is more complex than the early psychometric theorists believed, and it has not yet been adequately explicated. As an illustration of some of the difficulties, suppose we want to develop a test selection battery to predict employees' involvement in accidents. Very little is known about "accident proneness," but one possibility is that behavioral tendencies toward accidents overgird a dynamic and changing pattern of attitudinal and emotional components; that is, persons may be more and less "prone" toward accidents at different times. If so, we should seek a measure possessing high odd-even precision and sensitive to attitude changes over time; very likely this measure would possess low equivalent-form stability. Such a measure would probably need to be administered periodically—for example, each day—in order to assess each employee's level of "accident proneness" as he reported to work. The measure could conceivably be perfectly predictive of accident behavior; yet no simple or easy relation would exist between the precision and stability estimates and the accuracy of prediction. In contrast, if "accident proneness" consists of a heterogeneous but stable grouping of cognitive and attitudinal components, the requirements of a measure to predict accident behavior are quite different. The heterogeneity of the "trait" would argue for a measure with low internal precision as estimated by item comparison methods but with high stability over time.

The point of all this is that accuracy of prediction demands that we know a great deal about the human qualities or traits being measured and the relative precision of the measures developed to represent them. Perhaps the best way to obtain such knowledge is to compute the various kinds of estimates discussed above. But there is no assurance that predictive accuracy will depend in any known way on the size of any one of the estimates obtained.

Factor Analysis

Factor analysis is a mathematical procedure for identifying the minimum number of dimensions or factors that account for the total pattern or matrix of intercorrelations among a much larger number of measures. Because the correlation coefficient indicates the extent to which two tests measure the same thing,[4] it is the basic statistic for factor analytic studies. Thus, if many tests are administered to a number of persons and r's calculated between every possible pair of tests, the resulting matrix of correlations may be examined to discover groupings or clusters of highly correlated tests. In Table 2–2 we have presented the correlations between all pairs of supervisory ratings of nine different aspects of secretarial job behavior for the comely young ladies we have been discussing in this chapter. The first impression is that nearly all the ratings are positively correlated, but a more careful look shows that some are much more highly related (for example, for A and C, $r = .70$; for B and G, $r = .75$) than others (for example, for A and G, $r = .10$; for D and G, $r = .00$). Examination of the matrix reveals two prominent groupings of rather highly correlated job behaviors. These groupings are more clearly evident in Table 2–3 where the order of the duties has been rearranged. The duties A, C, D, and F are highly correlated, as are the duties B, E, G, and H. Correlations between the two groups (shown in the lower-left and upper-right quadrants) and with the rather specific job duty of coffee making are very low. In factor analysis, highly correlated groupings that also are relatively independent of one another are called *factors*. Examination of the content of the measures making up a factor usually suggests a label or name for the factor. For our data, Factor I (comprising duties A, C, D, and F) involves accuracy and orderliness; we might infer that tests of perceptual accuracy and of behavioral tendencies toward conscientiousness might predict success in Factor I activities. Factor II (comprising duties B, E, G, and H) involves learning ability and initiative; we might infer that tests of inductive reasoning and of behavioral tendencies toward confidence might predict success in Factor II activities. Note that coffee-making proficiency is essentially unrelated

---

[4] Granted, of course, that the necessary assumptions for using r are satisfied.

	A	B	C	D	E	F	G	H	I
A	—	.20	.70	.60	.15	.75	.10	.10	.10
B	.20	—	.30	.00	.50	−.05	.75	.60	.00
C	.70	.30	—	.75	.25	.55	.20	.10	.05
D	.60	.00	.75	—	.05	.60	.00	−.10	.15
E	.15	.50	.25	.05	—	.10	.80	.70	−.05
F	.75	−.05	.55	.60	.10	—	.20	−.10	.20
G	.10	.75	.20	.00	.80	.20	—	.50	−.10
H	.10	.60	.10	−.10	.70	−.10	.50	—	.15
I	.10	.00	.05	.15	−.05	.20	−.10	.15	—

A. Her typing (letters and manuscripts) is accurate and free from error.
B. She goes ahead on her own even when her supervisor is gone or unavailable.
C. She knows where to find things when they are needed.
D. Her work is neat and pleasing in appearance.
E. She almost always understands instructions the first time they are given.
F. She is extremely accurate in posting invoices.
G. She asks questions about things she doesn't understand.
H. She has suggested several improvements leading to increased departmental efficiency.
I. She makes excellent coffee.

TABLE 2–3. *Rearranged correlations from Table 2–2 to show clusters of highly correlated job behaviors.*

	A	C	D	F	B	E	G	H	I
A	—	.70	.60	.75	.20	.15	.10	.10	.10
C	.70	—	.75	.55	.30	.25	.20	.10	.05
D	.60	.75	—	.60	.00	.05	.00	−.10	.15
F	.75	.55	.60	—	−.05	.10	.20	−.10	.20
B	.20	.30	.00	−.05	—	.50	.75	.60	.00
E	.15	.25	.05	.10	.50	—	.80	.70	−.05
G	.10	.20	.00	.20	.75	.80	—	.50	−.10
H	.10	.10	−.10	−.10	.60	.70	.50	—	.15
I	.10	.05	.15	.20	.00	−.05	−.10	.15	—

FACTOR I

A. Her typing (letters and manuscripts) is accurate and free from errors.
C. She knows where to find things when they are needed.
D. Her work is neat and pleasing in appearance.
F. She is extremely accurate in posting invoices.

FACTOR II

B. She goes ahead on her own even when her supervisor is gone or unavailable.
E. She almost always understands instructions the first time they are given.
G. She asks questions about things she doesn't understand.
H. She has suggested several improvements leading to increased departmental efficiency.

I. She makes excellent coffee.

to the other important aspects of secretarial behavior; most husbands and most bosses will probably testify that the only sure way of predicting this highly complex skill is to conduct an actual on-the-job tryout.

We have tried to illustrate with the above greatly simplified example how correlation tables may be studied to yield factors summarizing the underlying similarities among highly correlated measures.

In actual practice, a factor analytic study is rarely so simple as the one we have presented. Usually, many more tests are correlated; electronic computers make possible the computation of correlation matrixes involving hundreds of measures, and the results are rarely so easily discerned through simple inspection as those shown above; it is almost always necessary to employ the more precise and more mathematically sophisticated procedures of factor analysis to discover the factors concealed in the data. Our simple visual analysis does, however, illustrate accurately the essential nature of the outcomes of factor analytic studies, and the method of interpreting factors is basically the same as we have shown for our clusters.

Sampling Variation, Statistical Inference, and Cross-Validation

To be most useful, selection research results from one group or sample of employees must apply also to subsequent applicants. Results obtained from subsequent groups may differ because of chance sampling variations. Thus, in interpreting a correlation coefficient, a difference between means, or any other statistic, it is necessary to estimate how its size might be expected to change in subsequent samples of persons. Two approaches may be taken to this estimation problem.

Statistical Inference

First, the theory and methods of *statistical inference* may be applied. The details of statistical inference are beyond the scope of what we wish to cover in this book, but the reader may refer to any of a number of standard statistics texts (40, 49, 61) for a thorough treatment of it. It is sufficient here to give a rough notion of the reasoning involved. Basically, it is assumed that any particular sample of persons on whom statistics have been computed was selected randomly from an infinitely large population of such persons—that is, each member had an equal chance of being selected. Then the representativeness of the data obtained from the particular sample depends solely on the theoretical amount of sampling variation to be expected among many samples of the same size selected from the hypothetical population. The magnitude of the sampling variation is *inversely* proportional to the square root of the sample size, N. Thus, according to statistical inference, the larger the sample, the smaller the sampling variation.

One of the most common uses of statistical inference by psychologists is to test the so-called *null hypothesis*. In the typical selection study, the null hypothesis assumes that *no* relationship exists between predictor and job behavior measures in the population from which subjects for the study were selected. Statistical inference prescribes methods for testing the tenability of this assumption. If the relationship in the sample is much greater than the amount of chance sampling variation, the null hypothesis is rejected and the results for the sample are said to be "statistically significant."

Null hypothesis testing is a necessary, but far from sufficient, procedure for evaluating the effectiveness of selection research studies. With large samples, even small relationships can be shown to be "statistically significant"; yet small relationships have little usefulness for making practical personnel decisions. It is far more important to decide whether a relationship between predictor and job performance measures is sufficiently large to warrant using the predictor for making personnel decisions than it is simply to show that the relationship is "significantly" greater than zero. Only after deciding that a relationship is large enough to have practical merit should we worry about testing it for "significance." When a relationship does appear to be of practical importance, it is then desirable to apply the methods of statistical inference to estimate its probable error and its expected magnitude in subsequent samples.

On the other hand, it should be clear that even extremely high and seemingly important relationships mean little if they are based on so small a sample (such as our small sample of fifteen secretarial applicants) that we can make no stable estimates of what to expect from future applicants. In selection research, we must strive for a middle ground between sample sizes too small to yield stable results and those so large as to use our resources wastefully and inefficiently.

A useful rule to follow—one spelled out in more detail in Chapter 7—is to base selection studies on about fifty or sixty persons. If a particular test yields a statistically significant relationship in a group of fifty to sixty employees, it is fairly certain that it also will be useful for making personnel decisions and that it will apply about equally well to subsequent groups of applicants. The results will be statistically significant, the relationship will be moderately large, and the chance sampling variation will be moderately small.

Cross-Validation

A far more pragmatic method used to estimate the magnitude of sampling variation is *cross-validation*. It consists simply of selecting another sample of persons and comparing the results obtained in it with those obtained in the first sample. In a sense, cross-validation is an empirical test of the rules of statistical inference. Results obtained on even a small sample can be checked against an independently selected group to confirm or disconfirm the stability of the relationships between tests and job behavior shown in the first sample. If confirmed, the results are said to have "held up" on cross-validation. If not confirmed, the results are said to have "washed out." A number of methods are used for obtaining cross-validation samples. Perhaps the most common is to divide the total sample into two groups—a validation or developmental group and a cross-validation group. Usually the validation group is somewhat larger (perhaps two-thirds of the total sample) in order to assure greater statistical stability due to the larger sample size. A second method is to develop or validate results on all applicants hired during one year and to cross-validate the results on applicants hired during another year. The actual method used in providing a cross-validation sample is not important as long as the two samples are comparable. But it is important to provide a separate and distinct sample in which to confirm or disconfirm the results obtained in another sample.

Cross-validation should be a part of every selection research study. It is the only way of testing directly how well results obtained on one group may be expected to apply to subsequent ones. No assumptions are made about the so-called randomness of either of the groups, and no theories or hypothetical sampling distributions are necessary for testing or inferring the relative stability of the statistics computed.

In summary, then, sampling variation should be handled in selection research by two major methods. First, the samples should be sufficiently large (fifty or sixty) to assure relatively good sampling stability of the statistics computed. Second, cross-validation should be employed in order to provide an actual empirical check on the stability of the results.

chapter three

Measuring
Differences
between
People

The Recognition of Human Differences

For centuries, philosophers speculated about the nature of man. Kant argued against a science of psychology because he believed that human feelings, sensations, images, and thoughts could never be accessible to observation and measurement. But this does not rule out the observation of human *behavior* and of the external conditions or stimuli under which the behavior occurs. The early Greeks were strongly aware of human differences in the ability to learn. Socrates developed and refined tests of how much his students learned, and he used the tests to assess and to enrich their learning. The Greeks also graded boys on an elaborate series of physical tests to keep tab on them as they matured and acquired the skills of manhood. Plato clearly recognized the differing abilities of men and saw the need for accurate assignment of individuals to the particular occupations (soldier, statesman, teacher, etc.) for which they were best suited so that they would make maximum contributions to society.

Measurement of Human Differences

However, true measurement of individual differences (that is, the assignment of quantitative values to observable differences in human behavior) had to await someone with a desire to understand differences between people and who had the wherewithal for developing mathematical methods for measuring such differences. Both the desire and the means were provided by the genius of Sir Francis Galton, who founded the study of individual differences. In his book *Hereditary Genius,* published in 1869, he presented the elements of a system for classifying men according to their eminence (abilities). He stated that true eminence was extremely rare, characterizing only one person out of every 4,000, that *all* human abilities were distributed according to the normal probability curve, and that persons could therefore be classified according to the known frequencies of the normal distribution.

Galton's first efforts (illustrated in Figure 3–1) simply ordered people in a number of broad categories. However, he also recognized the desirability of expressing each person's relative standing in the form of a single score or index, and, to do this, he invented the standard score.

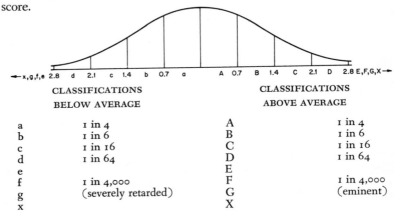

	CLASSIFICATIONS BELOW AVERAGE		CLASSIFICATIONS ABOVE AVERAGE
a	1 in 4	A	1 in 4
b	1 in 6	B	1 in 6
c	1 in 16	C	1 in 16
d	1 in 64	D	1 in 64
e		E	
f	1 in 4,000	F	1 in 4,000
g	(severely retarded)	G	(eminent)
x		X	

FIGURE 3–1. *Galton's classification of persons according to their abilities and the proportion of persons in each class.*

The Development of Psychological Measures

Galton's concern with eminence and the relative contributions made by men to society led him and others to seek ways of measuring human differences in learning ability. At first, it was expected that learning ability should be reflected in such things as sensory sensitivity, quickness of response, and various physical proficiencies. As a consequence, the "mental tests" of the late 1800s consisted of reaction times and measures of tactual sensitivity, keenness of vision and hearing, strength of grip, tapping speed, and the like. However, differences on these measures showed no relation to differences in the ability to learn as reflected by school grades or teachers' ratings of pupil performance.

Toward Complex Processes

In 1895, the French psychologist Alfred Binet published an article severely criticizing the practices of sensory and motor testing. With his colleague Henri, Binet argued that more complex mental processes should be studied; he emphasized the importance of studying and *measuring* the higher faculties such as memory, imagery, imagination, attention, and comprehension—an argument that probably would have been "laughed out of court" had it not been for the groundwork laid by Galton's earlier emphasis on the meaningfulness and importance of measuring individual differences and the classification of persons "according to their natural abilities."

During the next decade, Binet tried a number of short tasks designed to tap the complex mental processes of school children. He reasoned that as children grow they are exposed to similar things, and they have opportunities to learn and to develop skills in dealing with the world they live in. He thought mental ability might be estimated by simply observing how a child copes with tasks similar to the ones he has faced in his day-to-day activities. Binet asked youngsters to identify familiar objects, name the months in order, name coins, arrange scrambled words into meaningful sentences, and define abstract words. These tasks obviously were far more complex and closer to the kind of functioning demanded in the real world than the reaction-time, sensory, and motor tests being espoused by most of the laboratory psychologists of the time.

Binet was an *empiricist* who did not completely trust his own judgment for choosing test items. He demanded that children's responses to each of his test tasks be compared with other aspects of their behavior. He reasoned that, to be useful, a test item should yield different responses from children identified by their teachers as quick learners and those identified as slow learners. Thus, Binet was probably the first psychologist to use methods of *item analysis* to decide whether responses to any given item were or were not related to important behaviors outside the test. As we shall see, this *empirical* approach to test development has much to recommend it and is, in fact, the method used by the authors of nearly all our more widely used and most effective psychological tests today.

In Binet's approach, children of the same age were rated by their teacher as "quick" and "slow" learners, and these ratings were compared with the children's performance on several simple tasks. (See hypothetical data in Table 3–1.)

TABLE 3–1

| | PERCENTAGE OF CHILDREN PERFORMING TASK CORRECTLY | | DIFFERENCE |
	Quick Learners (N = 10)	Slow Learners (N = 10)	(Quick − Slow)
Task 1: Count to five without error.	60%	20%	+40%
Task 2: Follow a lighted match with the eyes.	90	100	−10
Task 3: Use the word *home* correctly in a sentence.	80	60	+20
Task 4: Define the meaning of the word *sorry*.	20	0	+20
Task 5: Point to objects of different colors, red, yellow, and blue.	70	20	+50

Tasks 1 and 5 discriminate sharply between quick and slow learners. Many more quick learners perform the two tasks correctly. Tasks 1 and 5 can be said, therefore, to be good indicators of whatever behaviors are involved in this particular teacher's rating of learning ability; tasks 2, 3, and 4 are poor indicators. Tasks 1 and 5 are worthy of further study as possible measures of learning ability or "intelligence." However, knowledge about these tasks would need to be extended in a number of ways. Since the numbers of children used for this comparison were so small, it would be well to repeat the study on other children to see whether the same two tasks prove to be best. This would provide other sets of teacher observations against which to compare the results. Moreover, it would be well to obtain information on other kinds of estimates of learning ability. Another one Binet used was a simple age comparison; he assumed that older children, because of their greater exposure to learning situations and because of their greater growth, should develop more ability to learn than younger children.

The Empirical Method of Test Development

We have gone into detail in describing Binet's approach because it so aptly illustrates the crucial steps in the empirical development of psychological measures.

First, people are observed to differ in a particular behavior—a behavior sufficiently important to society that it seems worthwhile to seek to understand it better. For Binet, the important behavior was *learning ability.*

Second, behavioral observations are made of a number of individuals; they are rated, labeled, or categorized according to the amount they show of the behavior being studied. For Binet, teacher's ratings, school attainment, and age comparisons served this purpose.

Third, a series of standardized tasks, questions, statements, or other stimuli are prepared which seem to be related to the behavior being studied. As we have seen, Binet rejected sensory and motor testing in favor of developing more complex tasks that seemed more accurate indicators of learning ability.

Fourth, the stimuli are presented to the individuals whose behavior has been observed; their responses are studied (item analysis) to discover which stimuli elicit behavior related to the behavior being studied. Most psychological measures *do not* measure the relevant behavior directly. As Chauncey and Dobbin (11) have pointed out, this method of empirically studying the responses to test items is very much like the methods used by physicists to detect the forces released by the atom. The cloud chamber does not measure the atom or its components directly, but the tracks of ionizing particles do permit deductions about the nature of the atom and the forces holding it together. In the same way, responses shown to be related to observations of the behavior we label *learning ability* enable the psychologist to deduce things about learning ability. Binet's greatest contribution was his application of empirical methods to the measurement of an important area of human behavior.

Measuring Intelligence

In 1905, the first Binet Test, consisting of thirty tasks ranging from very simple to rather difficult, was published and began to be used in the Paris schools. He called his series of tasks a *metrical scale of intelligence,* and with this contribution Binet set off an immediate worldwide response.

It was soon apparent to other investigators that the Binet Test yielded accurate estimates of children's mental status and good predictions of school accomplishment. In this country, Lewis Terman of Stanford University translated, revised, and greatly extended the Binet Test. In 1916, his Stanford-Binet Test was published; it consisted of ninety tasks arranged in order of increasing difficulty. Terman chose to express scores on the test as an Intelligence Quotient (IQ),[1] the ratio (multiplied by 100) between an individual's "mental age" (calculated from the tasks he successfully completed) and his chronological age. With this test, the measurement of individual differences came of age; an important aspect of human variation had been studied and a measure successfully developed. This development was met with a widespread response of research activity directed toward learning more about this new test and the nature of the underlying construct (intelligence) it was designed to measure.

The General Factor, Factor Analysis, and Multiple Factors

Charles Spearman, an English statistician and contemporary of Binet's, held (68) that humans possessed an underlying *general intelligence* or *g* factor accompanied by a myriad of *specific* abilities called *s* factors. He argued that a high correlation between grades in French and grades in the study of the classics was evidence of the common action of the underlying ability, *g*, but that the correlation was less than perfect because of the singular actions of abilities specific to the study of French and to the study of the classics.

The correlational procedures Spearman used to support his theoretical statements about intelligence marked the beginning of *factor analysis*. As we noted in the last chapter, factor analysis is a method for summarizing the correlations among a large number of measures in terms of a smaller number of clusters or factors. It is presumed that the factors constitute relatively more basic or fundamental dimensions underlying the many different measures on which the correlation matrix is based.

Subsequent factor analysts, notably L. L. Thurstone and J. P. Guilford, have argued that several factors are necessary to account for the range of observable differences among people. Intelligence appears to be many faceted, made up of a number of broad groupings of relatively

---

[1] The choice of IQ as a method of expressing scores was unfortunate, for it implied that "intelligence" was a global, all-encompassing, and unchanging human quality. The IQ came to be widely misinterpreted and misused. Finally, in 1960, it was decided to express scores on the third edition of the Stanford-Binet Test in terms of standard score units with a mean of 100 and a standard deviation of 16.

independent aptitudes. For example, Thurstone concluded that the major cognitive abilities of man could be grouped into seven categories:

Verbal comprehension: to understand the meaning of words and their relations to each other; to comprehend readily and accurately what is read; measured by test items such as:

Which one of the following words means most nearly the same as *effusive?*
1. evasive
2. affluent
3. gushing
4. realistic
5. lethargic

Word fluency: to be fluent in naming or making words, such as making smaller words from the letters in a large one or playing anagrams; measured by test items such as:

Using the letters in the word *Minneapolis,* write as many four letter words as you can in the next two minutes.

_____
_____
_____
_____

Number aptitude: to be speedy and accurate in making simple arithmetic calculations; measured by test items such as:

Carry out the following calculations:

346	8732	422 × 32 = _____
+722	−4843	3630 ÷ 5 = _____

Inductive reasoning: to be able to discover a rule or principle and apply it to the solution of a problem, such as determining what is to come next in a series of numbers or words; measured by test items such as:

What number should come next in the sequence of the following five numbers?

1   5   2   4   3

1. 7
2. 1

3. 2
4. 4
5. 3

Memory: to have a good rote memory for paired words, lists of numbers, etc.; measured by test items such as:

> The examinee may be given a list of letters paired with symbols such as:

> A *   E ?
> B ,   F ;
> C ☆   G :
> D !   H .

> He is given a brief period to memorize the pairs. Then he is told to turn the page and write the appropriate symbols after each of the letters appearing there.

Spatial aptitude: to perceive fixed geometric relations among figures accurately and to be able to visualize their manipulation in space; measured by test items such as:

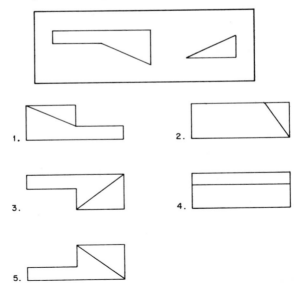

Which figure would result if the two pieces in the picture above were put together?

Perceptual speed: to perceive visual details quickly and accurately; measured by test items such as:

Make a check mark in front of each pair below in which the numbers are identical.

1. 367773————367713
2. 471352————471352
3. 581688————581688
4. 324579————334579
5. 875989————876898

Empiricism and Factor Analysis

At this point, it is well to note some of the differences between Binet's approach to measuring intelligence and the factor-analytic approach. First, even though Binet did believe that human cognitive ability (intelligence) consisted of a number of faculties such as imagination, memory, attention, and comprehension, he made no pretense of separately identifying and measuring each one. Instead, he found it more useful to define intelligence as the sum total of a student's proficiency on all the problems or test items. This approach differs from that of factor analysis because factor analysis seeks to classify human abilities according to the patterns of their similarities and differences as expressed by correlation coefficients.

Second, as we have seen, Binet's justification for the selection of test items was an empirical relationship between success on an item and some observation of nontest behavior such as teachers' ratings or other estimates of school success or intellectual growth. In contrast, factor analysis is directed toward sampling and classifying adequately a large domain of *tested* abilities. The names or labels given to factors (such as Inductive Reasoning, Number Ability, or Word Fluency) are based on the investigator's knowledge of or presumptions about the content of the tests making up a factor rather than on any effort to classify observed behavior outside the test. This characteristic of the factor-analytic approach is one reason why efforts to show relationships between scores on factorially developed tests and nontest behavior are often disappointing. As we shall see in Chapters 4 and 5, job behavior and behavioral observations of persons on jobs appear to be very complex factorially. We should not be surprised, therefore, to learn that any one factor of tested ability may be only a limited sampling and, therefore, a rather poor indicator of the complex behaviors demanded in most job situations. Because of this, it is often necessary to combine several of the factored tests of ability, and in many instances it is more efficient to use Binet's empirical approach.

Nevertheless, the classification of human tested abilities is important theoretically, and such a taxonomy may also take on added practical significance when more clearly defined and more complete classifications of nontest and job behaviors become available. Because of this, the work of factor analysts has continued unabated. By analyzing human tested abilities more and more thoroughly (for example, by factor analyzing sets of tests *within* each of the broad groupings defined by Thurstone), nearly 60 additional factors have been found.

The Three Faces of Intellect

In 1956 Guilford (38, 39) summarized his own and others' factor-analytic results, systematizing for the first time the many factors observed. He viewed mental organization as lying along three dimensions. Along one dimension are the *operations* (the things a person can do); along a second are the *contents* (the kinds of material or content on which the operations may be performed); and along the third dimension are the *products* (the outcomes or results of the operations being performed on one or more of the contents). The classifications within each of the three areas are as follows:

Operations

1. Cognition—becoming aware of the existence of something.
2. Memory—remembering what was once known.
3. Convergent Thinking—organizing content in such a way as to produce a single correct solution to a problem.
4. Divergent Thinking—utilizing content to produce a wide range or variety of possible solutions to a problem.
5. Evaluation—making judgments or decisions.

Contents

1. Semantic—contents involving language.
2. Symbolic—contents involving numerical ideas and concepts.

3. Figural—contents involving various configurations, patterns, or shapes.

4. Behavioral—contents involving the way persons behave toward one another.

Products

1. Units—bits of information.

2. Classes—groupings of units.

3. Relations—similarities, differences, and contingencies among classes.

4. Systems—groupings of relations.

5. Transformations—concepts of how things change.

6. Implications—projections of concepts to deduce events that have not yet been observed.

According to Helmstadter (50), a person performing successfully all the operations containing semantic content would be said to have high verbal ability; a person performing all operations containing symbolic content would have high mathematical ability; one performing effectively the operations with figural content would have high spatial or artistic ability; and a person who could recognize, remember, solve, and evaluate contents involving interpersonal behavior would be said to possess high social ability.

Obviously, Guilford's suggested taxonomy of human abilities is a far cry from the intentions of Binet when he set out rather simply to develop indicators of school learning ability. Even so, it is interesting that Binet's early tests and certainly the 1960 revision of the Stanford-Binet Test include items sampling many of the factors suggested by Guilford's classification. The most notable lack, perhaps, is in the Operations area of Divergent Thinking. School performance, teachers' ratings, learning ability, etc., have typically emphasized convergent thinking—that is, finding a single correct answer to problems. It is no surprise that Binet "missed" this important aspect of human ability; he based his selection of items on ratings of nontest behaviors that failed to emphasize divergent thinking abilities. Only recently have psychologists and educators come to recognize the potential importance of the divergent thinking abilities in jobs placing a premium on creativeness and originality. The rationally derived tests of divergent thinking may fill the gap caused by Binet's early dependence on behavioral observations that were incomplete estimates of the ability to cope successfully with problems. Raw empiricism may succeed in developing good indicators of nontest behaviors, but it may miss important aspects of human variation if the criterion observations of the nontest behaviors are deficient or limited in some way. Ideally, both methods should be employed as we seek to measure individual differences and to understand human behavior more fully. The history of the development of our present knowledge of what constitutes human intelligence and the specification of the wide variety of human abilities is a clear illustration of the interactive and additive contributions of the two methods.

Measuring Other Human Differences

Motor Skills

So far, we have traced and discussed the development of measures of human cognitive abilities—those abilities crucial in developing an awareness and understanding of the elements of our environment. We have said nothing about the physical manipulation of objects in the environment. This involves the specification and measurement of *motor skills,* many of which have obvious relevance to the world of work. For example, the job of secretary involves not only a wide range of cognitive abilities such as verbal comprehension, perceptual speed, memory, and reasoning, but also, possibly, whatever motor skills may be necessary to handle a typewriter adequately. Scores of other jobs could be named (for example, bricklayer, auto mechanic, and watch repairman) that require relatively greater amounts of motor proficiency. Thus, the measurement of motor abilities is also important if an effective job of personnel selection and placement is to be done.

The major conclusion from a wealth of research on motor skills is that these abilities are highly specific. Tests designed to measure skills such as finger dexterity, steadiness, speed of response, and eye-hand coordination show only low intercorrelations. Summarizing over a decade of factor-analytic results with motor skills tests, Fleishman (23) concluded that there are eleven fairly independent groupings of motor skills. These are:

> 1. *Control precision,* involving tasks requiring finely controlled muscular adjustments, such as moving a lever to a precise setting.

2. *Multilimb coordination,* involving the ability to co-ordinate the movements of a number of limbs simultaneously, such as packing a box with both hands.

3. *Response orientation,* involving the ability to make correct and accurate movements in relation to a stimulus under highly speeded conditions, such as reaching out and flicking a switch when a warning horn sounds.

4. *Reaction time,* involving the speed of a person's response when a stimulus appears, such as pressing a key in response to a bell.

5. *Speed of arm movement,* involving the speed of gross arm movements where accuracy is not required, such as gathering trash or debris and throwing it into a large pile.

6. *Rate control,* involving the ability to make continuous motor adjustments relative to a moving target changing in speed and direction, such as holding a rod on a moving rotor.

7. *Manual dexterity,* involving skillful arm and hand movements in handling rather large objects under speeded conditions, such as placing blocks rapidly into a form board.

8. *Finger dexterity,* involving skillful manipulations of small objects (such as nuts and bolts) with the fingers.

9. *Arm-hand steadiness,* involving the ability to make precise arm-hand positioning movements that do not require strength or speed, such as threading a needle.

10. *Wrist-finger speed,* involving rapid tapping movements with the wrist and fingers, such as transmitting a continuous signal with a telegraphic key.

11. *Aiming,* involving an extremely narrow ability defined by a test in which the examinee places dots in circles as rapidly as possible.

Unfortunately, not much research has been done on the relative importance of each of these basic motor skills in successfully performing various industrial tasks. However, tests are available to measure each of the above abilities, either singly or in combination, and one or several of them may be added to a selection and placement test battery on the basis of job analysis results (job analysis procedures and their implications for test selection are discussed in Chapter 4).

Typical Behavior Measures

Cronbach (12) has chosen the term *maximum performance* measures to denote tests of cognitive and motor abilities. Such tests are designed primarily to determine how much a person can do or how well he can perform on any given test. In contrast, a number of tests have been developed with no distinction between so-called right and wrong answers. Cronbach calls these tests *typical behavior* measures. These are the tests of attitudes, interests, personality, and the like; their prime purpose is to yield descriptions of an individual's typical behavior as he pursues his daily activities. There are no right or wrong answers except as they are descriptive of individual behavioral tendencies; instead of just one scoring key, such inventories tend to have several—each representing a mode or pattern of observed behavior relevant for describing differences between people. Information of this kind has obvious potential importance for making selection decisions because it indicates the pattern of behavior to be expected from a person after he has been placed on a job.

As a means of describing the kinds of typical behavior tests available, we can consider the methods used for developing such tests and some of the results obtained. The three major methods are *armchair theoretic, factor analytic,* and *empirical.*

THE ARMCHAIR THEORIST

Based on his pet theory of human behavior, a test developer might simply sit at his desk (or in his armchair) and devise a set of stimulus materials (such as verbal statements, ambiguous pictures, inkblots) to be used in eliciting responses from persons. He would then administer the test materials to a group of persons and decide, on the basis of his theory, what their responses might mean in terms of each person's major behavior tendencies. The final step would be to confirm or disconfirm the behavioral inferences by observing and measuring the actual subsequent behavior of the persons tested. However, this last step is very rarely undertaken by users of this method. Instead, evaluation of such tests usually occurs from the same place they were created—the armchair.

It should be obvious that the armchair approach has little to recommend it for developing tests useful in selection and placement programs. Most existing behavioral theories have at best doubtful validity, and it is unlikely that any test developer is so omniscient that he can accurately intuit what a person's responses to a set of stimuli may mean in terms of later observed behavior. Unfortunately, however, many tests and methods of this kind are still being used in industrial selection programs. Some examples of such methods are handwriting analysis, the Rorschach Test, and the Thematic Apperception Test.

THE FACTOR ANALYST

The factor-analytic approach should already be fairly familiar from our discussion of developing and defining cognitive and motor skill measures. Its use in developing typical behavior tests usually begins with a lengthy listing of terms (for example, all possible adjectives) or statements commonly used to describe human behavior. Observers then use the terms in rating or describing the actual behavior shown by persons who are well known to them. For example, sorority or fraternity members might describe each other, or clinical psychologists might describe their patients. The descriptions can then be correlated and factor analyzed to yield the basic dimensions (taxonomy) of typically observed human behaviors. This approach has been used in many studies and as a basis for developing many inventories. Eight such studies have recently been summarized by Tupes and Christal (76). The persons rated in the various studies ranged from airmen with only high school education to male and female college students and first-year graduate students. The observers carrying out the ratings ranged from psychologically unsophisticated persons (for example, the airmen) to clinical psychologists and psychiatrists with years of experience in observing human behavior. In spite of these wide differences among subjects and raters, the same five factors of typical behavior emerged from all studies.

1. *Surgency*—the tendency to be assertive, talkative, outgoing, and cheerful as opposed to being meek, mild, and reserved.

2. *Agreeableness*—the tendency to be good natured, cooperative, emotionally mature, and attentive to people.

3. *Dependability*—the tendency to be orderly, responsible, conscientious, and persevering.

4. *Emotional stability*—the tendency to be poised, calm and self-sufficient.

5. *Culture*—the tendency to be imaginative, cultured, socially polished, and independently minded.

The factor-analytic approach has a good deal to recommend it because it starts with observable behavioral tendencies and seeks to identify the minimum number of dimensions necessary for usefully describing the behavior shown by people in normal day-to-day intercourse. As suggested by the Tupes and Christal summary, factor-analytic studies have yielded a stable and useful classification of different modes of human interpersonal behavior. Tests designed to measure these behavioral tendencies are available and warrant inclusion in experimental selection and placement test batteries.

THE EMPIRICIST

The empiric approach follows much the same pattern of test development used by Binet and outlined in the early pages of this chapter. Whereas Binet was seeking a measure indicative of learning ability, the method has been employed to identify other patterns of behavior. The method has been used with notable success to identify the characteristic patterns of likes and dislikes of persons who have entered and persisted in a variety of professions (physician, lawyer, engineer, personnel director, etc.) and skilled trades (electrician, plumber, carpenter, etc.). In these instances, the behavior chosen for study has been occupational choice and occupational persistence, and the groups against which the statements of various kinds of likes and dislikes have been compared (item analyzed) are classified simply on the basis of occupational belonging. Two of the most widely used and successful measures of vocational interest were developed in this way— the *Strong Vocational Interest Blank* (SVIB) and the *Minnesota Vocational Interest Inventory* (MVII).

Other patterns of behavior, less easily defined and specified, have been used as a basis for test development. For example, the first scales of the widely used *Minnesota Multiphasic Personality Inventory* (MMPI) were chosen by comparing responses of groups of persons with different psychiatric disturbances (paranoia, schizophrenia, severe depression, etc.) with those given by emotionally undisturbed ("well") persons. Thus, the MMPI has come to play an important role in psychiatric diagnosis.

A similar test is the *California Psychological Inventory* (CPI).

In this test the responses have been validated against "normal" patterns of observed behavior (such as dominance, sociability, social maturity, achievement motivation, etc.). Here, the behavioral criterion consisted of ratings of observed behavioral patterns occurring in everyday life. Item responses differentiating persons with different rated behaviors were chosen and scored to form the various scales; thus, the typical behaviors measured by the CPI are potentially more relevant to the world of work than the psychiatrically relevant behaviors tapped by the MMPI. Table 3-2 shows the test author's listing of the kinds of behaviors that research has shown are associated with high and low scores on each of the CPI scales.

Since the empirical method is so strongly behaviorally based, it is the most desirable method for developing typical behavior tests. Consider, for example, the relative degree of confidence that may be attached to behavioral inferences based respectively on armchair and on empirically developed tests. Experience shows the chances to be extremely slight that inferences derived from armchair inventories will prove valid. This is because so many *untested* assumptions necessarily lie between the enunciation of a behavior theory and the ultimate observation of behavior in the real world. Even if the major elements of· a behavior theory undergirding a test were essentially correct (and this, unfortunately, is extremely unlikely for most of psychology's present "theories"), there would be no assurance that the stimuli (test items) chosen intuitively or the theorists' inferences about the behavioral meaning of an examinee's responses would have any semblance of reality or fact.

In contrast, the empirical method places no such burden on the shoulders of the test author. He simply accumulates experimental evidence that certain test item responses are or are not associated with certain defined patterns of behavior in the real world, and he chooses for his test those responses that are empirically related to the particular pattern of behavior he is interested in. There probably is no more clear example of the failure of the armchair method than of the failure of early sensory tests to reflect the real world of human behavior. Binet was successful because he broke with current theorizing and proceeded to select his test stimuli on empirical rather than on theoretical grounds.

POSSIBLE PROBLEMS WITH EMPIRICISM

It is imperative in the development of any test or specialized scoring key to determine the relative stability of the association between item responses and behavior patterns. It is possible, particularly if only

TABLE 3-2. *Class I: measures of poise, ascendancy, and self-assurance.*

HIGH SCORERS TEND TO BE SEEN AS:	SCALE AND PURPOSE	LOW SCORERS TEND TO BE SEEN AS:
Aggressive, confident, persistent, and planful; as being persuasive and verbally fluent; as self-reliant and independent; and as having leadership potential and initiative.	1. Do (*dominance*). To assess factors of leadership ability, dominance, persistence, and social initiative.	Retiring, inhibited, commonplace, indifferent, silent and unassuming; as being slow in thought and action; as avoiding situations of tension and decision; and as lacking in self-confidence.
Ambitious, active, forceful, insightful, resourceful, and versatile; as being ascendant and self-seeking; effective in communication; and as having personal scope and breadth of interests.	2. Cs (*capacity for status*). To serve as an index of an individual's capacity for status (not his actual or achieved status). The scale attempts to measure the personal qualities and attributes which underlie and lead to status.	Apathetic, shy, conventional, dull, mild, simple, and slow; as being stereotyped in thinking; restricted in outlook and interests; and as being uneasy and awkward in new or unfamiliar social situations.
Outgoing, enterprising, and ingenious; as being competitive and forward; and as original and fluent in thought.	3. Sy (*sociability*). To identify persons of outgoing, sociable, participative temperament.	Awkward, conventional, quiet, submissive, and unassuming; as being detached and passive in attitude; and as being suggestible and overly influenced by others' reactions and opinions.
Clever, enthusiastic, imaginative, quick, informal, spontaneous, and talkative; as being active and vigorous; and as having an expressive, ebullient nature.	4. Sp (*social presence*). To assess factors such as poise, spontaneity, and self-confidence in personal and social interaction.	Deliberate, moderate, patient, self-restrained, and simple; as vacillating and uncertain in decision; and as being literal and unoriginal in thinking and judging.
Intelligent, outspoken, sharp-witted, demanding, aggressive, and self-centered; as being persuasive and verbally fluent; and as possessing self-confidence and self-assurance.	5. Sa (*self-acceptance*). To assess factors such as sense of personal worth, self-acceptance, and capacity for independent thinking and action.	Methodical, conservative, dependable, conventional, easygoing, and quiet; as self-abasing and given to feelings of guilt and self-blame; and as being passive in action and narrow in interests.
Energetic, enterprising, alert, ambitious, and versatile; as being productive and active; as valuing work and effort for its own sake.	6. Wb (*sense of well-being*). To identify persons who minimize their worries and complaints, and who are relatively free from self-doubt and disillusionment.	Unambitious, leisurely, awkward, cautious, apathetic, and conventional; as being self-defensive and apologetic; and as constricted in thought and action.

HIGH SCORERS TEND TO BE SEEN AS:	SCALE AND PURPOSE	LOW SCORERS TEND TO BE SEEN AS:
Planful, responsible, thorough, progressive, capable, dignified, and independent; as being conscientious and dependable; resourceful and efficient; and as being alert to ethical and moral issues.	7. *Re (responsibility). To identify persons of conscientious, responsible, and dependable disposition and temperament.*	Immature, moody, lazy, awkward, changeable, and disbelieving; as being influenced by personal bias, spite, and dogmatism; and as under-controlled and impulsive in behavior.
Serious, honest, industrious, modest, obliging, sincere, and steady; as being conscientious and responsible; and as being self-denying and conforming.	8. *So (socialization). To indicate the degree of social maturity, integrity, and rectitude which the individual has attained.*	Defensive, demanding, opinionated, resentful, stubborn, headstrong, rebellious, and undependable; as being guileful and deceitful in dealing with others; and as given to excess, exhibition, and ostentation in their behavior.
Calm, patient, practical, slow, self-denying, inhibited, thoughtful, and deliberate; as being strict and thorough in their own work and in their expectations for others; and as being honest and conscientious.	9. *Sc (self-control). To assess the degree and adequacy of self-regulation and self-control and freedom from impulsivity and self-centeredness.*	Impulsive, shrewd, excitable, irritable, self-centered, and uninhibited; as being aggressive and assertive; and as overemphasizing personal pleasure and self-gain.
Enterprising, informal, quick, tolerant, clear-thinking, and resourceful; as being intellectually able and verbally fluent; and as having broad and varied interests.	10. *To (tolerance). To identify persons with permissive, accepting, and non-judgmental social beliefs and attitude.*	Suspicious, narrow, aloof, wary, and retiring; as being passive and overly judgmental in attitude; and as disbelieving and distrustful in personal and social outlook.
Co-operative, enterprising, outgoing, sociable warm, and helpful; as being concerned with making a good impression; and as being diligent and persistent.	11. *Gi (good impression). To identify persons capable of creating a favorable impression, and who are concerned about how others react to them.*	Inhibited, cautious, shrewd, wary, aloof, and resentful; as being cool and distant in their relationships with others; and as being self-centered and too little concerned with the needs and wants of others.
Dependable, moderate, tactful, reliable, sincere, patient, steady, and realistic; as being honest and conscientious; and as having common sense and good judgment.	12. *Cm (communality). To indicate the degree to which an individual's reactions and responses correspond to the modal ("common") pattern established for the inventory.*	Impatient, changeable, complicated, imaginative, disorderly, nervous, restless, and confused; as being guileful and deceitful; inattentive and forgetful; and as having internal conflicts and problems.

TABLE 3-2 (cont.). Class III: *measures of achievement potential and intellectual efficiency.*

HIGH SCORERS TEND TO BE SEEN AS:	SCALE AND PURPOSE	LOW SCORERS TEND TO BE SEEN AS:
Capable, co-operative, efficient, organized, responsible, stable, and sincere; as being persistent and industrious; and as valuing intellectual activity and intellectual achievement.	13. Ac (*achievement via conformance*). To identify those factors of interest and motivation which facilitate achievement in any setting where conformance is a positive behavior.	Coarse, stubborn, aloof, awkward, insecure, and opinionated; as easily disorganized under stress or pressures to conform; and as pessimistic about their occupational futures.
Mature, forceful, strong, dominant, demanding, and foresighted; as being independent and self-reliant; and as having superior intellectual ability and judgment.	14. Ai (*achievement via independence*). To identify those factors of interest and motivation which facilitate achievement in any setting where autonomy and independence are positive behaviors.	Inhibited, anxious, cautious, dissatisfied, dull, and wary; as being submissive and compliant before authority; and as lacking in self-insight and self-understanding.
Efficient, clear-thinking, capable, intelligent, progressive, planful, thorough, and resourceful; as being alert and well-informed; and as placing a high value on cognitive and intellectual matters.	15. Ie (*intellectual efficiency*). To indicate the degree of personal and intellectual efficiency which the individual has attained.	Cautious, confused, easygoing, defensive, shallow, and unambitious; as being conventional and stereotyped in thinking; and as lacking in self-direction and self-discipline.

TABLE 3-2 (cont.). *Class IV: measures of intellectual and interest modes.*

HIGH SCORERS TEND TO BE SEEN AS:	SCALE AND PURPOSE	LOW SCORERS TEND TO BE SEEN AS:
Observant, spontaneous, quick, perceptive, talkative, resourceful, and changeable; as being verbally fluent and socially ascendant; and as being rebellious toward rules, restrictions, and constraints.	16. *Py (psychological-mindedness). To measure the degree to which the individual is interested in, and responsive to, the inner needs, motives, and experiences of others.*	Apathetic, peaceable, serious, cautious, and unassuming; as being slow and deliberate in tempo; and as being overly conforming and conventional.
Insightful, informal, adventurous, confident, humorous, rebellious, idealistic, assertive, and egoistic; as being sarcastic and cynical; and as highly concerned with personal pleasure and diversion.	17. *Fx (flexibility). To indicate the degree of flexibility and adaptability of a person's thinking and social behavior.*	Deliberate, cautious, worrying, industrious, guarded, mannerly, methodical, and rigid; as being formal and pedantic in thought; and as being overly deferential to authority, custom, and tradition.
Appreciative, patient, helpful, gentle, moderate, persevering, and sincere; as being respectful and accepting of others; and as behaving in a conscientious and sympathetic way.	18. *Fe (femininity). To assess the masculinity or femininity of interests. (High scores indicate more feminine interests, low scores more masculine.)*	Outgoing, hard-headed, ambitious, masculine, active, robust, and restless; as being manipulative and opportunistic in dealing with others; blunt and direct in thinking and action; and impatient with delay, indecision, and reflection.

Table 3-2 is reproduced by permission from the Manual for the California Psychological Inventory by Harrison G. Gough. Copyright, 1957, by Consulting Psychologists Press, Inc.

a few persons have been used as experimental subjects, that apparent response differences may be the result of only random or chance fluctuations. The best way to check stability of any scoring key is *cross-validation,* as discussed in the last chapter. (A similar approach—the one used by Binet—is simply to carry out item analyses on several different groups and to select for the final test or scale only those items and responses showing consistent differences between persons with different observed behaviors—for example, high- versus low-rated learning ability.) The necessity for cross-validation is obvious; it is a safeguard for assuring that empirical results are based on real and not on chance differences. Even so, some tests on the market have *not* been properly cross-validated against the behavioral descriptions they are designed to measure. No confidence can be placed in a typical behavior test that has not been properly cross-validated.

A second problem with empirically developed tests grows out of the very strengths such tests possess. Such a test identifies certain specific behaviors used as the basis for item validation and selection, but little additional meaning can be attached initially to scores on the test. The lack of any cohesive theory during test development and the dependence of item selection on a rather narrowly specified behavior may result in interpretive sterility for scores. A critic of such a test might, for example, say, "Yes, I know that a high score means that a person has likes and dislikes similar to those of lawyers, but what does this *really* mean in terms of the behavior I might expect from such a person?" Such a critic is really asking for further definition of relationships between scores on the test and other observed behaviors. The initial empirical development of a test does not usually provide such additional information. Ordinarily, the test author should assume responsibility, along with other interested researchers, for seeking out and publicizing lawful relations between his measure and additional behavior observations and measures. The process is never ending, and a variety of research methods may be used.

Consider some of the research with the *Strong Vocational Interest Blank.* The first scales showed substantial differences between the likes and dislikes of persons in different occupations, but many questions about the scales remained unanswered. How stable over time were different patterns of response on the SVIB? Which, if any, patterns of occupational interests tended to be relatively more and less similar to one another? Given early in persons' educational or work careers, did occupational interest scales on the SVIB predict tendencies to enter and remain in an occupation or were they useful only for identifying the occupation that a person had already entered? Over many years of research, Strong (71, 72) and others have managed to answer these questions. It is known now that after age 18 or 19, measured interests *are* highly stable individual qualities. It is also known that on the average, male college students scoring high on a specific occupational scale of the SVIB are about four times as likely to be in that occupation nearly twenty years later than college men scoring low on the same scale. Moreover, men most satisfied with their chosen professions at ages 40–45 tend to be those whose measured interests in college were most compatible with their actual career choices. Factor analyses have also aided in understanding the way in which measured vocational likes and dislikes group together—that is, the basic dimensions of vocational interests. Summarizing the results of many such studies, Super and Crites (73) suggest the following major factors of vocational interest:

> Scientific activities
> Social welfare activities (a helpful interest in people)
> Literary, linguistic, and verbal activities (for example, journalism and law)
> Materials manipulation (such as carpentry)
> Systems interests (clerical and business detail jobs)
> Persuasive personal contact activities (a manipulative interest in people)
> Aesthetic expression
> Aesthetic appreciation

These lines of evidence add greatly to what we know about scores on the SVIB. Similar research has been done on many other existing typical behavior inventories, such as the CPI and MMPI. The important point is, that the empirical method of item selection, *crucial* as it is as a first step in test development, still needs to be supplemented by further empirical studies designed to round out the meaning and interpretive significance of scores on the test.

USING TYPICAL BEHAVIOR MEASURES IN SELECTION

Finally, a word should be said about the potential usefulness of typical behavior tests in personnel selection and placement. Though widely used as aids in making selection decisions, the evidence regarding their accuracy for predicting job behavior is far from impressive. Among the major reasons are the following:

1. Only a few of these tests have been developed empirically. Unfortunately, the armchair method still characterizes most of the tests currently being used. Since the initial development of many such tests was not behaviorally based, the odds are not highly in favor of their being related to important aspects of job behavior.

2. For the most part, job behavior has been inadequately studied in selection and test validation studies. At the worst, researchers have merely used global ratings or other crude measures to identify "successful" and "unsuccessful" employees with little or no attention to actual job behaviors making up so-called success or failure in any given setting. In such studies, the two groups have usually scored differently on tests of maximum performance (cognitive and motor tests), probably because the crude success classifications reflect, if anything, the *abilities* necessary for doing the job. On the other hand, the typical behavior measures have usually failed to show differences between the two groups—not an unexpected result in view of the failure to study and to specify carefully the kinds of job behaviors involved. (The importance and methods of careful job behavior observation and measurement are dealt with in detail in Chapters 4 and 5.)

3. Typical behavior tests, as opposed to maximum performance tests, can be slanted or distorted by the examinee. An applicant for any given job probably has a fairly definite impression (though possibly erroneous) of the typical behavior characteristics shown by persons in such jobs. Assuming that he is probably eager to get the job, he may try to convince the examiner, through his replies to the test, that his own typical behavior is consonant with what he perceives to be the desired behavior patterns on the job. This tendency is called "faking the test."

There are no easy or sure answers to this problem. Probably the best answer—not widely employed—is to develop such tests directly on applicant samples and to base item selection on empirical relationships to later observed job behaviors. A myriad of other methods have been tried, such as special item formats ("forced choice") and special faking detection keys. Unfortunately, these methods are too technical and too numerous to warrant further discussion in this brief book.

BIOGRAPHICAL INFORMATION

One of the most promising reasons for developing typical behavior inventories is that one of the best predictors of future behavior is past behavior. Nearly all programs of personnel selection seek to tap elements of past behavior by interviewing, checking references, analyzing application blanks and personal data sheets, reviewing scholastic records, and the like. Unfortunately, it is difficult to know exactly how past behaviors relate to specific future behaviors that may be of interest. The methods mentioned above are usually poorly standardized. The nature and extent of the information attained differ from applicant to applicant; predictions must be based on varying knowledge with the usual result that they can be little more than vague impressions, subjective hunches, and intuitive feelings.

The most commonly used method in selection, the personal interview, is notoriously bad in this regard. It is handled differently by each interviewer, who in turn probably uses different methods with each applicant. At its worst, the personal interview may bog down into merely "passing the time of day," with little time devoted to learning about an applicant's typical past behavior patterns. Under the best conditions, a highly skilled interviewer may be able to gather a wide range of fairly accurate information from the past, but even then it is difficult to interpret the meaning of this data for predicting future behavior; and again reliance must be placed on intuitive hunches and guesses. Some interviewers' hunches turn out to be much better than those of others, but it is difficult to know ahead of time who the better and more accurate interviewers are.

In spite of all this, no one would suggest dispensing with the interview in personnel selection; it is the only way of seeing what the applicant looks like, of getting a feeling for how his personality "clicks" with yours, and of getting acquainted with him as a person. Moreover, it is still the best way for "selling" the company to a promising applicant and of creating in him a good impression of how he was dealt with during the selection process. Thus, as a public relations device, the interview is crucial; as a means of predicting expected future job behavior, it often is not much good.

The best way to capitalize on past behavior for predicting future behavior is to use the empirical method with a standardized biographical inventory to learn what job behaviors may be predicted from various elements of past behavior. In effect, elements of a person's past behavior—marital history, jobs held, activities in high school and college, amount of education, hobbies, past successes and failures, etc.—are treated as separate items to be compared against defined job behavior categories in much the same way that Binet compared performance on test items with learning ability ratings. In this way, items of a biographical inventory may be scored to yield predictions of typical behavior in the future. The resulting typical behavior inventory does not suffer from many of the usual difficulties encountered by personality and interest tests. For example, (1) the inventory is empirically developed; (2) it is linked directly to job behavior, thereby forcing a more careful study of job behavior than has been done for most typical behavior inventories; and, best of all, (3) it is much less likely to be "faked" because it includes information of actual past behavior which can, if necessary, be checked by independent means.

Since biographical inventories first came into wide use about twenty years ago, they have been used in a wide variety of studies and in many selection programs. Very often, a carefully developed typical behavior inventory based on biographical information has proved to be the single best predictor of future job behavior. Thus, biographical information constitutes one of the most fruitful sources of predictive data, to be considered along with measures of cognitive abilities, motor skills, and personality and interest measures.

Conclusions

In this chapter, we have presented a brief history and described the current status of the measurement of individual differences. It may seem that we have strayed far afield from our intended discourse on personnel selection and placement. This is not true, however, for psychology's concern with individual differences broadly summarizes the steps involved in any program of selection research or test validation. Analyzing jobs and job circumstances, and observing and measuring significant job behaviors necessarily precedes the choice of tests in any selection program.

Now, sixty years after Binet's contributions, psychology has available a vast array of tests—some carefully developed and backed by years of research, others hastily thrown together and poorly researched. In this brief chapter, we have presented what we believe to be the major dimensions of human variation. We hope that the reader now possesses a framework for structuring his inferences concerning the cognitive abilities, motor skills, or patterns of typical behavior necessary for getting any particular job done. We urge him to turn to any of a number of standard reference works (2, 4, 9, 12, 29, 41, 50, 70) as aids for choosing the actual tests to be tried in a selection program.

chapter four

Studying
Jobs and
Job Behavior

The prime purpose of personnel selection and placement is to predict job behavior. To do this demands a thorough understanding of jobs and the patterns of job behavior necessary to get them done properly. Compared with psychology's significant accomplishments in measuring human differences, the study of jobs may seem rather unexciting and mundane, beset by difficulties of definition and by dynamic fluctuations in job content that often make careful study seem thankless and never ending. Consider, for example, the problems involved in studying even such a seemingly straightforward job as that of salesman.

Job Analysis

The term *salesman* is too broad to mean very much. As a job label, it encompasses a great diversity of job duties, products, markets, customers, and human endeavors. The label itself is behaviorally sterile, suggesting almost nothing about actual job behaviors or job requirements. Thus, a first step in studying the job of salesman would necessarily involve learning about the content of the particular sales job in which we might be interested. We would gather background information about the firm's products, its customers, sales objectives, and sales organization. Persons currently employed as salesmen could provide data about specific job objectives, job duties, work situations, and characteristic patterns of behavior necessary for getting the job done. The result of all this data gathering would be a systematic account of the sales job, usually called a *job description*.

The job description could be used, in conjunction with our knowledge of measurable human differences, to infer the kinds of abilities, interests, experiences, and background factors desirable in any applicant. These inferences would be highly subjective, but they could at least shape the direction for further inquiry to include a study of the degree of relationship between predictor measures and sales job behavior measures. The central role of job analysis information is to provide the basic clues for choosing potentially useful predictor measures and for developing the measures of job behavior we desire to predict.

Problems and Definitions

To be maximally useful, however, the information must be *behavior-centered*. Let us consider briefly some of the major issues, problems, and obstacles that must be resolved if we are to do an adequate job of pinpointing the actual behavioral requirements of any job.

1. WHAT IS A JOB?

Our casual use of the term job up to now has probably implied an easy answer to the question. Yet job titles in industry may have little behavioral meaning; for our purposes, *A job is a relatively homogeneous cluster of work tasks carried out to achieve some essential and enduring purpose in an organization.* A job is a grouping of tasks that appear to "go together" in some meaningful sense—tasks similar in kind or content, tasks posing common requirements, or tasks for which the only common ground is that employees who perform one task X are likely also to perform another task Y. Defining jobs at the level of work tasks assures greater attention to actual job behaviors and behavior requirements; this in turn aids us in looking beyond existing job labels when we carry out selection research.

2. WHAT IS JOB ANALYSIS?

Job analysis consists of defining the job and discovering what the job calls for in employee behaviors. A job analysis focuses on observable employee behavior. For example, after defining a sales task cluster, a job analysis would proceed to pinpoint the behavioral requirements for the job. Some or all of the following might be listed:

1. Presenting ideas forcefully.
2. Operating comfortably under time pressure.

3. Originating new approaches to selling.

4. Showing no reluctance in asking for the order.

5. Discerning accurately the reactions and feelings of customers and prospects.

Specified in a job analysis, then, are the actual behaviors to be measured and predicted by our selection and placement methods. At the same time, the behavioral specifications derived from job analyses will prove unusually useful in other personnel procedures—for example, in specifying training needs, designing compensation procedures, and developing performance evaluation methods.

3. JOB DYNAMICS

Even when great care has been taken to identify relatively homogeneous task clusters and to list the defining behaviors of a job, we are still faced with the likelihood that the job will change over time. Job analysis must take account of and seek to estimate the effects of potential agents of change. There are at least three major agents:

Time-determined changes. Farmers, guides, part-time workers, and Santa Claus have jobs that change with the seasons. Most other jobs also change with time. An executive does things when he is preparing the annual budget that are different from what he does when conducting labor contract negotiations. Similarly, the tasks of factory workers change according to production schedules, and research or engineering jobs show a wide range of content from the beginning to the end of a development project. These kinds of changes are not difficult to handle in a job analysis because they can usually be anticipated and varying behavioral requirements specified ahead of time.

Somewhat more difficult to handle are job changes due to the employee's acquisition of experience. For example, behavior specifications on entry jobs might emphasize observing the work of others, seeking supervisory assistance when necessary, and avoiding self-initiated job short-cuts. Later on, these behaviors would diminish in favor of more productive activities. The job analyst must take account of changes such as these, and the design of selection research should specify the exact job behaviors to be predicted.

Employee-determined changes. Without a doubt, the behavioral demands of most industrial jobs are modified by what different employees bring to their jobs. In these instances it is unreasonable to assume that a task cluster is fixed and unchanging or that duties are not defined in part by the persons assigned to the jobs. Many managers are assigned broad administrative goals, for example, but are allowed a considerable latitude in the way they accomplish them. Jobs in areas such as selling, teaching, engineering, and research are invariably of this type. By contrast, there are other jobs—precision assembly or inspection tasks, for example—that permit only a minimum of employee-determined changes.

When the activities of a job are defined to any significant degree by the specific persons assigned to the job, it is necessary to take account of this during the job analysis. The best way to do this is to sample many employees doing the same job and to enumerate the several methods used to accomplish the broad goals required by the job. Selection would then be devoted to identifying employee characteristics predictive of *any* of the broad acceptable behavioral patterns.

Situation-determined changes. The *job situation* may be defined as the total environmental context within which a job occurs. It is easy to suggest examples of changes in job situations resulting in changes in job behavior requirements. For example, a machine breakdown would necessitate a shift from production to repair duties and might stimulate the addition to the job of preventive maintenance tasks; daily crises would change a supervisor's job away from planning duties and toward more trouble-shooting and problem-solving tasks; changes in the product, the market, or competitors' efforts could stimulate marked changes in the requirements of a sales job.

Situation-determined changes are usually difficult to anticipate during a job analysis. Often they are simply wished out of the picture, and potentially significant factors in the job situation are ignored. As a step in the right direction, it is necessary to identify and describe aspects in the job setting that could potentially alter job content. Such aspects might include any or all of the following:

1. Physical variables—such as safety hazards, illumination, noise level, unique characteristics of work area, and equipment used.

2. People in the situation—such as the supervisor and other persons interacted with, and goals and needs of typical participants in these interactions.

3. Group influences—such as size and nature of work group, informal group goals and norms, social circumstances, and institutional values.

4. Historical antecedents—such as sources of prior job changes, successes or failures of previous job occupants, and past trends and developments in areas like labor relations and recruitment.

5. Qualitative character of the situation—such as the work climate, nature of supervision received, extent of job pressures, and crises.

Anything appearing to be significant earmarks of a given job setting should be included as part of the job definition. Obviously, complex job settings make it difficult to incorporate all elements into a job definition; even the most careful effort to do this will still not rule out situation-determined changes in job content. If a job changes due to situational factors and we have been able to anticipate them, our selection strategies will obtain people who respond successfully to the changes. On the other hand, failure to anticipate such changes can result in hiring persons whose behavioral repertoires are too sparse for successful response.

What Job Analysis Seeks to Discover

The foregoing discussion of job dynamics and our definitions of *job* and *job analysis* may now be used while we consider more specifically the questions that job analysis seeks to answer.

What is the job?

1. What are the broad goals of the larger organization—department, plant, company—of which this job is a part?

2. How is the organization structured to accomplish these goals?

3. What work tasks lead to accomplishing the organizational objectives?

4. How do the work tasks cluster together in terms of similar behaviors or common requirements?

5. Which tasks may be meaningfully grouped together and defined as a job?

Obviously job identification is judgmental. As we have said repeatedly, the job analyst should give major attention to behavioral requirements and not be misled by existing job titles or traditional organizational structures and strictures.

What are the static and dynamic features of the job? As discussed above.

What employee behaviors are demanded by the job? To specify these, the job analyst must consider both present and future demands and, as we have said, possible requirements due to situational changes. He may draw on the experience and judgment of others who know the job and who may be able to specify which employee behaviors are most important.

What "man requirements" may be inferred from these behavior requirements? The prime purpose of job analysis is to learn more about the job behavior we wish to predict with selection and placement procedures. However, we cannot analyze jobs or study the behavior of persons on jobs without forming rather definite opinions about the personal qualities necessary for getting the jobs done. At the most subjective level, we may merely form impressions of what qualities employees on a given job should possess. For example, it might seem that salesmen ought to be extroverted; secretaries, beautiful; jockeys, tiny; artists, creative; and driving teachers, fearless. Such impressions, even though subjective, *do* provide a preliminary basis for choosing the measures to be tried out in a selection program, but they cannot guarantee the utility of the measures tried.

In an effort to reduce the subjectivity involved in inferring man requirements from job analysis data, several far more objective procedures have been developed. For example, the United States Employment Service (USES) has used vocational counselors and trained job analysts for estimating (from job descriptions) the worker trait requirements for 4,000 different jobs. The raters, working independently, agreed well with one another in estimating worker requirements in six broad areas; training time, type of aptitude required, temperamental requirements, interest requirements, physical capacities necessary, and special demands due to unusual working conditions. Based on these ratings, the USES provides job analysis and rating manuals for anyone who desires to follow a more objective method in inferring man requirements from job analyses (20, 21).

How may the desired employee behaviors be observed and measured? Throughout his job analysis, the analyst must be aware of later needs in his selection research, particularly the need to observe and measure job behavior and to compare these measures with the individual differences measures to be used as predictors.

Are there other implications for the overall selection study? The job analysis step in selection or placement studies is a *design phase,* setting the pattern for steps ahead. Answered adequately, each of the questions above will aid in the proper design of the study. But there are other design implications in addition to those intended most directly by our questions. As the job analysis unfolds, any of a number of implications for the broader selection study may appear.

1. The study's feasibility may be questioned. The problem may prove to be too complex to be unraveled in the time available; jobs may be found to be in a rapid state of flux because of organizational changes or external conditions; potential situational factors might be found to contaminate greatly any job behavior measures; or the individuals on the job might be relatively unimportant in determining how well or how poorly the job gets done.

2. Alternatives to the study may appear desirable. Evidence may point to other approaches (such as improved training, an organizational realignment, or changes in recruiting methods) that might prove more profitable than conducting a selection research study.

3. Modifications in the broad, original design may be considered. There are endless examples; for one, if the jobs analyzed were found to provide quick and clear lines of promotion or transfer to other jobs, the personnel decision maker might want to extend his study to cover the "from-to" categories. This would imply the need to study additional jobs and required behaviors to broaden over-all selection or placement goals.

Methods of Job Study

Because many of the traditional and widely used methods for conducting job analyses do not really provide the kind of information we want for selection research, we present them only briefly; methods defining actual job behavior are considered in greater detail.

Where does the job analyst get information about jobs? The sources include the following:

1. Direct observation or on-the-job experience.
2. Interviews with job incumbents and their supervisors.
3. Meetings with higher management and representatives of the personnel function.
4. Questionnaires or checklists completed by job incumbents, their supervisors, or others familiar with the job.
5. Psychological tests and ratings of man requirements.
6. Other sources of available information, such as may be found in training manuals, existing job guides and descriptions, process specifications, various records and reports, and the *Dictionary of Occupational Titles* (77, 78).

The above sources provide starting points for job analyses. Essentially, the first step is to try to get a rough idea of exactly what the job consists of. Our first assumption is that the job is relatively static—that it stays the same over limited periods of time and that it is not changed greatly by different situations or different people. As we have seen, this is usually an oversimplified point of view but it provides a starting point for the more descriptive types of job analysis methods— methods which, because they make static assumptions about jobs, may be called job-centered methods (in contrast to behavior-centered methods).

Job-Centered Methods

Most of the job-centered methods are of historical interest only. Their major purpose is to describe a job as thoroughly as possible in writing. As mentioned above, they deal with the job primarily as a static entity and tend to neglect important elements of job dynamics.

NARRATIVE DESCRIPTIONS

This most widely used job-centered method was first applied to a few factory jobs just before World War I and extensively used during the war by the Army Committee on Classification of Personnel. The general aim is to describe the nature and scope of jobs as currently constituted and apart from the persons performing them. The work is observed, job incumbents are interviewed, and other sources of information are tapped to write job definitions and descriptions. The description of the job of housewife, shown in Figure 4–1, is an

Form USES-546
(2-44)

U. S. DEPARTMENT OF LABOR
BUREAU OF EMPLOYMENT SECURITY
UNITED STATES EMPLOYMENT SERVICE

Budget Bureau No. 44-R577.3

JOB ANALYSIS SCHEDULE

1. Job title ___ Bank Clerk's Wife ___

2. Number ___ 102 ___

3. Number employed M ___ 0 ___ F ___ 1 ___

4. Establishment No. ___

6. Alternate titles ___

5. Date ___ 1944 ___

Number of sheets ___

___ Spouse ___

___ Darling ___

8. Industry ___ Family ___

___ Battleaxe ___

9. Branch ___ Local ___

7. Dictionary title and code ___

10. Department ___ Uxorial ___

11. WORK PERFORMED:

Under supervision of Husband (101) and/or Children (104, 105, 106) maintains household. Allocates funds. Purchases supplies. Contrives, invents means and methods of making Bank Clerk's (101) salary support family. (This is considered impossible, or at least improbable, by careful statisticians.) Entertains intelligentsia (friends and own family) and Morons (husband's friends and family). Supervises Dog (103) and other livestock including Husband (101) and Children (104, 105, 106).

Daily Duties:

1. Awakes Clerk (101). Selects suit (selection limited to one). Selects shirt (selection limited to one clean, one soiled and two frayed). Searches for shoes, keys, handkerchiefs, studs. Gives detailed instructions for day's program.
2. Prepares meal. Disburses carfare and/or lunch funds.
3. Dresses children (104, 105, 106).
4. Washes dishes. Scrubs floors, windows, paintwork. Polishes silver, brass, furniture.
5. Plans day's marketing. Calculates expenditures. Compares calculations with available funds. Recalculates. Goes to market with Children (104, 105, 106). Destroys market list as impractical. Improvises new menu according to availability of materials.
6. Arbitrates differences of opinion expressed vociferously and belligerently by Children (104, 105, 106).
7. Washes and irons sheets, shirts, blankets, rugs, underwear.
8. Mends and repairs sheets, shirts, blankets, rugs, underwear, tables, chairs, beds, radio.
9. Compromises differences of opinion. Accepts her own opinion. Rejects Husband's.
10. Exercises Dog (103). Wards off seasonal acquaintances. Takes Dog out when Dog prefers to stay in. Takes Dog in when Dog insists upon staying out. Separates Dog from fights and other turmoils. Relegates Husband (101) to dog-house.

(CONTINUE ON SUPPLEMENTARY SHEETS)

Analyst ___ A. Clurk ___

Reviewer ___

FIGURE 4-1. *Narrative description of the job of wife.* (Used by permission from Laurence Siegel, *Industrial Psychology.* Copyright 1962 by Richard D. Irwin, Inc., Homewood, Illinois.)

12. Experience: None .... Acceptable ..Charm,_poise,_amatory_efficiency_--_past_
.........experience_not_divulged._Complete_knowledge_of_French,_piano;_ballet,_opera,_
.........literature._Ability'_to_handle_butlers,_personal_servants_etc.

13. Training data: Minimum training time—(a) Inexperienced workers.   Varies
                            (b) Experienced workers.   Varies

TRAINING	SPECIFIC JOB SKILLS ACQUIRED THROUGH TRAINING
In-plant (on job) training Continual during the period of employment.	Ability to render first aid, medical advice and treatment and minor surgical assistance. Veterinarian ability. Ability to haggle, wash diapers, iron shirts etc.
Vocational training Continual prior to employment.	twelve hours a day and still look lovely in the evening. Ability to do the work of carpenter, painter, electrician, plumber, cleaning woman, dishwasher, chef, CPA,
Technical training Varies	arbitrator, fashion designer, advisor.
SRW Eng. General education Ability to please, charm and fascinate.	
Activities and hobbies	

14. Apprenticeship: Formal ..No.. Informal .No.. Length required ....
15. Relation to other jobs:
    (a) Promotions from and to, transfers, etc.: ...Promotion_from_'Teen._Eventual_promotion_to_
.........mother-in-law.

    (b) Supervision received: General .... Close ....X....... By ...Husband_(101)........................
                                                      (Title)

    (c) Supervision given: None .... Number supervised ....5..... Titles ..Husband_(101),_Children_
....(104,_105,_106)_and_Dog_(103).
The following items must be covered on supplementary sheets.

PERFORMANCE REQUIREMENTS

    16. Responsibility (consider material or product, safety of others, equipment or process, cooperation with others, instruction of others, public contacts, and the like).
    17. Job knowledge (consider pre-employment and on-the-job knowledge of equipment, materials, working procedures, techniques, and processes).
    18. Mental application (consider initiative, adaptability, independent judgment, and mental alertness).
    19. Dexterity and accuracy (consider speed and degree of precision, dexterity, accuracy, coordination, expertness, care, and deftness of manipulation, operation, or processing of materials, tools, instruments, or gages used).

COMMENTS

20. Equipment, materials, and supplies. : Electrical equipment, vacuum cleaner, duster, mop, broom,
21. Definition of terms.   sewing machine, rolling pin, pressure cooker, snow shovel,
22. General comments.   ash cans, washing machine, black lace and other deceptive
                                devices, eyelashes, girdles, sweaters, lipstick and
                                  perfumes.

FIGURE 4–1 (cont.).

example of the kind of narrative account that might result from this method.

The search and task-finding character of this method promises most—simply because no one has found a way to replace conversation and ordinary observation in job analysis. Even so, the verbal descriptions developed from such conversations are often loosely written, subject to many differences in interpretation, and usually poorly standardized. It is difficult to glean behavioral implications from them and even harder to infer the important human traits necessary for doing the job.

POSITION GUIDES AND TASK SPECIFICATIONS

While a narrative is designed to describe a job as it exists currently, position guides and task specifications provide general outlines and specific details of ideal job content—that is, how a job might better be constituted to eliminate certain deficiencies or to meet certain desired objectives. An example of a position guide would be the outlines sometimes developed to clarify the broad duties of managerial jobs. Task specifications are illustrated by the detailed, step-by-step procedural outline that might be developed for a laboratory technician. These methods may be a starting point for selection studies, but they usually include much that is either difficult to pin down or irrelevant—stated either too broadly to have behavioral meaning or in such detail that the important behavioral elements are difficult if not impossible to discern.

CLASSIFYING DUTIES AND WORK TASKS

We have defined a job as a homogeneous cluster of work tasks directed toward achieving a particular organizational purpose. Thus, perhaps the most promising of the job-centered methods are those that attempt to organize work into more fundamental job units or groupings. As a beginning, this classification process might be accomplished by judgment, grouping together on some rational basis tasks that appear to go together—such as tasks with a common purpose or those dealing with the same objects or work materials or those that seem to involve the same actions or behaviors. But human judgment is very likely to err either by overclassifying (placing tasks together that *really* are different behaviorally) or by underclassifying (not grouping tasks that *do* belong together).

What is really needed for developing task clusters is evidence that the behavior necessary to accomplish the tasks is similar for all of them. One approach is illustrated by the example we gave in our discussion of factor analysis in Chapter 2. In that example, nine specific job tasks were rated in terms of their importance to the job of secretary. The ratings for every possible pair of tasks were correlated and the matrix of correlations factor analyzed. You will remember that the result showed just two broad groupings of tasks—one involving detail work and accuracy, and the other involving doing things on one's own and exercising good judgment. Inferences based on such findings would need to be tested by studies relating predictor measures to actual job behavior measures, but task clustering is very useful and meaningful because it defines *empirically* the basic job behavior groupings that we want to predict in programs of selection and placement. Another distinct advantage is that the ambiguity and poor standardization of verbal descriptions is dissipated and replaced with more objective and behaviorally based statements denoting actual job requirements.

In practice, the starting point for carrying out an empirical task clustering of this type would usually be verbal job descriptions gleaned from any or all of the sources listed previously. From these, job behavior checklists would be developed and utilized, as with the short secretarial checklist. Thus, although beginning with job-centered information, the result is behavior centered. Still, since the basic approach does not *start* with behavior-centered information, it would probably fail to detect many of the possible dynamic qualities of jobs.

Behavior-Centered Methodology (Critical Incidents)

Behavior-centered methods seek to specify the kinds of job behavior satisfying job demands, which are in turn set by organizational purposes and goals. In other words, behavior-centered methods define the job in terms of those behaviors necessary for successfully performing it.

The most direct attack on defining jobs behaviorally has been made in Flanagan's Method of Critical Incidents (22). This method asks supervisors, employees, or others familiar with a job to record critical incidents of job behavior. The incidents are just what the name implies—actual outstanding occurrences of successful or unsuccessful job behavior. Such occurrences are usually recorded in stories or anecdotes. Each one describes (1) what led up to the incident and the setting in which it occurred, (2) exactly *what* the employee did that was so effective (or ineffective), (3) perceived consequences of the critical behavior, and (4) whether such consequences were actually within the control of the employee. After a large number of such incidents are collected, they may be abstracted and categorized to form a composite picture of job essentials. These categories, in turn, form a behaviorally based starting point for developing checklists of task behaviors regarded as crucial to either effective or ineffective performance. The critical incidents method will typically yield both static and dynamic aspects of a job. The anecdotal accounts of what actually happened or of what an employee actually did force attention on situationally determined elements and also on modes of behavior that might be relatively unique to the person being described. Thus, the stance of the typical critical incidents analysis is to "get the whole truth and nothing but the truth" behaviorally speaking. It is a brilliant search technique—startlingly simple in conception, yet fulfilling perfectly the behavioral description requirements of our definition of job analysis. To satisfy these requirements demands a broad sampling of observations of a large number of employees doing their jobs. Thus, the typical critical incidents study may accumulate hundreds or even thousands of incidents in order to assure sufficient coverage of the entire job behavior domain.

A good study to illustrate the use of the approach is the one by Kirchner and Dunnette (54). They asked a large number of sales managers to describe critical incidents in selling. From over 100 such incidents, the following behavioral categories were developed:

1. Following up
   a. on customer complaints.
   b. on special requests.
   c. on orders.
   d. on leads for new business.

2. Planning ahead.

3. Communicating important information to sales managers.

4. Being truthful with customers and managers.

5. Carrying out promises.

6. Persisting with "tough customers."

7. Telling customers about other useful company products.

8. Keeping up with new sales techniques and methods.

9. Initiating new sales approaches.

10. Learning customer requirements and trying to fulfill them.

11. Defending the company's policies.

12. Calling on all accounts.

13. Showing a nonpassive attitude.

Note that the above categories describe actual job behaviors, not broad and ambiguous goals or ultimate purposes. Since the categories also include (by definition) behaviors making the difference between effective and ineffective selling, the listing is particularly useful for selection research. The listing encompasses the situational, time, and man dynamics discussed earlier. This is both an advantage and a disadvantage—a disadvantage because the listed behaviors apply to no one specific job, an advantage because the listing provides the base from which comprehensive task checklists may be developed to discover the relatively homogeneous task clusters for empirical definition of jobs and job behaviors. The beginnings of such a checklist would look like the following:

1. Calls on customers immediately after hearing of any complaints.

2. Discusses complaints with customers.

3. Gathers facts relevant to customers' complaints.

4. Transmits information about complaints back to customers and resolves problems to their satisfaction.

5. Plans each day's activities ahead of time.

6. Lays out broad sales plans for one month ahead.

7. Gathers sales information from customers, other salesmen, trade journals, and other relevant sources.

8. Transmits sales information to manager.

9. Is truthful in dealing with customers.

10. Is truthful in dealing with superiors.

11. Suggests new approaches to selling.

12. Systematically calls on all customer accounts.

It is important to recognize that the job analysis would still not be finished. The checklist simply serves as the basic research instrument for answering the specific job analysis questions outlined earlier. For example:

> 1. *Which tasks may be grouped into relatively homogeneous task clusters?* Answering this question is crucial to the whole enterprise, for the behavior categories will be the major groupings for developing behavior measures and for making job behavior predictions during selection. Factor-analytic methods are perhaps the best for deriving empirical groupings, but it will often be impracticable to carry out the ratings, correlations, and computations demanded by factor analysis. When this is the case, it is still meaningful to group the tasks on *a priori* or logical grounds and to use these categories to structure our observations and predictions of job behavior. In fact, it may often be desirable to predict behaviors related to specific tasks directly and not necessarily undertake any broader grouping of tasks. Thus, it would be meaningful to attempt to predict the sales behavior of "systematically calling on customer accounts" without worrying what other sales tasks the behavior might be related to. The choice of what behaviors to attempt to predict in selection studies and whether to cluster or not to cluster obviously demands good judgment on the part of both the psychologist and management. At this stage management must tell the personnel decision maker just what aspects of job behavior it (management) regards as most important for observation, measurement, and prediction. And the psychologist must educate management in the most sophisticated methods for making accurate and meaningful job behavior predictions.

> 2. *What job dynamics must be taken into account? How does the job change over time? Which tasks are important for new employees? Which are more important for experienced employees? How does the job change situationally? What situations may facilitate or inhibit carrying out tasks? How do different persons effect changes in the job? Which tasks must be performed by all persons? What particular patterns of job behavior have various previous employees shown?* All questions related to job dynamics may best be answered by further inquiry from supervisors, from the employees themselves, or from others who know

the job intimately. In seeking to answer questions about job dynamics, it is well to be armed with the job behavior checklist and to obtain actual estimates on the checklist of the kinds of changes that might be expected over time, under different situations, and with different persons.

3. *What employee behaviors are demanded by the job?* This, of course, has already been answered implicitly by gathering critical incidents. However, a limited sampling might miss some important aspect of job behavior. Thus, a first step after developing the job behavior checklist should probably be to show the checklist to supervisors and employees with the request that they add any important behaviors missed. For example, one obvious area of sales job behavior that fails to appear in the above categories based on critical incidents is "asking for the order." Any good sales manager or salesman would call this to our attention and direct us to supplement our job behavior list with tasks related to asking for the order.

4. *What "man requirements" may be inferred?* Inferences about man requirements will naturally be made throughout job analysis. However, as we have seen, it is best to avoid jumping to conclusions about their accuracy; it is best to use these inferences instead solely as a basis for selecting predictors to be tried out in the selection study.

5. *How may employee behaviors be observed and measured?* Answering this question is the subject of our next chapter. It is sufficient here to say that a behaviorally based checklist will provide a rich source for developing the job behavior measures against which applicant performance on predictor measures will be compared.

6. *Are there other implications for the selection study?* Critical-incidents analysis provides a great potential for learning more about the total job situation and implications for selection research. It could be discovered, for example, that *no* ineffective incidents are reported, in which case we would conclude that existing selection procedures are adequate and that no new ones need be tried. Many other needed actions might also be discovered, such as the need for job redesign, equipment modification, or reorganization. Again, the critical-incidents method is ideally suited for discovering such additional implications—quite apart from implications related to selection research per se.

After considering the above questions and doing the additional research necessary to answer them, the job analyst should end up with jobs defined as relatively homogeneous behavior groupings dependent not only on static job characteristics but also on behavior patterns of those assigned to the jobs. This is essentially what Hemphill (51) found after factor analyzing the responses given by ninety-three executives to a 575-item job behavior checklist. He identified ten behavior groupings; the men in each group were similar to one another in important job behaviors yet different from men in each of the other groups. Hemphill succeeded, therefore, in identifying ten dimensions of executive work to be used in describing objectively the patterns of behavior involved in executive jobs. His study is a good illustration of a behavior-based job analysis because these complex jobs were analyzed not only in terms of the static demands of different jobs but also in terms of what different executives brought to each job. Hemphill's executive job-behavior groupings may now be used to develop behavior measures against which to compare individual characteristics in the effort to learn what personal measures may be useful for predicting different job outcomes in executive jobs. When we undertake a job analysis as part of a selection study, we are not interested in long verbal descriptions, broad statements of organizational goals or purposes, or long and detailed accounts of actual job duties. We are interested solely in a fairly complete checklist of essential job behaviors, and we want them to be observable and measurable so that predictor measures can be compared with them.

chapter
five

Observing
and Recording
Job Behavior

Since the essential purpose of selection and placement is to predict job behavior, job behavior must be observed and recorded. Behavior-based job analyses tell us which behaviors are desired on the job and which are necessary for getting the job done properly. In turn, this information forms the basis for developing objective observational methods showing whether or not employees actually do the things defined and specified by the job analysis.

In this chapter we consider some of the problems in observing accurately the job behavior of others and spell out some of the methods for making such observations. The major scientific requirement is to observe, record, and measure events so that independent observers can obtain the same or very similar results. In developing methods for job observation and measurement we must specify the conditions and procedures with such precision that they may be communicated readily and accurately to whoever may make the observations.

Obviously, unless considerable time and effort is devoted to this phase of selection research, the outcome is likely to be a set of predictors (tests, interview information, biographical data, etc.) related to only marginally relevant behaviors or to nothing. To avoid such untoward outcomes, we need answers to at least the following questions:

1. What job behaviors should be observed and recorded?

2. What are the psychometric characteristics of an adequate measure of job behavior?

3. What problems or sources of error are often encountered in observing and recording job behavior and how may they be overcome?

4. What kinds of "instruments"—rating forms, checklists, etc.—may be used to record job behavior observations, and how well do they satisfy the requirements of an adequate measure?

5. How do the records or measurements of job behavior relate to other important organizational consequences, and what relevance do such relationships have for personnel selection and placement programs?

We consider answers to the above questions throughout this chapter.

Deciding What to Observe

As we have said, the result of job analysis is a listing of job behaviors grouped by either rational or empirical means into clusters of relatively homogeneous duties and activities. If the duties have been collected comprehensively by rather extensive sampling, interviewing employees and supervisors, and recording critical incidents, we will know the relative frequency of behaviors and the extent of their individual and situational determinants. Deciding whether to include infrequent behaviors depends almost entirely on their relative importance. Embezzling money from a bank, though infrequent, is important to avoid, and we might seek to predict it in selection. Falling down while dealing with a depositor is also infrequent, but it does not really warrant attention in selection. We would ordinarily drop from further consideration any job behaviors determined *entirely* by situations over which the individual employee has no control. Those determined only *in part* by the situation would be retained and described in the statement of the job behavior—for example, "Works even harder when others in his work group give him competition."

After deciding whether to include certain job behaviors, we still are faced with a myriad of possible job behaviors from which to choose for observation and measurement. As a general rule, it is better to err on the side of including too many than on the side of including too few. It is a distinct advantage to learn how accurately we can predict *several* aspects of job behavior and then to decide later, for any given selection situation, which aspects to predict. Thus, the broader our sampling of relevant job behaviors during selection research, the greater is our flexibility when we decide which predictors to use and which behaviors to predict. Job "success" is many faceted and must be recognized as such. The longer we retain in our selection research analyses the many facets of job behavior, the greater and more diverse will be the knowledge we accumulate about predictor-job behavior relationships. As Guion (41) states:

> If judgment [about the relative importance of various job behaviors] comes first, the entire superstructure of personnel research rests, not on an empirical foundation or even a theoretical one, but upon judgment. If it comes at the end, however, the judgment can be made with the twin advantage of knowing the relative validity with which the various [behaviors] can be predicted and of knowing also the current needs of the organization (p. 116).[1]

Our answer then to the question "What behaviors should be observed and recorded" is really very simple and straightforward. We should measure the job behaviors relevant and important for getting the job done properly. It is desirable to observe and to attempt to predict the many relatively discrete behaviors rather than group them unrealistically into some single or global measure of so-called job "success." (One important qualification is outlined in the following section.)

Psychometric Considerations

In working with people, all of us are continually making job behavior observations and judgments. We are prone to express such observations about co-workers with comments like the following:

> Jim really came through in the clutch on that last account.
>
> Henry should have finished the job he was doing instead of going fishing—even if it was opening day.
>
> Erica is really great when it comes to figures.
>
> Sophia talks so much, it's a wonder anybody gets any work done around here.

Such comments are, of course, inadequate for evaluating the usefulness of a set of predictors because they are casual, impressionistic, and rather opinionated. To be useful, job behavior observations must possess

---

[1] From *Personnel Testing* by R. M. Guion. Copyright © 1965. McGraw-Hill Book Company. Used by permission.

certain of the psychometric characteristics that we demand of other psychological measures.

Most important, job behavior observations should reflect stable aspects of behavior. We presented in Chapter 2 the major methods for estimating test precision and trait or behavior stability; these methods are directly applicable to measures of job behavior and should always be used to evaluate them. Thus, the *stability* of job behavior observations can be estimated by comparing the results from observations made on two or more different occasions, and the *precision* of job behavior observations can be estimated by comparing the results of observations made by two or more equally well-qualified observers on the same occasion.

An instrument designed for recording job behavior observations ought to yield high agreement between two or more equally well-qualified observers. If it does not, we can quite legitimately be uneasy about both the observability and predictability of the job behavior it is designed to measure. In contrast, if measures of a given job behavior obtained on two or more different occasions fail to show high agreement, this may be due to the imprecision of the measuring instrument or to actual changes in the pattern of behavior being observed. In the latter case, we could be confident in the observability of the behavior, but we would also need to devise predictors that would accurately pinpoint fluctuations. At any rate, for any instrument, we need estimates of test-retest stability and estimates of inter-observer agreement that may be obtained with it. At the very least, we must require high inter-observer agreement if we are to have confidence in our ability to predict job behavior.

A major basis for deciding which behaviors to observe is their relative stability. It is quite likely, for example, that the behavior denoted by the statement "goes out of his way to be friendly with everyone" might be highly relevant in the job of umpire; yet two observers might differ in the way they would rate any given umpire on the statement, and therefore the statement does not describe umpiring precisely enough to warrant its continued use in a job observation instrument. Information about inter-observer agreement and test-retest stability can, however, form the basis for grouping statements into broader dimensions. Such groupings may be suggested by logical or factor-analytic studies. Thus, observers' responses to a series of similar (for example, highly intercorrelated) behavioral statements can be taken together and summed to form a "behavior dimension rating score" such as friendly behavior on the job. Nearly always, the inter-observer agreement and stability of scores based on such a dimension or grouping of statements will be considerably higher than on any single statement taken singly.

Sources of Error in Behavior Observation

The variety and nature of the possible errors in making job behavior observations is frightening. Yet such measures are essential if we are to identify successfully and utilize predictors of job behavior; thus, we must recognize these potential errors and overcome them.

At this point, the reader should review our discussion in Chapter 2 of the four major sources of error in psychological measurement, for errors of behavior observation may be classified in essentially the same way.

Inadequate Sampling of the Job Behavior Domain

Observations of job behavior depend on defining completely and exhaustively the domain of relevant job behaviors. If the domain is only sketchily or incompletely defined, the resulting observations are said to be *deficient;* if job elements are included that do not really belong there (for example, behaviors not necessary for doing the job properly), the resulting observations are said to be *contaminated*. Both these extremes must be avoided; the only sure means of doing so is to give careful and exhaustive attention to job analysis.

Response Sets and Chance Response Tendencies

The most pervasive source of error in job behavior ratings and the one most diligently ignored by persons designing rating instruments is due to observers' lack of knowledge, understanding, or rapport. The one most often asked to observe and record job behavior is the immediate supervisor of the employee whose behavior is being described. The supervisor-observer alone—not the test developer, not the psychologist, not the president of the firm, not even the personnel man responsible for screening applicants—must view the job-behavior description form as understandable, relevant, practical, and acceptable. Thus, if a supervisor-observer fails to understand the statements or items of a rating form, if he regards them as irrelevant or as unimportant, if he does not feel like cooperating with those who ask him to complete the form, or if he has had little or only limited opportunity to observe either the employee or his job behavior, he may adopt one or several of the following tactics:

1. *Central tendency.* He may simply complete all the forms in about the same way for all the people he describes, failing to discriminate either among different persons or within the behavioral repertoire of a single person.

2. *Leniency tendency.* In this special type of central-tendency error, the observer says only "good" things about everyone.

3. *Halo.* The observer, in filling out the form, may make an over-all evaluative judgment about each employee and then proceed to describe him with all "good"-sounding or "bad"-sounding statements or ratings, irrespective of the actual behavioral content of the items in the form.

4. *Other tendencies.* Any number of other response tendencies are possible, depending upon special dispositions of each observer. One rather common tendency is to give very variable and inconsistent responses, still without regard to the behavioral content of the items, but giving the false impression that care has been taken to describe differentially the job behavior of each employee.

It is easy to state but less easy to implement the steps for overcoming observer errors due to response tendencies. Somehow we must be assured that observers understand the job-behavior description form, regard it as important, and observe systematically and accurately the job behaviors of persons they are asked to describe. Assessing the inter-observer agreement for statements in a form is one way of estimating whether or not they convey the same meaning to different observers. Better yet, the observers should actually develop the form; then they cannot help but understand it and be committed to using it properly. Securing critical incidents from supervisors is most certainly a first step in this direction, but it must be carried much further. (Observer-developed forms are outlined later in the section discussing job-behavior description instruments.)

Changes in the Job or Job Environment

As discussed in the last chapter, different behaviors may be required at different times on any job. The most usual change is that due to the changing pattern of job demands while an employee is "learning the ropes" on a new job. For example, Fleishman and Fruchter (24) showed that different behaviors are involved during the early and late stages of learning Morse code. In a somewhat similar study, Ghiselli and Haire (35) showed that the job behaviors related to high over-all production (dollar volume of fares collected) during cab drivers' first few weeks of employment were different from the job behaviors leading to high production after 4½ months on the job. To prevent serious observational errors, it may be necessary to investigate possible temporal changes in job demands and the effect of such changes on predictors and job behavior measures.

Changes in Employee Behavior

Just as job demands need to be sampled at different times, so must the observations of employee behaviors. It would be extremely misleading for a supervisor-observer to base his job behavior descriptions on only a single day's observations. Yet such an occurrence is far from unlikely, because most observers remember recent events most clearly. To assure a much better sampling of an employee's behavior, Guion (41) suggests keeping a Job Anecdote File in which the supervisor would systematically and periodically record each subordinate's significant job behaviors during a specific period. This file, according to Guion, could then serve as a "memory jogger" when the supervisor is asked to complete a job-behavior description form.

Ridding the Observational System of Error

Job behavior observation is fraught with potential error. The most serious source of difficulty is very fundamental—stemming primarily from a common tendency for psychologists to impose their own beliefs about job behavior and their own systems for recording it upon the persons who observe that behavior. According to Smith and Kendall (66), and we most certainly concur, this has almost always resulted in observers' lack of understanding and lack of commitment to the observational task. As a consequence, they tend to fill in the forms with little conviction and little agreement; the records, therefore, contain large and for the most part inestimable errors—errors that can only serve to attenuate seriously any empirical relationships between predictor measures and job behavior observations. Below, we suggest the means for removing these errors from the observational system.

Methods for Recording Job Behavior

Global Assessment Methods

Many methods have been tried for describing or assessing employees' job behavior or their relative job proficiency. Several methods have sought merely to accomplish an over-all ranking of employees on a given job with no intention of describing their actual job behaviors. The simplest is the *ranking method* in which the observer or rater simply picks out the employee he considers best, the one he regards as next best, and so on. Some forms ask the rater to alternate between selecting highly effective and less-effective employees—first picking the best, then the worst, the next best, the next worst, and so on. The ranking method is simple and easy to understand, and different raters usually agree fairly well on their placement of employees. But the results obviously are not based on behavior-centered analyses; job success is treated as unidimensional, which is usually unrealistic; and each rater is given free rein to utilize whatever bases for judging job "success" as may appeal to him. The result is a behaviorally undifferentiated listing of employees that seriously ignores that "success" is many faceted and that the behaviors leading to any given level of success are many and diverse.

Another commonly used approach for judging employee proficiency is the *rating scale*. Rating scales come in many forms, shapes, and sizes. Perhaps the simplest is illustrated by the hypothetical one for judging over-all proficiency of an exotic dancer:

Poor and Inadequate	*Below Average*	*Average*	*Above Average*	*Absolutely Top Notch*

Such a scale depends heavily on each individual rater's idiosyncratic definition of effective job behavior. It suffers from the same shortcomings as the ranking method.

A type of rating scale more often found in industry is shown in Figure 5–1. Here an effort has been made to "dimensionalize" job proficiency into a number of *a priori* factors such as quality and quantity of work and estimates of dependability and compatibility. It is amazing that scales such as this have received such widespread and uncritical use in industry; obviously, such a scale is unusually prone to *all* of the observational errors discussed previously. The sooner that such methods of "rating" the job proficiency of employees disappear from the industrial scene, the better off we will be.

Job Behavior Checklists and Other Approaches

An excellent basis for describing job behavior is provided by the critical-incidents method. A particular advantage is that the persons best

PROGRESS RECORD

Name_____Dept._____Div._____Date_____

Employee's Position_____Job Class_____

Note: This rating will represent in a systematic way your appraisal of the employee in terms of his ACTUAL PERFORMANCE ON HIS PRESENT JOB. In the interests of furthering careful analysis, the following suggestions are offered regarding the use of this form.

1. Consider only **one** factor at a time.
2. Study each factor and the specifications for each grade.
3. Review upon completion to see that the rating of each factor applies exclusively to the individual's ACTUAL PERFORMANCE ON HIS PRESENT JOB.
4. Comment fully at bottom of page and on reverse side upon any matter which in your opinion needs explanation.

PERFORMANCE FACTORS	PERFORMANCE GRADE				
	Far Exceeds requirements of this job	Exceeds requirements of this job	Meets requirements of this job	Partially Meets requirements of this job	Does Not Meet requirements of this job
QUALITY OF WORK Accuracy Economy of Materials Economy of Time (his own and others) Neatness Thoroughness	Consistently superior ☐	Sometimes superior ☐	Consistently satisfactory ☐	Usually acceptable ☐	Consistently unsatisfactory ☐
QUANTITY OF WORK Productive Output	Consistently exceeds requirements ☐	Frequently exceeds requirements ☐	Meets requirements ☐	Frequently below requirements ☐	Consistently below requirements ☐
DEPENDABILITY Follows Instructions Judgment Punctuality and Attendance Safety Habits	Consistently dependable ☐	Dependable in most respects ☐	Ordinarily dependable ☐	Frequently undependable ☐	Consistently undependable ☐
COMPATIBILITY Attitude Towards the Company Attitude Towards Supervision Co-operation with Fellow-Employees	Inspires others to work with and assist co-workers ☐	Quick to volunteer to work with and assist others ☐	Generally works well with and assists others ☐	Seldom works well with or assists others ☐	Does not work well with or assist others ☐

COMMENTS:_____

_____

_____

_____

_____

FIGURE 5–1. *A typical multiple-step rating scale used in industry.* (Joseph Tiffin & Ernest J. McCormick, *Industrial Psychology,* fifth edition, © 1965. Reprinted by permission of Prentice-Hall, Inc., Englewood Cliffs, N.J.)

equipped for observing and recording job behaviors are the ones who already have provided the anecdotal accounts comprising the critical incidents. Thus, the incidents are behavior based; they are in the language of the supervisor-observers and are therefore much more likely to be meaningful to them. Most important, the incidents include many different examples of unusually effective and ineffective job behavior rather than assuming a single or global job-success dimension. Critical incidents can be translated rather easily into descriptive job-behavior statements. Examples, drawn from the critical sales-job incidents in the last chapter, are the following:

1. Gossips about customer's confidential information.
2. Follows up quickly on requests from customers.
3. Shows lackadaisical attitude.
4. Promises too much to customers.
5. Is familiar with competitive products and sales methods.
6. Writes very poor sales reports.
7. Assists fellow salesmen with displays when needed.

Another set of statements developed by Knauft (55) for describing the job behavior of bake-shop managers is:

1. His window display always has customer appeal.
2. Products dropped on the floor are sometimes sold.
3. He seldom forgets what he has once been told.
4. He does not anticipate probable emergencies.
5. He pays little attention to customers.
6. He encourages his employees to show initiative.
7. His shop is unusually neat and clean.
8. He is slow at making decisions.
9. His bakers do not respect him.
10. He often has vermin and insects in his shop.
11. No baking is done in his shop after twelve noon.

12. His sales per customer are relatively high.

13. He occasionally runs a selling contest among his sales-
girls.

Such statements can be used by raters to describe the typical pattern of an individual's job behavior. Ideally, the raters should be able to pinpoint specific areas of strengths and weaknesses, and these can be compared with predictors to develop guidelines for selecting future applicants. For example, descriptions on the above statements might identify a group of bakery managers who keep their shops neat and clean and have good window displays but who do not maintain the confidence of their bakers and do not have particularly high sales volumes. The predictor information on such a group (test scores, interview information, etc.) might then be studied in order to identify personal characteristics associated with this particular pattern of job performance. The great advantage of such a checklist stems from its basis in actual job behavior and from the fact that the supervisors reported the incidents on which the statements are based.

Unfortunately, work with such checklists suggests that supervisor-observers do *not* typically use them in the diagnostic fashion for which they seem to be so well fitted. Instead, raters usually fall prey to the halo effect just as readily with checklists as with less carefully developed procedures such as rating scales. Raters apparently form an over-all global evaluation of the person being rated and then proceed to check either the "good" statements or the "bad" statements without thinking critically or analytically about the behavioral descriptions. This probably occurs because the supervisors have not typically been involved in all phases of the checklist development; the editing of the critical incidents and their abstraction into statements apparently "sterilizes" or "psychologizes" them so that they no longer convey universal and unambiguous meaning to the many supervisor-observers who use them. It is easier to check the items according to a broad evaluative dimension than to discern the intent of the person who edited the incidents and wrote the items.

Solving the Riddle

Many additional efforts have been made to rid the observational system of error, including elaborate sorting techniques and *forced-choice* items especially developed to "force" the supervisor-observer to choose which of two or more equally desirable phrases most accurately describes the employee. None of these methods has lived up to initial high hopes for them. The sorting methods still are prone to leniency and other biasing tendencies. The forced-choice approach, though controlling fairly effectively for leniency and halo effects, still ends up with an over-all or global rating. Moreover, since it utilizes a hidden or disguised scoring system, the forced-choice method has often proved to be unacceptable to the raters asked to use it; the experience with it in the United States Army led to its abandonment in 1950 because "raters . . . found it so unacceptable to rate without knowledge of the final outcome that they concentrated on finding ways to beat the system" (64, p. 51).

Until recently, the riddle remained: How could standardized job-behavior rating forms be developed that would possess necessary psychometric characteristics and that could be completed accurately and enthusiastically by relatively untrained observers? Very recently, Smith and Kendall (66) developed a method for describing the job effectiveness of nurses that promises to help solve this enigma.

Smith and Kendall built their observational system around the assumption that errors could only be avoided by "selling" the observers upon the desirability of completing the ratings honestly and carefully. From this, it follows that the job behavior forms must have an appearance of obvious usefulness to the observer as well as to the selection researcher. The most effective way of assuring this happy outcome was to involve nursing supervisors in each step of scale development and to take unusual pains to maintain clear and nonambiguous scales and behavior descriptions. The following comment by Smith and Kendall is indicative of the principles guiding them in developing the job behavior form:

> Better ratings can be obtained in our opinion, not by trying to trick the rater (as in forced choice scales) but by helping him to rate. We should ask questions which he can honestly answer about behaviors which he can observe. We should reassure him that his answers will not be misinterpreted, and we should provide a basis by which he and others can check his answers (66, p. 151).

The actual steps employed by Smith and Kendall were as follows:

1. Several groups of head nurses participated in conferences devoted to discussing the use of personnel evaluations for

improving nursing performance. Information was gathered by mail from additional groups.

2. Each group listed the major qualities in successful nursing, and critical incidents were gathered and classified to illustrate examples of behavior related to each quality. Throughout, the nurses' own terminology was retained.

3. The groups also formulated general statements defining high, low, and acceptable performance for each quality, and additional examples of actual performance incidents were suggested for each quality.

4. The head nurses then indicated *independently* what quality was illustrated by each incident. *Incidents* were eliminated if there was not clear agreement concerning the quality to which it belonged. *Qualities* were eliminated if the incidents were not consistently reassigned to the quality for which they were originally chosen as illustrative.

Smith and Kendall made certain that the meaning of both the job qualities and of the behavioral incidents chosen to illustrate them would be tightly specific and nonambiguous. This step, the crucial innovation in their approach, is basically similar to procedure ensuring that translations from one language to another adhere to the connotations as well as the denotations of the original. Material is translated into a foreign language and then translated back into the original by an independent translator.

5. The incidents were then judged by another group of head nurses on a scale ranging from 0.0 to 2.0 according to the proper behavior for nursing. Incidents were eliminated if the judgments showed a large dispersion or if they fell into more than one distinct group. This procedure provided another safeguard assuring absolute agreement and lack of ambiguity.

The outcome of this painstaking work was a job-behavior evaluation form including scales for judging six major qualities—knowledge and judgment, conscientiousness, skill in human relationships, organizational ability, objectivity, and observational ability—each firmly defined behaviorally and anchored at various points by incidents stated in the nurses' own language and rigidly fixed according to scale location. Figure 5–2 shows the scale for judging skill in human relationships.

SKILL IN HUMAN RELATIONSHIPS *(with patients, families, and co-workers)*
behaves in a manner appropriate to the situation and individuals involved.

← 2.00 ↑

Even when there is considerable emotional self-involvement, behavior with others is so skillful and insightful that it not only smooths but often prevents difficult emotional and social situations; this implies the ability to recognize the subtle as well as the more obvious components of basic emotional reactions in self and others (e.g., anxiety, fear, frustration, anger, etc.).

1.75 — This nurse could be expected, whenever possible, to sit down and talk with a terminal-cancer patient who is considered to be "demanding."

1.50 — If two aides asked this nurse, acting as team leader, if they could exchange assignments because of rapport problems with the patients assigned, would expect this nurse to discuss the problem with the aides and make certain changes which would be satisfying to them.

If this nurse were admitting a patient who talks rapidly and continuously of her symptoms and past medical history, could be expected to look interested and listen.

1.25 — If this nurse were assigned for the first time to a patient who insists upon having her treatment done in a certain order, could be expected to do as the patient wishes without making an issue about it.

98

If emotional self-involvement is minimal, behavior with others is such that it does not complicate difficult emotional and social situations; this implies the ability to recognize the more obvious components of basic emotional reactions in self and others.

1.00

If the husband of a woman, who is postoperative and in good condition, asks about his wife, this nurse could be expected to reply as follows: "Her condition is good."

0.75

If a convalescent patient complained about the service in the hospital, this nurse would be likely to tell the patient that the hospital is short of nurses and the needs of the sickest patients have to be met first.

If this nurse were assigned to care for a terminal-cancer patient, in a 2-bed room, who is depressed and uncommunicative, could be expected to carry on a conversation with the other patient while giving care to the terminal-cancer patient.

0.50

In the presence of a woman who is crying because her husband is dangerously ill, this nurse would be expected to tell the woman not to cry.

0.25

If this nurse were told by an ambulatory patient that a patient in the ward was having difficulty in breathing, could be expected to tell the ambulatory patient that his help in caring for the patients was not needed.

0.00

Behavior with others is such that it tends to complicate or create difficult emotional or social situations; this implies an inability to recognize even the obvious basic emotional reactions of self and others.

FIGURE 5-2. *Example of job behavior scale for describing nurses' skills in human relationships.*

(National League for Nursing, Research and Studies Service. A Method for Rating the Proficiency of the Hospital General Staff Nurse; Manual of Directions. New York, 1964.)

Even a cursory examination indicates the degree of precision in its development and the probable ease with which it can be completed for any given nurse.

Finally, in order to check the consistency of scale judgments, Smith and Kendall correlated the judgments made by the several different groups of judges. The lowest value obtained was .972, suggesting an extremely high degree of agreement. Although results are not yet available for the operational use of these scales, it appears that the method has great promise for overcoming many of the problems and potential errors believed for so long to be inherent in most systems of behavior observation. The scales are rooted in and referable to actual observed behavior; behavior observations have been supplied by observers highly similar to those expected to use the scales; and the qualities covered by the scales are rigorously defined and have been shown to be easily and accurately distinguished from one another by the raters.

Although we cannot present his results in detail, Sprecher (69) has used essentially the same method for developing job behavior description forms for engineers. He has found that the major aspects of engineering job performance can be described along six major dimensions: loyalty, friendship, and teamwork; thoroughness and analytical ability; technical knowledge; problem-solving orientation; cost consciousness; and communication skills.

This approach appears to allow us to eat our cake and still have it. The job behavior domain is sampled exhaustively in the same way as for other careful critical-incidents analysis; however, the grouping of the incidents is not left up to the psychometrist. Instead, they are developed specifically to illustrate the broad behavior qualities of greatest importance for doing the job properly. Happily, the result is a series of relatively independent scales based on actual job performance incidents that reflect, not a global or unidimensional assumption about job "success," but instead the several different dimensions and behavior patterns that can lead to "success" in any job.

Organizational Consequences as Indicators of Job Performance

Once we have developed a job-behavior description form according to the standards and methods outlined above, it should be used to study relationships between employees' job behavior and other more

global measures of individual "success" and organizational consequences. As we have already implied, industrial managers and supervisors do not typically do a good job of observing the actual job
behavior of subordinates. Their personnel decisions about promotions,
job transfers, discharges, salary increases, etc., are more often influenced
by whether employees have or have not been associated with realizing
certain broad organizational outcomes. For example, a salesman is
bound to be judged by his sales volume, even though it is widely
known that for nearly all industrial sales jobs many other factors either
enhance or delimit the over-all sales volume that any salesman can
realize—for example, differing potentials and competitive advantages
of sales territories, relative effectiveness of different advertising cam-
paigns, types of customers and firms called upon. During World War
II, psychologists investigating bombing accuracy as a possible measure
of the skill of bombardiers found that the measure was contaminated
by a myriad of factors outside the control of the bombardier—air tur-
bulence, condition and calibration of the bombsight, altitude and length
of the bombing run. Yet even though bombing accuracy had practically no relevance for estimating bombardiers' job "success," higher
officers gave it great attention and used "scores" on practice runs for
judging the over-all effectiveness of different bombardiers.

We are confronted with an interesting and rather surprising
paradox. In industry today, job behavior is not typically observed and
recorded with care or precision. Instead, decisions about people are
made on the basis of over-all impressions and global judgments apt to
be influenced by many irrelevant factors or by a few outstanding incidents that may seem to be related to broad organizational goals and
outcomes. Actual job behavior is being observed and measured much
less effectively than we know how—in favor, unfortunately, of using
measures that "everyone knows" are both deficient and contaminated
to unknown amounts by factors irrelevant to getting the job done
properly.

We need to give greater attention to developing systematic procedures for observing and measuring job behavior and using them to
learn exactly how employee job behaviors are related to other organizational measures such as over-all rankings of "success," promotion rates,
productivity indices, quality measures, work sample "scores" (such as
bombing accuracy), job satisfaction and morale, and the many other
gross performance measures of interest and readily available in most
firms.

Results from this type of research will have important implications for personnel decision making in the future:

1. Systematic procedures for observing and recording actual job behavior will become much more widespread and will serve to "educate" management in the complex art of observing and making judgments about employees.

2. Managers will become aware of the behavioral patterns and behavioral mechanisms leading to the broad designations that have traditionally been labeled "successes" and "failures." Presumably, such knowledge will be invaluable for making much more fully informed and wiser personnel decisions.

3. Finally, armed with empirical evidence of how organizational consequences and over-all success patterns are moderated by specific employee behaviors, the personnel decision maker will be able to make much firmer selection and placement recommendations based on a thorough understanding of the complex linkages between predictors, job behaviors, and organizational consequences.

part two

Strategies for
Personnel Decisions

A Model
for Test
Validation
and Selection
Research

A Research Framework

So far we have discussed the major steps undergirding any program of personnel selection and placement—individual differences measurement, job analysis, and job behavior observation. In selection, we seek to predict later job behavior from the results of measures administered when candidates apply for the job. To do this, we need a *blueprint* summarizing all the things to take into account as we seek to establish predictive and stable relations between the attributes of people, their jobs, and the behavior they show on their jobs.

The Traditional Approach

For years, psychologists have relied on a rather oversimplified model to structure their selection research. This model has sought to link *predictors* (that is, various measures of individual differences) directly with so-called *criteria* (that is, various measures of organizational consequences or job "success") through a simple index of relationship, the correlation coefficient. This traditional validation model directed that persons on any given job be divided on some global measure (such as sales volume, over-all rating of "success," or potential for promotion) into successes and failures and that they be compared on test scores, biographical information, or any other personal measurements available. Such a simplified approach tends to ignore the careful methods designed to pinpoint jobs and job circumstances and the methods of job behavior observation discussed in the last two chapters. Moreover, such a simple linkage of predictors and "criteria" is seriously oversimplified when viewed against the many complexities in predicting human behavior outlined in Chapter 1.

There has also been a tendency to ignore that any given level of job "success," defined globally, can be the consequence of any number of interacting factors. For example, two salesmen selling exactly the same amount of life insurance (and, therefore, equally "successful") may have achieved their goals by widely differing patterns of job behavior—the one perhaps being a persistent and diligent worker, the other possibly "winning the sale" by his glowing personality and strongly persuasive tactics. Certainly the two would differ sharply from one another in personal characteristics; yet the classic model, for purposes of analysis, would lump them together in the same "success" group. Nor does the classic model take proper note of job differences, possible changes due to training in the man-job interaction, or the differing situational and social circumstances of the jobs. In every instance, the effect is to classify together persons who do not really belong together. In these very heterogeneous groupings of "successes" and "failures," the difference among persons within the groups has often exceeded the difference between the means of the two groups. The result has been that attempts to predict job "success" and job "failure" have yielded disappointing outcomes, rarely exceeding correlation coefficients of .50.

A New Model for Selection Research

In order to do justice to the complexities of real prediction situations and to assure the more homogeneous grouping of persons by job behaviors, situations, and predictability, a new and more complicated model is needed. Such a model has been presented by Dunnette (16). It is shown in Figure 6–1.

The brackets and arrows serve as reminders of the many pos-

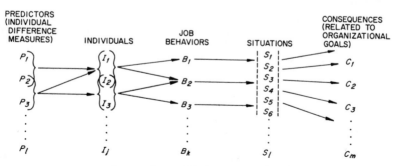

FIGURE 6–1. *A model for test validation and selection research.*

sibilities for different prediction strategies that should be considered in any personnel selection or test validation study. The brackets in the diagram signify different groupings of tests for different groups of persons, depending upon the patterns of job behavior to be predicted. The arrows in the diagram show that different avenues based on various groupings of predictors, persons, and behaviors may be utilized. For example, predictors P_2 and P_3 might be tried for individuals I_2 and I_3 or for individuals I_1 and I_2, but they probably would yield differentially accurate predictions for different job behaviors. The diagram also portrays the possibility of different job behaviors leading to various organizational consequences depending upon differing situational contexts. Thus, the prediction model calls attention to the likelihood of complex interactions between predictor groupings, groups or types of individuals, job behavior patterns, and broadly defined organizational consequences. Moreover, the model makes explicit the necessity for predicting actual job behavior and studying it in the context of different job situations rather than simply contrasting groups formed on the basis of over-all organizational outcomes.

Selection research, based on this model, becomes a series of investigations designed to discover the optimal groupings or subsets of predictors, persons, job behaviors, and situations within which to study patterns of predictability and to validate and cross-validate prediction strategies. As we have said, most previous selection research has been rather fixedly concerned with predicting organizational consequences directly without first seeking to learn the nature of possible linkages between such consequences and all that goes before in the model—notably the patterns of situational circumstances and the possible differences in job behavior. Our model implies no lessening of interest in predicting organizational outcomes but it does direct research efforts toward a more careful analysis of their behavioral and situational correlates with the hope of understanding these organizational outcomes better, and of predicting them more accurately.

Our rather abstract description of the selection model may not have given the reader an exact view of the model's implications. Therefore, we turn to a concrete illustration.

A Hypothetical Selection Research Study

We have concocted data for a hypothetical group of seventy-four employees who were tested six months ago and hired by a firm as bottle inspectors. The job involves standing at the end of a beer-bottle production line, rapidly inspecting the bottles for imperfections (such as bubbles, dented lips, and odd shapes), and packing the good ones into shipping cases holding twenty-four bottles each. Records are kept, showing the number of cases packed per day by each employee and also the number of bottles inspected by each person which were later rejected as imperfect by the bottling firms purchasing the bottles. The test used at the time of hiring was a fifteen-minute test of speed and accuracy of perception; the only other information available at the time of hiring was the educational level and sex of each applicant. Thus, the job behavior observations include simply the amount (average number of bottles packed per day) and quality (number of bottles rejected by bottling firms) of work done, and the predictor is the score on the perceptual speed and accuracy test.

The relationship between predictor scores and the work-volume measure for all seventy-four employees is shown in the scatter diagram in Figure 6–2. High work volume tends to be associated with high test scores, and low volume is associated with low scores. This is reflected by the relatively high correlation coefficient of .60 obtained for the data in Figure 6–2. However, not *all* the employees follow the general trend. A small group (in the lower right-hand corner of the scatter diagram) scores highly on the test but shows low work volume.

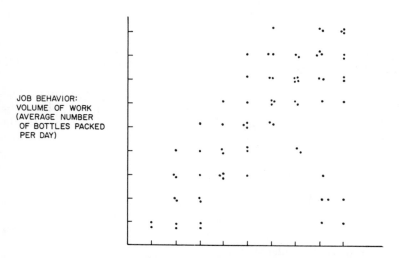

JOB BEHAVIOR:
VOLUME OF WORK
(AVERAGE NUMBER
OF BOTTLES PACKED
PER DAY)

PREDICTOR: TEST OF SPEED AND ACCURACY OF PERCEPTION

FIGURE 6–2. *Scatter diagram depicting relationship between test score and job behavior.*

There appears also to be a spreading or fanning effect in the upper-right portion of the scatter diagram; the relationship between test scores and work volume is less marked in this portion than in the lower-left part of the scatter chart. How are these effects related to our selection research model?

Looking again at Figure 6–1, we note that the model directs us to investigate the nature of relationships for different subsets of individuals and for different predictors and job behaviors. Men and women constitute two obvious groups to be studied separately, and it is possible that high school and non-high school graduates might show different patterns of predictability. One of the best ways for studying these possibilities is through multidimensional scatterplotting, a method described by Rimland (63). This simple graphic technique uses different symbols to identify separate groupings of persons in a scatter diagram. It is necessary, of course, to provide for validation and cross-validation groups to check the stability of relationships discovered. In our example, the group of seventy-four employees was separated into groups of forty-eight and twenty-six to serve, respectively, as validation and cross-validation samples. In the group of forty-eight, there were (1) a dozen male high school graduates, (2) a dozen female high school graduates, (3) a dozen male nongraduates, and (4) a dozen female nongraduates. For the four groups, Figure 6–3 shows different patterns of relationship between test scores and job behavior. Work volume for nongraduates, both men and women, is linearly and highly related to test performance. Since the relationship is linear, a correlation coefficient appropriately describes the magnitude of relationship. For all non-high school graduates, $r = .87$; the separate values for men and women in this group are .93 and .89, respectively. In contrast, high school graduates, both men and women, show no linear relation between work volume and test score. For the women who applied for this job, simply having a high school diploma seems sufficient to assure high work volume, but there is no useful relationship *within* the group between test scores and work volume. For the men, the middle scores show a moderate, though not outstanding, work volume, and *both* high and low scores on the test show low work volume. Since the relationship between test score and work volume for the men is so obviously nonlinear, r is inappropriate for estimating its magnitude; therefore, it was not calculated.

The foregoing illustrates very nicely the gain in predictive efficiency that can often be realized by the more careful analyses of sub-

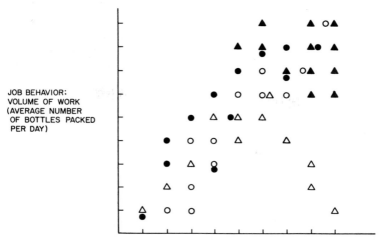

JOB BEHAVIOR:
VOLUME OF WORK
(AVERAGE NUMBER
OF BOTTLES PACKED
PER DAY)

PREDICTOR: TEST OF SPEED AND ACCURACY OF PERCEPTION

△ Male, High School Graduate
▲ Female, High School Graduate
O Male, Non−High School Graduate
● Female, Non−High School Graduate

FIGURE 6–3. *Multidimensional scatterplot de-picting relations among test scores, job behavior, sex, and educational status for validation group.*

group relationships suggested by our selection research model. However, the apparent gain could be due to the spurious effects of chance sampling errors—particularly for such small samples as these. Cross-validation is doubly necessary when carrying out a set of subgroup analyses of this kind. The multidimensional scatterplot (Figure 6–4) based on the remaining twenty-six employees (cross-validation group) confirms and strengthens the conclusions drawn from the validation group.

Implications for Strategies of Selection

Figure 6–5 shows the decision rules, selection strategies, and job behavior predictions suggested by the relationships discovered in the previous analyses. The test would not be administered at all to female high school graduates, since a direct prediction of high work volume may be made for them. It could be argued also that the test should not be administered to male graduates either, for none become high-

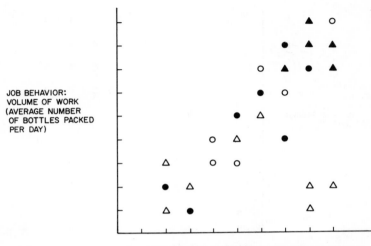

PREDICTOR: TEST OF SPEED AND ACCURACY OF PERCEPTION

△ Male, High School Graduate
▲ Female, High School Graduate
○ Male, Non-High School Graduate
● Female, Non-High School Graduate

FIGURE 6–4. *Multidimensional scatterplot depicting relations among test scores, job behavior, sex, and educational status for cross-validation group.*

volume workers, and it is somewhat inefficient to use a test solely as a negative screening device. The test is, of course, clearly useful and a highly efficient predictor of work volume for all non-high school graduates. Thus, the pattern of data analysis suggested by our selection research model has led to a sort of selection prescription tailored individually for each applicant, using only those predictors most efficient for him.

Conclusions

This example is of course greatly simplified, illustrating only the potential gain to be realized from considering different types of persons separately. Next steps would normally include a similar analysis against other available job behavior measures (for example, the bottle reject rate); and if sufficient numbers of employees were available for

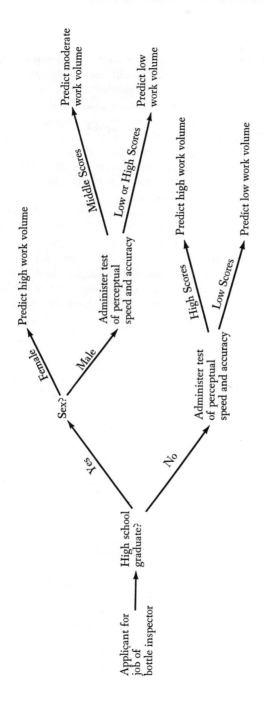

FIGURE 6–5. *Selection strategies, decision rules, and behavior predictions based on selection research study of bottle inspectors.*

study, situational differences (for example, nature of supervision, relative adequacy of job training, and social conditions on the production line), and other tests or predictors that might be used with different subsets of persons. In effect, then, the selection research model directs us to develop an array of prediction equations showing the patterns of predictability for different combinations of predictors, applicants, job behaviors, and situations. Selection strategies may then be designed to take account of the accumulating information on any given applicant so that the tests and procedures known to be optimal will be applied at each stage of the selection or placement process.

In Chapter 8 we will present additional methods for subgrouping people, predictors, situations, and job behaviors. It has been our intention in this chapter simply to present and illustrate the use of this new selection research model and to clarify its implications for research design and analysis and for forming selection strategies. In Chapter 7 we will give more detailed attention to expressing relationships between predictors and job behaviors and translating these into behavioral predictions.

The Strategies and the Statistics of Validation

What Does a Test Measure?

The choice of which tests to use for personnel selection and placement demands that an adequate answer be given to this question for each of the tests in the battery. Test authors often become over-zealous in choosing titles for their tests; because of this, it is best to assume that a test's title tells us *little* about what the test measures. In order to learn *what* a test actually measures, it is necessary to carry out a series of *validation* studies. *Validation* refers broadly to the process of learning more about the *meaning* or total network of inter-pretations that may be attached to an individual differences measure. Test validation is never ending, because each new research study may provide some new information about relationships between test be-haviors and nontest behaviors. At any given time, the meaning of a particular test score can be derived only from the total accumulation of research information available for that test. Such information helps in choosing measures to be "tried out" in any given personnel selection or placement situation. Presumably, of course, it is more efficient to try well-researched methods or measures rather than those about which little is known. But even for well-researched methods, it is necessary to see how the tests work for specific job circumstances. The evidence gained from additional study of the tests tells us how useful they actually are for predicting the job behaviors we are interested in, and the evidence may also add to the accumulating body of research in-formation about the tests and extend knowledge of their meaning, inter-pretability, and potential uses.

This chapter outlines and discusses the experimental strategies in test validation and presents some of the statistical procedures commonly used for expressing the linkages or relationships between test behaviors and nontest behaviors. Our purpose, then, is to describe the research evidence that gives meaning to a test and to present the procedures and statistics for developing such evidence.

The Strategies of Validation

Generally, we want to learn enough about the meaning of various scores on a test so that we may make inferences about present and future behaviors. Essentially, we are asking what sort of person has just taken this test, what are his typical patterns of behavior, how will these behaviors be reflected on a job, and how might he react to different situations and people that may confront him in the job? To answer these questions, the lines of evidence about a test must include information about concurrent relationships between test behavior and other behaviors, relationships between test behavior and later or future behaviors, and the possible effects of various intervening experiences on test behavior and other correlated behaviors. These necessary kinds of evidence suggest various research strategies for use in validation studies. There are five major strategies—concurrent, predictive, experimental, correlational, and content-analytical. These are discussed in the sections following.

Concurrent Validation Strategy

Figure 7–1 is a schematic representation of a concurrent validation design. The design is essentially equivalent to that used by Binet in his initial development and validation of intelligence test items. A concurrent study yields information about behaviors concomitantly related to test responses. It is not strictly correct to infer predictive usefulness for a test if it has been submitted only to concurrent validation. However, in personnel selection, concurrent studies are often the only means available for test validation; unfortunately, such studies probably underestimate the degree of relationship between test scores and job behaviors because the sample of subjects will not usually include potentially less effective employees who were not hired or who have failed and been discharged. It may also fail to include the highly effective persons who, through success, have been promoted to more responsible and more demanding jobs. A concurrent study tells us only what the present

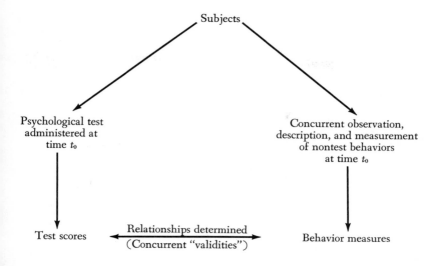

FIGURE 7–1. *Validation strategy for determining concurrent relationships between test measures and nontest behaviors.*

relationship may be between the test behavior and other concurrently observed behaviors. Nothing is necessarily implied about the usefulness of the test for predicting later nontest behavior, although investigators commonly imply that they have demonstrated predictive utility by carrying out concurrent validation strategies. Actually, many test responses (particularly those made to typical behavior inventories) may be *due to* rather than *predictive of* current aspects of a person's behavior. A highly successful salesman would probably be more likely to use the adjective "successful" in describing himself than he would have been when he was first applying for a job fresh out of college. It would be unwise to infer predictive accuracy from such a concurrent finding.

Predictive Validation Strategy

Figure 7–2 is a schematic representation of a predictive validation design. Applied to a personnel selection study, this design dictates that all applicants would be tested and all would be hired without regard to their showing on the tests. Their job behaviors would be observed and measured, and careful records would be maintained of what happened to each person—how he did in training, whether or not he failed and was discharged or was so successful as to be promoted, his style or pattern of job behavior, how he "got on" with his boss and with other employees, etc. At some later date, then, relationships would

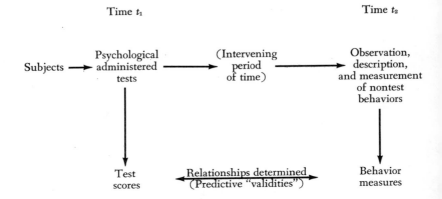

FIGURE 7–2. *Validation strategy for determining predictive relationships between test measures and nontest behaviors.*

be determined between the test scores and the various behavior patterns or outcomes shown by the employees. The predictive strategy is the preferred strategy for any personnel selection study because it is always our intention in the operational use of psychological tests to infer from the test results *future* job behavior outcomes. The predictive strategy also has the advantage of including test and job behavior information about *all* the applicants rather than a restricted sampling of them, as in the concurrent strategy. Unfortunately, however, practical difficulties in industrial settings often may rule out the use of the predictive design. A major difficulty is that the approach obviously involves a substantial delay before results become available. Moreover, hiring *all* applicants regardless of their measured capabilities is a potentially wasteful procedure because of the potentially detrimental effects to the organization and the ineffective utilization of human resources. Modern philosophies of effective management-employee relations do not typically include the idea of hiring any large number of applicants solely for validating psychological tests; thus, efforts are usually made to do the best possible job of personnel selection and placement even if the tests have not first been "properly" validated in a predictive study. Of course, the predictive strategy is definitely necessary because it yields a kind of information about test responses impossible to obtain from strictly concurrent comparisons. Therefore, predictive information should be obtained whenever possible in order to give a full account of a test's meaning and range of possible interpretations.

Experimental Validation Strategy

Figure 7–3 is a schematic representation of an experimental strategy designed to yield information about the personal attributes or constructs measured by a psychological test. A glance at the chart reveals that the experimental strategy is much more complicated than the concurrent and the predictive strategies. However, the experimental approach yields a greater wealth of information which, when based on a well-designed and carefully conducted experiment, can usually be generalized to more situations and circumstances than can result from either of the previous validation strategies. Because the method is complicated, let us illustrate how it has been used in industry.

During the early 1950s, a team of psychologists at Ohio State University developed a typical behavior inventory called the Leadership Behavior Description Questionnaire (LBDQ). It was scored for two behavioral tendencies found to be very nearly independent of each other. The first was *consideration* and included statements describing the leader as one who shows respect for individual employees, engenders mutual trust and respect, and maintains an easy and effective rapport with his subordinates. The second was *initiating structure* and included statements describing the leader as one who plans ahead, does an effective job of organizing and delegating responsibilities, and gives heavy emphasis to getting things done. Supposedly, responses to such an inventory *ought* to be related to the actual behaviors shown by supervisors in carrying out their jobs. Working in one of the plants of the International Harvester Company, Harris and Fleishman (47) asked at least three subordinates of each of ninety-eight foremen to describe their boss' behavior with the LBDQ. During the next eleven

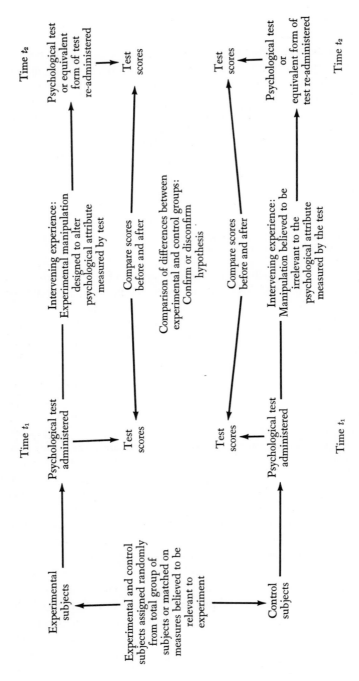

FIGURE 7–3. *Experimental strategy for studying hypothesized constructs or attributes measured by a psychological test.*

months, thirty-nine of the foremen were sent to an intensive two-week supervisory training program; the remaining fifty-nine foremen did not receive any training. The training session thus constituted the intervening experimental manipulation shown in Figure 7–3. The expectations (hypotheses) were that the training should change the supervisory behavior of the foremen and that this change should be reflected in descriptions on the LBDQ. At the end of eleven months, other groups of subordinates were asked to describe their supervisors' job behavior. The results are shown in the table on page 120.

It is apparent that scores on the inventory do not reflect changes in the behavior of the supervisors in either of the two groups. The experimental and control subjects are described by their subordinates in essentially the same way, both before and after the intervening experimental manipulation. Thus, neither of the hypotheses was confirmed. There are two possible explanations for these negative results: (1) no immediate change in supervisory behavior occurred as a result of the intensive training program or (2) the LBDQ is not valid for describing actual supervisory behavior. Had the results been positive (that is, the LBDQ descriptions changed for the experimental but not for the control group), both hypotheses would have been confirmed, and Harris and Fleishman would have had strong evidence for both the validity of the LBDQ *and* for the usefulness of the training procedure. As it is, the results constitute no evidence for the validity of the LBDQ; either additional experiments or other validational strategies would be necessary to confirm the behavioral validity of the inventory. As we shall see, other types of validational studies done with the LBDQ confirm its usefulness for measuring both *considerate* and *structuring* supervisory behavior.

The usual method for assessing the results of an experimental validation study is to compare the differences between means before and after the experimental manipulation for the experimental and control groups. To be meaningful, such comparisons must be expressed in relation to the amount of variation (measured by the standard deviation) present in the groups. The usual approach in psychology has been to "test" the null hypothesis (see Chapter 2) and to label as *positive* those results yielding mean differences that are significantly different statistically from zero. However, this approach is not really very rewarding as a way of learning more about what a test measures, because with large samples even very small differences can be statistically "significant." We are far more interested in the absolute magni-

| | | TIME 1 | | ELEVEN MONTHS | TIME 2 | |
| | | MEAN LBDQ SCORES | | | MEAN LBDQ SCORES | |
		Considera-tion	Initiating Structure		Considera-tion	Initiating Structure
Experimental Group:	Group I (N = 39 foremen)	71	43	Intervening Experience: Intensive Supervisory Training	72	41
Control Group:	Group II (N = 59 foremen)	74	42	Intervening Experience: No Special Training	74	40

tude of the changes occurring as a result of an experimental manipulation than we are in simply showing a statistically significant difference between the means. Therefore, for most purposes of test validation (that is, for learning what we can legitimately say about the behavioral meaning of test scores), the size of the mean difference should definitely be assessed in terms of the amount of overlap between the total distributions of test scores before and after the experimental manipulation. The less the overlap, the more confident are we in the behavioral interpretations that may be attached to the scores on the test. The reader will find a more detailed discussion of the overlap coefficient in the section on the statistics of validation.

Correlational Validation Strategy

CORRELATING TESTS

The correlational strategy takes a number of forms. Its most usual form consists of computing correlations between scores on the test and scores on other tests that already have been well researched and about which a good deal is known. Useful information about a test may be obtained by both inclusion and by exclusion; for example, correlating a new test with an existing and well-researched measure of verbal ability will yield meaningful information regardless of the magnitude of the correlation obtained. A high positive r would suggest that the new test is, to some degree, also measuring verbal ability, and an r close to zero would indicate that the new measure probably is independent of verbal ability. It is important, however, to guard against a common error in interpreting r's. Unless the correlation between two measures is 1.0, it is not proper to attribute identicalness to the two measures; yet, many investigators, upon obtaining a "high" correlation (say, an r of .60 or greater) between two measures, behave as if the two are perfectly interchangeable and functionally equivalent.

FACTOR ANALYSIS

A second form of the correlational strategy is factor analysis. As we have seen in Chapter 2, factor analysis is a mathematical procedure for identifying the minimum number of dimensions or factors necessary to account for the total matrix of correlations among a larger number of measures. Thus, in order to learn more about the meaning of a new test, one can correlate it with a large number of well-known tests, then carry out a factor analysis to learn something of what the test is measuring by examining the validational evidence available for the various tests correlating highly with the factor or factors with which the new test also is highly correlated. Here again, caution must be observed in interpreting correlations between measures.

COMPARING GROUPS OF PERSONS

A third strategy is to correlate or to compare test scores against nominal designations (categories) of persons. In developing a new test, the test author usually has some expectations of what he wants the test to measure, and he should be able to express these expectations in the form of hypotheses about how different groups of persons should score on the test. For example, graduate engineers should obtain higher scores than sophomore engineering students on a test designed to measure engineering knowledge; Negroes should obtain more favorable scores than Southern whites on a scale designed to measure attitudes toward integration; and salesmen should score higher than research chemists on a typical behavior inventory designed to measure assertiveness. Groups such as these can be compared simply by calculating their mean scores on the tests; but again the differences between groups should be expressed in terms of the overlaps between the various distributions of scores rather than in terms of the mean differences for statistical significance. Better yet, correlational procedures especially adapted for categorized data can be employed.[1] If the relationships are in the hypothesized direction and of reasonably high magnitude, our view of what the test is measuring is confirmed and extended; if the hypotheses are not confirmed, we are then forced to alter somewhat our view of what the test is measuring and to establish new hypotheses to be tested in subsequent studies.

An excellent example of this approach to test validation was undertaken by Fleishman and Harris (25) in another investigation of the behavioral correlates of the Leadership Behavior Description Questionnaire. On the basis of earlier pilot studies, they reasoned that foremen described by workers as low in *consideration* and high in *initiating structure* would have work groups with higher grievance and turnover rates. To test these hypotheses, they gathered information from fifty-seven production foremen and their work groups employed in a motor truck manufacturing plant. Three workers, drawn randomly from each foreman's department, described his supervisory behavior on the LBDQ.

---

[1] For example, the correlation ratio, eta (η), may be computed. This statistic makes no assumptions about the nature of the relationship (for example, linear) between two measures. It is discussed in the section on the statistics of validation.

The mean consideration and structure scores were computed for the foremen and compared with the work groups' grievance and turnover indices for the past eleven-month period. Tables 7–1 and 7–2 give the mean grievance and turnover measures for foremen with scores at different points on the two scales of the LBDQ. The original hypotheses are confirmed. Foremen described as low in consideration have groups with higher grievance and turnover rates; similarly, foremen

TABLE 7–1. *Mean grievance and turnover indices for work groups of foremen with scores at different levels on consideration.*

CONSIDERATION SCORE (MEAN OF THREE WORKERS' DESCRIPTIONS)	MEAN GRIEVANCE INDEX (NUMBER OF GRIEVANCES/SIZE OF WORK GROUP)	MEAN TURNOVER INDEX (NUMBER OF TERMINATIONS/SIZE OF WORK GROUP)
86–90	.06	.05
81–85	.11	.08
76–80	.07	.05
71–75	.17	.06
66–70	.15	.07
61–65	.23	.10
Below 60	.40	.22
Correlation (eta) with consideration	−.51	−.69

TABLE 7–2. *Mean grievance and turnover indices for work groups of foremen with scores at different levels on initiating structure.*

INITIATING STRUCTURE (MEAN OF THREE WORKERS' DESCRIPTIONS)	MEAN GRIEVANCE INDEX (NUMBER OF GRIEVANCES/SIZE OF WORK GROUP)	MEAN TURNOVER INDEX (NUMBER OF TERMINATIONS/SIZE OF WORK GROUP)
50 and above	.39	.18
45–49	.17	.10
40–44	.10	.09
35–39	.11	.06
30–34	.02	.07
29 and below	.05	.06
Correlation (eta) with structure	.71	.63

described as high in initiating structure have groups with higher grievance and turnover rates. Unfortunately, Fleishman and Harris did not present the N's or the standard deviations associated with the mean indices shown in Tables 7–1 and 7–2; thus, we cannot express the results in terms of the amount of overlap between distributions. However, they did calculate correlation ratios (eta coefficients), and these are shown in the last rows of the two tables. The correlations are moderately high, indicating a fairly substantial relationship between subordinates' descriptions of their foreman's behavior on the LBDQ and two behavioral measures of their work group members. Certainly this study adds meaning to scores on the LBDQ and may be taken as evidence tending to confirm the behavioral validity of supervisory descriptions derived from it.

In fact, this study shows not only the desirability but also the necessity of gathering many lines of evidence when validating a test. The high relationship between subordinates' LBDQ descriptions of their supervisor's behavior and their grievance and turnover records suggests rather strongly that the negative results obtained in Harris and Fleishman's previous study were due *not* to invalidity of the LBDQ but instead to the lack of the training program's effectiveness. As more studies of different types are conducted with any given test, we gain better understanding of the behavioral meanings that may be attached to various scores on that test.

Content-Analytic Validation Strategy

A final approach for determining the meaning of scores on a test is to conduct a careful content analysis of the items comprising the test and to infer from their content what the behavioral correlates of various responses might be. Obviously, such an approach rests heavily on expert judgment and more or less subjective impressions or guesses about the behavior associated with responses to the items or statements of the test. We have already argued in Chapter 3 that this armchair approach to test validation is, at best, only a starting point. It may serve as an aid during the initial specification and writing of test items, but it must be supplemented with information from most, if not all, of the other validation strategies before a broad range of interpretations from test scores can be made with confidence. The LBDQ is, of course, an example of a measure initially "validated" by content analysis. The two scales comprising the questionnaire—*consideration* and *initiating structure*—were named simply by looking at the nature of the statements comprising each one. However, before attributing actual behavioral meaning to scores on the test, other validational studies had to be conducted. Obviously, the task is not yet completed, but the results, so far, suggest some degree of behavioral "validity" for scores on the LBDQ.

In many instances, efforts to gain additional validational evidence for a test yield essentially negative results. This is not unusual when too great a reliance is placed on content-analytic validational procedures. Accurate personnel selection and placement demands direct empirical evidence of relationships between test scores and job behaviors. Such relationships are *not* obtained through content analysis; they can only be obtained by resorting to the other validational strategies, which require in turn the specification of the relationships through one or more of a number of statistical methods.

The Statistics of Validation

Requirements for Test Validation

Any number of methods are available for computing statistical relationships. We could easily get bogged down in a seemingly endless array of correlational indices, tests of statistical significance, and other numerical manipulations. Instead, we will limit the domain of discourse by first presenting a brief statement of exactly what we seek to accomplish in validating an individual differences measure; this will automatically exclude many of the more esoteric statistics and should ease considerably the burden of confusion often accompanying a statistical presentation.

The goal in validation is to learn what can be stated about the job behavior to be expected from a person who has obtained a certain score on the measure being validated. Validation seeks to determine the ways a test may classify people into different categories and the behaviors to be expected from these people. Though it is not always explicitly stated, validation must also provide estimates of the confidence associated with such classifications and behavioral predictions. We hope to discover and to utilize psychological measures yielding statements of high accuracy—tests which, over the long run, will lead to correct designations and predictions more often than not.

Thus, in order to judge how useful any given test may be for personnel selection or placement, we need to know at least two things: (1) the relative odds that persons with various test scores will exhibit particular job behaviors or job outcomes; and (2) the degree of confidence that can be placed in these odds.

Scatter Diagrams and Expectancy Charts

A good starting point for the first type of information is to draw a scatter diagram depicting the relationship between test scores and behavioral observations. A scatter diagram is simply a "picture" of the way in which two sets of measures co-vary. Suppose, for example, that a short adjective checklist has been given to fifty applicants for a summer job of selling magazine subscriptions door to door and that their responses have been "scored" for *dominance* by giving them a point for every one of the following adjectives they use in describing themselves: aggressive, ascendant, assertive, dominant, forceful, influential, leading, outgoing, persuasive, and talkative. Imagine further that the study uses a predictive validation strategy, so that all the applicants are hired and given a chance to try their hand at magazine selling. All fifty are given a one-week training program consisting almost entirely of "role playing" or practicing the face-to-face sales contact. At the end of the week's training, the instructors use the same set of adjectives to describe the behavior of the applicants during their training period, and these descriptions are also scored on the ten-point scale for *dominance*. Thus, each sales trainee has two scores—one based on his own description of his level of dominance, the other based on his instructor's observation of his actual behavior during the training period.

Figure 7–4 shows the scatter diagram based on the two sets of scores for all fifty trainees. The diagram is fan shaped—the handle of the fan extending toward the lower-left corner and the open fan extending toward the right part of the diagram. This means that applicants who described themselves as nondominant did actually appear to be nondominant during their training period and were described as such by their instructors. However, applicants describing themselves as highly dominant also included many who were seen by their instructors as rather nondominant. Let us restate these general remarks in the form of behavioral odds associated with various test scores. It might be agreed that persons receiving scores of 7 or higher on the instructor's ratings could be designated as highly dominant and that those receiving scores of 3 or lower can be called nondominant. We may then use the scatter diagram to form the table of frequencies depicting the behavioral outcomes of applicants scoring at various points on the self-description measure of dominance:

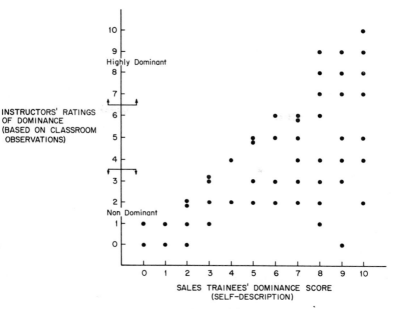

FIGURE 7–4. *Scatter diagram depicting relationship between fifty sales trainees' self-description of dominance at time of hiring and instructors' ratings of their dominance after a one-week sales training course.*

		INSTRUCTOR'S	
APPLICANT'S SCORE ON DOMINANCE AT TIME OF HIRING		TRAINEE BEHAVIOR RATING	
Score	Number with Score	"Highly Dominant"	"Nondominant"
10	7	4	1
9	7	3	2
8	8	3	3
7	6	0	2
6	4	0	2
5	4	0	2
4	2	0	1
3	4	0	4
2	4	0	4
1	2	0	2
0	2	0	2
Totals	50	10	25

This table may then be summarized further to yield the expectancy chart in Table 7-3. Interpretations based on the chart are straightforward. If a sales applicant obtains a score of 9 or 10 on the adjectival measure of dominance, the chart informs the interviewer that only about half of previous applicants with such scores were actually seen as dominant by their instructors. An applicant scoring 7 or 8 is shown by the chart to have slightly greater odds of showing nondominant behavior than of being highly dominant. Thus, the behavioral meaning (validity) of scores of 7, 8, 9, or 10 on this simple measure of dominance is not really very great—probably because it takes no great wisdom on the part of a sales applicant to discern that he probably should choose dominant-sounding words to describe himself; both dominant and nondominant people perceive this fact, with the result that the simple adjectival measure of dominance does not pinpoint people who really show dominant behavior. On the other hand, the adjective checklist does appear to be effective for identifying nondominant people. The chart shows that one can with almost complete certainty predict that an applicant with a very low score (0, 1, 2, 3) will not be seen as dominant by other persons.

Thus, the expectancy chart yields exactly the sort of information needed for making selection decisions and for learning more about the behavioral meanings of different scores on a test. Such a chart is simple to develop and easy to interpret; moreover, it emphasizes the usefulness of actually examining the validational data on which selection and test interpretation decisions are to be based. Our example illustrates the usefulness of examining the relationships between tests and behavioral observations. If some summary statistic such as the correlation coefficient (r) had been computed for these data without first drawing the scatter diagram, we would not have become aware of the differing interpretations and predictions to be attached to very high and very low scores on the dominance measure.

As we have said, validation is never ending. Although the above study would give us some basis for interpreting the scores on the adjective checklist, it would be only a beginning and would need to be supplemented by many other investigations. For example, one important job behavior often investigated in validation studies is staying on the job. In our example of the magazine salesmen, the employing organization desires to avoid investing recruiting time, training time, and costs on persons who will not continue working the entire summer. Thus, another kind of validational evidence might compare the ad-

TABLE 7–3. *Expectancy table and chart depicting odds of two behavioral outcomes (high dominance and nondominance) associated with applicants' scores on "dominance" on an adjective checklist.*

APPLICANT'S SCORE	NUMBER OF PERSONS	NUMBER RATED "HIGHLY DOMINANT"	NUMBER RATED "NONDOMINANT"	ODDS OF HIGH DOMINANCE	ODDS OF NONDOMINANCE
9, 10	14	7	3	1 in 2	1 in 5
7, 8	14	3	5	1 in 5	1 in 3
4, 5, 6	10	0	5	0	1 in 2
0, 1, 2, 3	12	0	12	0	1 in 1

jective checklist dominance scores with job tenure and with reasons for leaving. Figure 7–5 and Table 7–4 show the hypothetical scatter diagram and the corresponding expectancy chart that might be derived from such information. It can be seen that this study adds further mean-

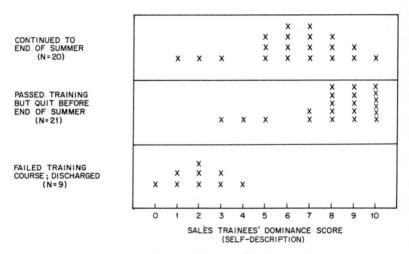

FIGURE 7–5.   *Scatter diagram depicting relationship between sales applicants' dominance scores and job tenure.*

ing to the scores on the crude adjectival self-description of dominance. The table below summarizes the validity information obtained for various score ranges on the measure:

SCORE RANGE	BEHAVIOR RATING	JOB TENURE
9, 10	Chances *even* of being highly dominant	Very unlikely to finish summer
7, 8	Chances *low* of being highly dominant	Chances *even* for finishing summer
4, 5, 6	Chances *even* of being non-dominant	Chances *high* for finishing summer
0, 1, 2, 3	Almost certain to be non-dominant	Very unlikely to finish summer or even to finish training successfully

From the table, we would very likely recommend that applicants scoring at the extremes on the dominance measure (0, 1, 2, 3 or 9, 10) be rejected. The studies have shown rather conclusively that the mea-

TABLE 7-4. *Expectancy table and chart depicting odds of completing entire summer's work for applicants with different dominance scores.*

APPLICANT'S SCORE	NUMBER OF PERSONS	NUMBER COMPLETING SUMMER WORK	ODDS OF COMPLETING SUMMER
			0.25 0.50 0.75 1.00
9, 10	14	3	1 in 5
7, 8	14	7	1 in 2
4, 5, 6	10	7	7 in 10
0, 1, 2, 3	12	3	1 in 4

sure *is not* a valid indicator of dominant behavior, though it does apparently pinpoint nondominant behavioral tendencies. Also, persons scoring in the middle ranges (4, 5, 6, 7, 8) have better than even odds of sticking the job out for the whole summer, and this is important knowledge on which to base a selection decision.

Implications for Validation

The foregoing discussion and our hypothetical example point up a number of facts about validation studies deserving special emphasis.

1. As in the hypothetical example just cited, validation studies are typically conducted in order to learn how test scores should be interpreted for future examinees. Because of this, subjects in a validation study should bear a close resemblance to the kinds of persons who will be taking the test in the future. It is necessary to describe the subjects taking part in the study rather carefully so that future users of a test will be able to judge how applicable previous research studies with the test may be to their own intended uses.

2. It is best to resist any prior assumptions about the nature of possible relationships between the measure being validated and other behaviors. Our simple example illustrates relationships that are nonlinear and nonhomoscedastic.[2] It is important to examine the nature of the relationship

[2] A nonhomoscedastic relationship is one in which the variability differs in different parts of the scatter diagram. The effect of this is that decision rules differ from one part of the scatter diagram to another.

directly rather than being content with using statistics such as the correlation coefficient which may demand assumptions (such as linearity) not satisfied by the data being analyzed.

3. It is well to accumulate as much information as possible bearing on the interpretability of scores on a test. We have seen how just two lines of evidence can enrich the validity or the meaning of scores on a test over that available from one study. Every new study can add new information about the inferences we can make from test scores.

4. Finally, since human behavior is so complex, we should remember in test validation that we are really seeking to learn the meaning of different scores and score ranges on the test rather than the meaning of the test as a whole. It is rather uncommon to find a monotonic relationship between test scores and other behavior—the situation where low scores denote a "little bit" of a certain behavior and high scores denote "a lot" of the behavior. It is more usual by far to obtain results similar to those obtained with our so-called dominance measure where low scores did indeed denote nondominant behavior but where high scores *did not,* with much precision, denote dominant behavior.

The studies described in the boxes on the pages 133–134 are examples of how expectancy charts have been used to express the relationship between test scores and job behavior measures in several different personnel selection situations.

Correlation

We have already noted that the relationship between two variables (such as a test score and a rating of job behavior) is most readily and most accurately examined by plotting a scatter diagram. However, it is often desirable to express the relationship between variables statistically rather than pictorially. For example, if large numbers of relationships involving many test scores and many job behavior measures are being examined, the burden of drawing so many scatter diagrams might make the task impracticable. Moreover, it is often desirable to try combining the test scores to give a single composite prediction of job behavior, and this usually requires statistical expressions of the relationships among the variables. Of course, the use of any single statistic to summarize data will result in a net loss of information, but this is no great

The chart* below summarizes the predictive accuracy for the battery of tests administered to thousands of airmen during World War II. Scores from the tests were combined into a single index (Pilot Aptitude Score) ranging from 1 to 9. It is readily apparent that the large majority (nearly 90 per cent) of airmen with high scores (7, 8, and 9) did successfully complete pilot training. At the other end of the scale, fewer than 40 per cent with low scores (3, 2, and 1) completed training successfully. Since the chart was developed after observing the behavior in training of airmen with different composite test scores, it proved extremely useful for interpreting the test scores of future pilot aspirants.

PILOT APTITUDE SCORE	PER CENT COMPLETING PILOT TRAINING	NUMBER WITH THIS SCORE	APPROXIMATE ODDS OF SUCCESS
	0 10 20 30 40 50 60 70 80 90 100		
9		14,682	9 in 10
8		15,286	9 in 10
7		24,367	8 in 10
6		30,066	8 in 10
5		31,091	7 in 10
4		22,827	6 in 10
3		11,471	4 in 10
2		2,239	3 in 10
1		904	2 in 10

* Chart showing relation between Pilot Aptitude Score and successful completion of pilot training ("Psychological Activities in Training Command AAF," *Psychological Bulletin*, 42, 1945, p. 46). Used by permission.

disadvantage because the human mind is incapable of properly collating and interpreting great masses of information anyway. In fact, for this very reason, summary statistics are usually computed in a selection study—that is, to aid in the difficult job of properly understanding the mass of information usually available to us about test scores, job behaviors, and their interactions. What we hope to avoid, of course, in the use of any statistic is the possible *distortion* of information. Thus, in using the correlation coefficient (r) as a measure of the degree of relationship between two variables, it is important to check on the plausibility of the important assumptions of linearity and homoscedasticity. When these two assumptions are satisfied, we may be reasonably certain that r accurately portrays the nature and magnitude of the relationship between two variables and that its use is justified.

Perhaps the major use for the correlation coefficient in selection studies is as a screening statistic. When many variables are included in

The chart* below shows results of studying the biographical histories of female office workers who had proved to be long-term (eighteen months and longer) or short-term (less than nine months) employees. By comparing the application blanks of short-term girls with those of long-term girls, several factors (for example, education, birthplace, age, marital status, previous work experience) were discovered which differentiated between the two groups. Points were assigned to the factors characterizing the long-term girls, and these were summed to form the distribution of scores shown in the chart below. Clearly, higher scores are associated with higher odds of staying with the firm eighteen months or more.

SCORED APPLICA- TION SCORE	PER CENT STAYING WITH COMPANY OVER 1½ YEARS	NUMBER SCORING IN THIS RANGE	APPROXIMATE ODDS OF STAYING WITH FIRM 1½ YEARS OR MORE
20 and above	0 10 20 30 40 50 60 70 80 90 100	18	9 in 10
15–19		20	6 in 10
10–14		21	4 in 10
9 and below		24	1 in 10

* Chart showing relation between biographical "score" and long service for female office employees ("Development of a Weighted Application Blank to Aid in the Selection of Office Employees," Research Report No. 7, *Personnel Research,* Minnesota Mining & Manufacturing Co., 1956).

The chart* below shows the concurrent relationship between a composite of a number of tests and biographical responses and an "over-all success" index for Standard Oil Company executives. The Success Index reflected the men's promotion rate in the firm and a job effectiveness rating. A high relationship exists between scores on the tests and the job behavior ratings for these executives.

	NUMBER OF PERSONS	CHANCES IN 100 OF BEING IN TOP HALF ON OVER-ALL SUCCESS INDEX	ODDS
Highest 20% on tests	88	0 10 20 30 40 50 60 70 80 90 100	9 in 10
Next 20% on tests	89		7 in 10
Middle 20% on tests	89		5 in 10
Next 20% on tests	89		3 in 10
Lowest 20% on tests	88		1 in 10

* Expectancy chart showing chances of being in the top half on the overall success index for Standard Oil managers with different composite test scores (H. Laurent, *Early Identification of Management Potential.* Social Science Research Report. New York: Standard Oil Co. [N.J.], 1961). Used by permission.

a study, it is a good first step (and an easy one with the use of electronic computers) to calculate r's between all the predictors (test scores, interview ratings, biographical information) and the various measures available of job behavior. The resulting set of correlations can then be handled in several ways:

1. The highest values will identify predictor and job behavior variables that merit more thorough study. It will usually be useful at this point to draw scatter diagrams for these variables and to develop expectancy charts depicting the relationships between the test predictors and the job behaviors.

2. Predictor variables showing low correlations with job behavior measures might also merit additional examination, particularly if there is reason to believe that a curvilinear relationship or a nonhomoscedastic one may be present. Ordinarily, however, a low correlation obtained at this stage of the screening procedure will result in the variable being discarded from further consideration.

3. After identifying the highest correlations, regression or prediction equations may be computed and used as a basis for predicting various job behaviors from the relevant predictors. The line of best fit for any predictor–job behavior combination is usually defined as the line that cuts through the scatter diagram so that the sum of the squared deviations of the actual values from the line is the lowest possible value. The equation for this line is:

$$Z_y = r_{xy}Z_x,$$

where

$Z_y =$ the standard score corresponding to any given value of y,

$Z_x =$ the standard score corresponding to any given value of x,

$r_{xy} =$ the correlation coefficient between the variables x and y.

Thus, if scores on the two variables are expressed in standard score form, the value of r_{xy} may be interpreted directly as the slope of the regression line drawn through the array

of points in the scatter diagram—that is, the ratio between
the amount of change in y on the regression line and the
amount of corresponding change on the x measure.

Let us take a look once more at the scatter diagram
shown in Figure 7–4 and compute the regression line for it.
It is shown in Figure 7–6.[3] The equation of the line may

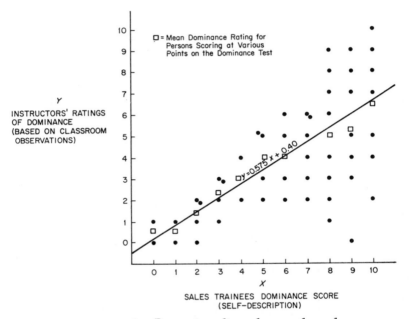

Y
INSTRUCTORS' RATINGS
OF DOMINANCE
(BASED ON CLASSROOM
OBSERVATIONS)

SALES TRAINEES DOMINANCE SCORE
(SELF–DESCRIPTION)

FIGURE 7–6. *Regression line drawn through
the scatter diagram relating trainees' dominance
scores to instructors' ratings of dominance.*

be used to predict or to "interpret" the various scores on the
dominance test in terms of dominant behavior as observed
by the classroom instructors. Thus, the mean rating of all
persons scoring 1 on the test would be expected to be

[3] The relevant statistics and the computation of the regression line for the
scatter diagram shown in Figure 7–6 are as follows:

$$M_x = 6.26; \; M_y = 4.00; \; r_{xy} = .64; \; SD_x = 2.98; \; SD_y = 2.68; \; Z_y = r_{xy}Z_x.$$

$$\frac{y - 4.00}{2.68} = \frac{[.64][x - 6.26]}{[\;2.98\;]}$$

$$y = 0.575X + 0.40.$$

0.975 [0.575(1.0) + 0.40], and the mean rating of all persons scoring 9 on the test should be expected to be 5.575 [0.575(9.0) + 0.40].

The regression line follows very closely along the points designating the mean values of Y (dominance ratings) for persons with different scores on X (the dominance test). If the regression between X and Y were *perfectly* linear, the line would pass exactly through each of the mean values. The regression does not depart far from being a linear one. The interested student may want to compare this scatter diagram with Figure 2–2, where a straight line would pass through *none* of the mean values; in other words, a correlation coefficient and a linear regression line clearly do not fit the data shown in Figure 2–2. Even the regression line in Figure 7–6 is rather a poor substitute for the expectancy chart based on the same data (shown in Table 7–3). This is because the relationship shows rather sharp departures from homoscedasticity. Regression lines and regression equations should be employed with great caution. It is preferable to resist "summarizing" the data in regression equations and use instead expectancy charts for more accurate portrayal of relationships.

Combining Measures

Two or more tests can be used in combination to predict job behavior more accurately than any of the tests can singly. For example, let us suppose that the adjective checklists completed by the sales trainees in our previous example could also be "scored" for persistence and affiliation[4] on a scale ranging from 1 to 7, and that these two scores were correlated with the rated "success"[5] of ten of the trainees at the

[4] The persistence score might consist of the number of adjectives chosen from among the following: hard working, determined, persistent, persevering, industrious, thorough, and stick-to-ative; and the affiliation score might similarly consist of the number chosen from among the following: friendly, sociable, warm, outgoing, kind, sensitive, and affiliative.

[5] As a very arbitrary and global measure of job "success," and solely for the purpose of illustration, let us assume that ratings were made on the following four-point scale:

1	2	3	4
One of the poorest summer sales trainees we have ever had.	He is definitely below average. I would probably not hire him again.	He is definitely better than average. I would hire him again if possible.	One of the best summer sales trainees we have ever had.

end of the summer job. The results obtained in this hypothetical study are shown in the three scatter diagrams of Figure 7–7. The correlation coefficient between the ratings and the persistence scores is +.36; that between the ratings and the affiliation scores, +.72; and between the persistence scores and affiliation scores, +.05. Scores on each of the two tests are moderately related to the ratings of the relative over-all success of the ten trainees. Yet the two tests are almost entirely independent of one another, and thus they are measuring quite different behavioral tendencies for the ten trainees. We might expect that a combination of the two measures would be more predictive of the "success" ratings than either taken alone. In fact, a low score on one of the tests might be compensated for by a high score on the other test. Perhaps a nonpersistent trainee could make up for lack of persistence by being friendly and affiliative and thereby be perceived as "successful" after all. The compensatory action of the two tests is illustrated in the third scatter diagram (Diagram C), particularly for subjects 4 and 7 who obtained only moderate scores on persistence and high scores on affiliation and who were rated in the top categories on over-all success.

Multiple Correlation

How should the scores for the two tests be combined? A simple expedient would be to add them together. Doing this yields a correlation coefficient of +.76 between the sum of the two and the job behavior rating, a value greater than the correlation based on either test taken singly. However, a simple summing of the two predictors does not account for possible differences in the degree of relationship shown by each, nor is the level of correlation between the two predictors considered. Thus, a simple sum is usually an oversimplification. A higher net relationship can nearly always be achieved by using multiple regression[6] to account for the factors mentioned above. Multiple regression procedures use all the information available about interrelationships among a set of measures. The method yields a *multiple correlation coefficient* (R) that describes the relationship between a measure

---

[6] A detailed account of multiple regression procedures is beyond the scope of this text. The best single source for a clear and accurate account of multiple regression, the derivation of appropriate formulae, and their use is E. E. Ghiselli, *Theory of Psychological Measurement* (New York: McGraw-Hill Book Company, Inc., 1964).

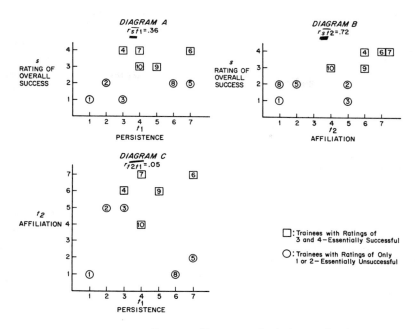

FIGURE 7–7. *Scatter diagrams depicting relationships between persistence, affiliation, and over-all success rating for ten summer sales trainees.*

(in our example—the "success" ratings) and the optimal linear combination of two or more predictors. The application of multiple regression to our homely example yields an R equal to +.79, a value higher than the value of +.76 obtained from the simple summation of the two scores. The method also yields a *multiple regression equation* analogous to the simple regression equation discussed previously and illustrated in Figure 7–6. For our data, the equation (using words to describe the variables) is the following:

$$[\text{Rating of Job "Success"}] =$$
$$.19 \, [\text{Persistence Score}] + .36 \, [\text{Affiliation Score}] + .22.$$

The above equation can be used to compute the best-guess prediction for the later-rated "success" for an applicant with any combination of scores on the two tests of persistence and affiliation. In this equation the two tests are now weighted differently (instead of the same, as they were when we simply summed them), taking account of their differing relationships to the "success" rating, their differing variabilities, and their intercorrelation. The reader should be cautioned again that the proper use of such an equation and of multiple regression procedures in general still depends on the underlying assumptions that all relationships are linear and homoscedastic. To the extent that these assumptions are not fulfilled, decisions based on multiple regression analyses will be inaccurate, and they will distort rather than accurately portray the data on which they are based.

Suppressor Variables

Occasionally a measure correlating nearly zero with a job behavior rating may still be useful when employed with a predictor measure with which it is highly correlated. Suppose a verbal reasoning test and a test of spatial relations reasoning are tried out as possible predictors for selecting auto mechanics. Against a job behavior rating based on over-all proficiency as a mechanic, the following pattern of correlations might be obtained:

$$r_{sp} = +.40$$
$$r_{vp} = .00$$
$$r_{sv} = +.70$$

where,

s = spatial reasoning test,
v = verbal reasoning test,
p = job proficiency rating.

At first glance, it seems extremely unlikely that the verbal reasoning test would be of any use; yet when it is combined (via multiple regression) with the spatial test, the value of R is found to be .56, and the corresponding regression equation (in standard score form) is

$$Z_p = .78\, Z_s - .55\, Z_v.$$

How can this apparent paradox be explained? Spatial reasoning ability apparently is predictive of mechanical proficiency, but scores on the test of spatial ability probably also depend on other factors, such as test taking "knowhow" and general intelligence, that may be irrelevant to mechanical proficiency; thus, in combination with the spatial test, the verbal test serves to "correct for" or to *suppress* the unwanted or irrelevant parts of the spatial reasoning measure. This is accomplished by the negative weighting of the verbal test in the regression equation, and this suppression effect is the basis for labeling such variables *suppressor variables*.

The combination of circumstances yielding suppressor variables occurs only rarely; yet the potential of such variables for increasing the predictive efficiency of a predictor combination is substantial, and patterns of correlation coefficients should always be studied with this in mind. A predictor correlating zero with a job behavior observation may prove highly useful *if* it is highly correlated with some other predictor showing a substantial relationship with the job behavior measure.

Mean Differences

Correlation and multiple regression analyses yield single indices indicative of the relationship between predictors and job behavior measures when each measure is treated as a continuous distribution of scores. However, it is more usual to classify job behavior outcomes in categories rather than along a continuum. The descriptive categories of different job outcomes shown in Figure 7–5 are examples of this. When job behavior observations are categorized, it is useful to express the relationship with predictor measures by simply calculating the mean predictor score for each of the behavior rating categories. Thus, for the data in Figure 7–5, the means and standard deviations are:

| | SUMMARY STATISTICS FOR TRAINEES' DOMINANCE SCORES | | |
	Number	*Mean*	*Standard Deviation*
1. Persons continuing to the end of summer	20	6.25	2.26
2. Completed training but quit before end of summer	21	8.14	1.97
3. Failed training course and were discharged	9	2.00	1.15

It is apparent that a relationship exists between the job outcome groupings and the predictor scores, but it is obviously not a simple linear one. Comparisons between the mean scores for the various groups show that the "quitters" (Group 2) obtained very high scores on the "dominance" test, the "failures" (Group 3) very low scores, and the "successes" (Group 1) middle to moderately high scores. The table above is really just another way of looking at the information presented via the expectancy chart in Table 7–4.

Percentage Overlap

The calculation of means does not really yield much information about the power of the predictor test for accurately identifying different job behavior groups. We need a statistic telling us how effectively the predictor can separate groups characterized by different job behavior outcomes. For example, in Figure 7–8 we show the score distributions for two groups classified according to different job behaviors. The shaded area designates the overlapping portion of the two distributions. The greater the amount of overlap, the less effective is the predictor in separating the two distributions; the less the overlap, the more effective is the predictor. Thus, the percentage of scores obtained by one group that may be matched by scores obtained in another group constitutes a very useful and meaningful index of the test's accuracy (validity) for separating any two groups defined on the basis of different job behaviors. If the two groups overlap completely—that is, the test is completely ineffective in separating them—the percentage of matching scores will be 100 per cent. In contrast, if the two groups show *no* overlap—that is, the test is completely accurate in separating them—the percentage of matching scores will be 0 per cent. The crucial question thus becomes: How shall the size of the shaded portion shown in Figure 7–8 be estimated?

Tilton (75) has provided one very simple estimate based on the ratio of the difference between the means of the two groups to the average of the two standard deviations. Table 7–5 shows the relevant

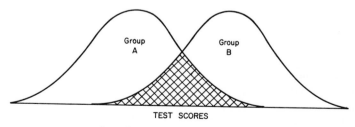

FIGURE 7–8. *Overlapping of test score distributions for two groups (A and B) with different job behavior outcomes.*

TABLE 7–5. *Estimation of percentage overlap, O, between two distributions from means and standard deviations.* (From Tilton, 75.)

DIFFERENCE* SD_{av}	PERCENTAGE OVERLAP, O	DIFFERENCE* SD_{av}	PERCENTAGE OVERLAP, O	DIFFERENCE* SD_{av}	PERCENTAGE OVERLAP, O
0.000	100%	0.880	66%	1.948	33%
0.025	99	0.908	65	1.989	32
0.050	98	0.935	64	2.030	31
0.075	97	0.963	63	2.073	30
0.100	96	0.992	62	2.116	29
0.125	95	1.020	61	2.161	28
0.151	94	1.049	60	2.206	27
0.176	93	1.078	59	2.253	26
0.201	92	1.107	58	2.301	25
0.226	91	1.136	57	2.350	24
0.251	90	1.166	56	2.401	23
0.277	89	1.197	55	2.453	22
0.302	88	1.226	54	2.507	21
0.327	87	1.256	53	2.563	20
0.353	86	1.287	52	2.621	19
0.378	85	1.318	51	2.682	18
0.403	84	1.349	50	2.744	17
0.429	83	1.381	49	2.810	16
0.455	82	1.413	48	2.879	15
0.481	81	1.445	47	2.952	14
0.507	80	1.478	46	3.028	13
0.533	79	1.511	45	3.110	12
0.559	78	1.544	44	3.196	11
0.585	77	1.578	43	3.290	10
0.611	76	1.613	42	3.391	9
0.637	75	1.648	41	3.501	8
0.664	74	1.683	40	3.624	7
0.690	73	1.719	39	3.762	6
0.717	72	1.756	38	3.920	5
0.744	71	1.793	37	4.107	4
0.771	70	1.831	36	4.340	3
0.798	69	1.869	35	4.653	2
0.825	68	1.908	34	5.152	1
0.852	67				

* Difference = Difference between means = $M_2 - M_1$

$SD_{av.}$ = Average of the Standard Deviations = $\dfrac{SD_2 + SD_1}{2}$

information for estimating Tilton's overlap statistic, O. The table was developed by assuming that the two distributions of scores are random samples from normally distributed populations with the same standard deviations. The value of O must, therefore, be interpreted with some caution, particularly if the groups show severe departures from normality or if their standard deviations are strikingly different. For most practical situations, however, Tilton's estimate provides a very useful index of how well a test separates two comparison groups. The value of O obtained from Table 7–5 can be regarded as a theoretical value approximating the percentage overlaps to be expected when the same test is used in future situations with similarly constituted groups.

In order to illustrate the usefulness of Tilton's overlap coefficient, we have calculated it for the comparisons between groups shown in Figure 7–5. The basic statistics for the computations are the means and standard deviations shown on page 143. The results are given below:

COMPARISON	MEAN DIFFERENCE	$\dfrac{\text{DIFFERENCE}}{SD_{av.}}$	O (FROM TABLE 7–5)
Group 1 (Successes) versus Group 2 (Quitters)	1.89	0.891	66%
Group 2 (Quitters) versus Group 3 (Failures)	6.14	3.935	5%
Group 1 (Successes) versus Group 3 (Failures)	4.25	2.500	21%

Groups 1 and 2 show a rather high degree of overlap on the dominance measure; thus, it is not highly accurate for pinpointing or predicting who among a group of applicants may quit the job after successfully completing training. Group 3, on the other hand, shows very low overlap with both groups; the dominance measure is highly effective for predicting which applicants will fail to complete the training program successfully.

Point Biserial Correlation

Another convenient index for expressing the relationship between measures when one measure is expressed in two categories is the *Point*

Biserial Correlation Coefficient (r_{pb}). This statistic may be computed by assigning the score of 1 to all the persons in one category and the score of 0 to the persons in the other, and then proceeding to calculate the correlation coefficient (r) between the dichotomized score and the continuous score. It can be shown that the formula for the correlation coefficient under these conditions reduces to the following expression:

$$r_{pb} = \frac{(M_1 - M_0)\sqrt{P_1 P_0}}{S_y}$$

where,

r_{pb} = point biserial correlation coefficient,

M_1 = mean on the continuous distribution of scores for persons in Category 1,

M_0 = mean on the continuous distribution of scores for persons in Category 0,

P_1 = proportion of persons who are in Category 1,

P_0 = proportion of persons who are in Category 0,

S_y = standard deviation of all scores on the continuous distribution.

Applying the above computational formula to the previous data yields the following values for r_{pb}:

MEAN	COMPARI-SON	$M_1 - M_0$*	P_1	P_0	S_y	r_{pb}
6.25	Successes versus	1.89	$21/41 = .51$	.49	2.32	.41
8.14	Quitters					
8.14	Quitters versus	6.14	$21/30 = .70$	.30	3.36	.86
2.00	Failures					
6.25	Successes versus	4.25	$20/29 = .69$	.31	2.82	.70
2.00	Failures					

* Note that 1 is assigned to the persons with the higher mean on the dominance measure; 0 is assigned to those with the lower mean.

The values of r_{pb} accurately reflect the other types of comparisons between the groups; that is, a relatively large difference between means corresponds with a high value of r_{pb} and with a low amount of overlap, O. Smaller differences between the means correspond with lower values of r_{pb} and larger degrees of overlap.

Although all these measures give similar information, perhaps the best is the overlap measure, O. It is interpretable directly as the degree of separation between two groups and thus yields an extremely useful index of the power of a test to identify different categories of job behavior. The point biserial coefficient is not so easily interpreted; it gives one only a rough notion of the magnitude of relationship between a test and categorical assignments based on job behavior observations. The difference between means is meaningless unless compared with the standard deviations of the two distributions; and once this is done, the overlap coefficient might just as well be computed.

Correlation Ratio (η)

We have emphasized rather strongly that the correlation coefficient, r, is only appropriate when the regression between two measures is linear. Thus, when the scatter diagram between two measures (for example, Figure 2–2 or the data depicted in Tables 7–1 and 7–2) clearly indicates that a straight line will not fit the data, a more appropriate estimate of relationship is necessary. Such a measure is the *correlation ratio*, η (eta). It is a general index of association particularly adapted to data in which there is curvilinear regression.

As we saw in Figure 7–6, when the regression between two measures X and Y is *linear*, a straight line can be drawn almost exactly through the mean values of Y corresponding to different values of X. In a similar way, when the regression is *curvilinear*, it is possible to fit a curved line to the data by connecting the mean values of Y corresponding to the various values of X. Note, however, that if *no* relationship exists between the two measures, *all* the mean values of Y are the same corresponding precisely to the over-all mean for all values of Y, and the resulting standard deviation of the Y means is zero. In contrast, if Y is completely determined by knowing X, there is no "scattering" of Y values within arrays corresponding to X values, and the standard deviation of the predicted (or mean) values of Y is fully as great as the standard deviation of all the Y values. Thus, a general way of defining the degree of relationship between two measures is as follows:

$$\text{relationship} = \frac{SD_y'}{SD_y}$$

where,

$SD_y' = $ standard deviation of mean values of Y corresponding to various X values,

$SD_y = $ over-all standard deviation of all Y values.

The above ratio is the defining formula for the correlation ratio. Note that its value ranges from 0 (when the means of the Y values are all the same, showing zero standard deviation) to 1.0 (when the standard deviation of Y means is exactly the same as the over-all standard deviation of Y).

The actual calculation of η may be illustrated with the data shown in Figure 7–6. The values of the Y means for each X value and the number (n) of scores on which each is based are shown below in columns 2 and 3:

(1)	(2)	(3) NUMBER OF Y SCORES,	(4)	(5)	(6)
X	M_y'	n	$M_y' - M_y$	$(M_y' - M_y)^2$	$n(M_y' - M_y)^2$
0	.5	2	−3.50	12.2500	24.5000
1	.5	2	−3.50	12.2500	24.5000
2	1.25	4	−2.75	7.5625	30.2500
3	2.25	4	−1.75	3.0625	12.2500
4	3.00	2	−1.00	1.0000	2.0000
5	3.75	4	− .25	.0625	.2500
6	4.00	4	.00	.0000	.0000
7	4.33	6	.33	.1089	.6534
8	5.00	8	1.00	1.0000	8.0000
9	5.14	7	1.14	1.2996	9.0972
10	6.42	7	2.42	5.8564	40.9948
Over-all Y mean = 4.00.				Total =	152.4954

The calculation of the standard deviation of the Y means is carried out simply by squaring the deviations of each from the over-all Y mean, weighting each square according to the number of scores, summing them, and determining the square root of the mean of the total. These operations are illustrated in columns 4, 5, and 6 of the above table. The value obtained is 1.75, which is then compared with the over-all standard deviation of Y (2.68) to calculate η. Hence,

$$\eta = \frac{SD_y'}{SD_y} = \frac{1.75}{2.68} = .65.$$

The value of η is almost identical to the value of r (.64) calculated for these same data. The near identity of the two values (r and η) confirms that a straight line accurately fits the relationship between the two variables.

We have also calculated η for the data shown in Figure 2–2. The resulting value is .96, *markedly* different from the r value for the same data of $-.03$.

The correlation ratio is, therefore, an extremely useful statistic because it yields not only a direct general index of how closely two measures are associated but also because one may, by comparing values of r and η, gain a good idea of the extent of any departure from linear regression. As a general rule, we strongly recommend calculating *both* r and η on every set of data for which scatter diagrams have not been plotted. When curvilinear regression is shown to be present, appropriate scatter diagrams can be drawn and examined to determine with precision the pattern of predictability possible between any two variables.

Interpretation of Percentage Overlap

Let us discuss briefly how to interpret O. How low should the value be in order for us to conclude that a meaningful and useful relationship exists between the test scores and job behavior information? How can O be used to "validate" or to add meaning to the interpretation of a test? What upper limit of O (short of 100 per cent) renders a test useless for making behavioral interpretations based on its scores? All these questions are considered below.

First, O is a percentage and may be interpreted directly as such. If it is high, we know that the measure being studied has not done a good job of accurately identifying or classifying persons belonging to different behavior categories. But how high is high? As a somewhat arbitrary "rule of thumb," we can say that any value of O exceeding

75 per cent does not offer much hope for the measure being studied. This value is equivalent to a separation between means of about one-half to two-thirds of a standard deviation, indicative of fairly good separation between the two distributions. Values of O between 50 per cent and 75 per cent may generally be taken as indicating moderately good relationships between a measure and a dichotomous behavior classification; and O values below 45 per cent denote unusually high accuracy for using a measure as a classificatory device. As examples of some typical values for O, the data illustrated in the boxes on pages 133–134 yield O values of 70 per cent, 53 per cent, and 54 per cent, respectively. Most vocational-interest scoring keys show O values of about 35 per cent when persons belonging to the keyed occupation are compared on the scoring key with men-in-general. Thus, if used strictly as a measure of relationship, the overlap coefficient may be interpreted roughly as follows: Values above 80 per cent show little, if any, useful relationship; the accuracy of classification is too low. Values between 50 per cent and 75 per cent denote fairly good separation between two groups and usually denote a practically useful relationship. Values below 45 per cent suggest a highly useful relationship; the accuracy of classification is high and the test or measure may be used with confidence that it is a valid indicant of the behavior against which it has been compared.

Other Factors Affecting the Usefulness of Predictors

In the actual use of tests for personnel selection or placement, the interpretation of the degree of relationship between the tests and the job behavior measures depends on certain additional factors. Two of the most important are the *base rate* and the *selection ratio*. *Base rate* refers to the relative incidence of any given behavior in the total population. In our example involving summer magazine salesmen, relevant base rates were the proportions of persons showing different job behavioral outcomes—for example, the proportion failing to complete the training program, the proportion quitting before the summer was over, etc. Unfortunately, it is usually extremely difficult to estimate the base rates of various behaviors in the total population because we so rarely have the total population or even a reasonably good sample of it available for study. The alternative is to use whatever data are at hand. In most selection studies, the data "at hand" are based either on present employees or on applicants. Thus, for the magazine salesmen, our best estimate of the base rate for quitting the job even after training had been successfully completed would be $21/50 = .42$ (see Figure 7–5), and the estimate for successfully completing both training and sticking it out for the whole summer would be $20/50 = .40$.

Why is a knowledge of the base rate important for estimating the usefulness of a predictor? This is easily answered. If either a very high or a very low proportion of applicants shows a particular behavior, it is not too likely that even an extremely good test will help much for improving our prediction of that behavior. For example, if 95 per cent of men over age twenty-five are married, we would need an extremely good test of the predisposition to marry (that is, one showing extremely low overlap between marrieds and nonmarrieds), before we could improve on the accuracy of the simple prediction that by the time a man reaches twenty-five he will be married. At the other extreme, the base rate for becoming involved in a fatal hunting accident is extremely low, probably less than ten instances for every 100,000 hunters—a base rate of .0001. The best prediction one can make is that a person will *not* accidentally shoot another hunter, and this prediction will be correct .9999 of the time. Thus, a test for measuring some of the behavioral concomitants of involvement in fatal hunting accidents would not be valuable as a screening device for granting hunting licenses, because anything less than a completely perfect test would misclassify as "poor accident risks" an extremely large number of hunters who will never actually be involved in such accidents. The result would be a substantial decrease in the over-all accuracy of prediction, and thousands of aspiring hunters would rise up in anguish at having been misclassified by the test and denied their licenses to hunt. When the base rate of any behavior is either very low or very high, a test, if it is to increase the accuracy of behavioral predictions, will need to be far better (lower O) than when the behavioral base rate is close to .50.

The *selection ratio* must also be taken into account in interpreting and in estimating the usefulness of a predictor. The *selection ratio* in any particular selection situation is the proportion of applicants or candidates selected and placed on a job. If the supply of job candidates is very large, it might be possible to set a low selection ratio—that is, select only a small proportion of the total number of candidates available. The persons selected would, of course, be the "cream of the crop"—those with the highest test scores—and the probability of these high scorers achieving desired job outcomes would very likely be much higher than if we were forced to adopt less stringent selection standards (for example, because of a limited supply of job candidates or because of a limited budget for recruiting and screening candidates).

The effect of the selection ratio on the usefulness of a test is illustrated in Figure 7–9. There, we show the distributions of scores on the scored biographical inventory obtained by the two groups of female clerical workers who were the subjects of the study described on page 134. The information in Figure 7–9 can be used to estimate job outcomes for girls hired under various different selection ratios. If the selection ratio were set at .10, only the girls with scores in the highest 10 per cent of the total distribution would be hired; thus, only those applicants with scores of 23 or above would be hired, and nearly all of these (90 per cent) would be predicted to be long-term employees. (Note that nine of the ten girls scoring 23 or above were long-term employees.) A selection ratio of .50 (that is, one out of every two applicants) would result in hiring all girls with scores of 15 and above, and of these, only 73 per cent (32/44) would be predicted to be long term. Finally, if applicants were in extremely short supply, we might be forced to hire just about everyone—say, nine out of ten (selection

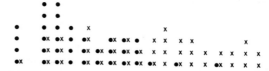

$\bullet$: *Short-term Girls* (N = 40)   x: *Long-term Girls* (N = 45)

Mean = 12.32   Mean = 17.69
Standard Deviation = 3.95   Standard Deviation = 4.89

Difference = 17.69 − 12.32 = 5.37

$$SD_{av.} = \frac{8.84}{2} = 4.42$$

$$\frac{\text{Difference}}{SD_{av.}} = 1.215$$

From Table 7–5, O = 54%

FIGURE 7–9. *Biographical score distributions for long-term and short-term girls in cross-validation sample and estimation of percentage overlap.*

ratio = .90). Then, the cutting score would be 9 or above and the estimated proportion of long-term girls would be 57 per cent, only slightly higher than the base rate of 53 per cent (45/85) for the total group. With a high selection ratio, a test needs to be much better (lower O) in order to maintain the same proportion of employees with certain desired behavioral outcomes than when the selection ratio is low.

In summary, to do an equally effective job of selection (that is, maintain a given level of accuracy in predicting that applicants will show certain desired job behavior outcomes), we need better and better tests (showing lower and lower overlap coefficients) as the selection ratio increases and as the base rate departs further and further from .50.

Estimating Stability of Validation Results

Earlier in this section on the statistics of validation, we said that two kinds of information are necessary for judging the usefulness of a test in personnel selection: (1) the relative odds that persons with various scores on the test will show particular behavioral outcomes and (2) the degree of confidence that can be placed in these odds. So far, we have discussed possible methods and related statistics for getting at the former, but we have thus far avoided discussing the latter in order first to gain a clear overview of available strategies for learning about the behavioral meaning of tests. Now, however, we must discuss the possible instability of test results.

Chance Errors

First, it is important to recognize the ubiquitous operation of chance sampling errors. If you obtain five heads upon tossing six coins, you would probably be surprised, and you might even question the "fairness" of the coins. Yet, over the long run, nearly 10 per cent of such tosses will yield five heads purely through chance. Even tosses yielding *all* heads on six coins can be expected to occur nearly 2 per cent of the time. It is exactly the same when we seek to determine the odds of certain behaviors being associated with test scores. A rather "unusual" relationship may turn out to have been determined by chance. It is necessary, therefore, to estimate the relative stability of the results of test validation studies.

Cross-Validation

It is not enough simply to establish that a difference between means or a certain size correlation coefficient or a given overlap coefficient is "statistically significant." It is far more important to know the stability of the magnitude of the relationship and particularly the stability of the figures in expectancy charts or cutting scores based on the relationship. Such matters are best handled by cross-validation. As we have said in Chapter 2, cross-validation simply involves checking our findings on another group of persons. Usually the second group is comprised of persons who were randomly set aside or "held out" from the major group. A somewhat more rigorous form of cross-validation (usually called *validity generalization*) is to select a second independent sample of subjects and to determine how well results obtained in the first sample apply to it. For example, results based on a concurrent study of present employees might be generalized by conducting a predictive study on all employees hired during the ensuing six months. Or results based on salesmen, clerical workers, or engineers working in one division of a company might be submitted for verification to a similar group of employees working in another division. It is important to realize that cross-validation is not complicated or operationally complex. It is just an obvious and easy step to confirm that both the magnitude and form of a test relationship hold up when applied to a second group of subjects. But without this simple step, little assurance can be placed in the stability of the results of a test validation study. Cross-validation is particularly necessary when item analysis procedures are used to select the "best" items for a specially developed scoring key or when several tests are combined by multiple regression procedures. In both cases, the possibility of chance events is greatly magnified, and cross-validation must be used to estimate the "shrinkage" to be expected when applying the scoring key or multiple regression equation to subsequent samples.

Locke (59) has vividly illustrated the necessity for cross-validation and the potentially illusory nature of results obtained without cross-validation. He administered a checklist of eighty-one adjectives to fifty-nine students at Cornell University. He randomly selected twenty-nine subjects for preliminary analysis, setting aside the remaining thirty for cross-validation. This preliminary group was then divided into those with longer (seven or more letters) and shorter (six or fewer letters) last names, and their responses to each adjective were analyzed to determine how the two groups might differ in their self-descriptions. Of the eighty-one adjectives, eighteen clearly $(r's \geq .36)$ discriminated between the two groups. A scoring key based on these eighteen "significant" adjectives succeeded in separating almost perfectly $(O = 8$ per cent$)$ long- and short-named persons; the difference in means between the two groups was highly significant statistically. Unfortunately, when the scoring key was cross-validated on the "hold out" group of thirty subjects, it showed absolutely no relationship $(O = 95$ per cent$)$ with the length of name.

This study may seem at first to be somewhat ridiculous; certainly, no one is interested in developing a test to predict the length of a person's last name. However, the illusion that such a test—and a very good one—had been developed was very strong until it was dissipated by trying the "test" on another sample. Similarly, in test validation and selection research, the illusion of a test's validity can be very great, particularly when a researcher is trying with all his might to develop a useful and accurate predictor of some significant aspect of job behavior. Thus, cross-validation is crucial. And, earlier in this chapter, the methods for depicting or estimating relationships between tests and job behaviors would need to be cross-validated before being employed to give meaning to the tests studied.

Statistical Significance versus Practical Importance

Throughout this chapter, we have emphasized that the primary aim of validating a test is to learn about the behavioral meanings and interpretations of scores on the test. We are not interested in inconsequential differences between mean scores, small correlation coefficients, or excessively high overlap coefficients. Small differences and inconsequential correlations, even if they are statistically "significant," do not provide a sufficient yield either for making potentially accurate predictions about expected behavioral tendencies or for understanding theoretically the functional relationships between behavior and other factors. Thus, we have chosen to say little about statistical inference and the practice of testing relationships for statistical significance. It is not enough merely to be able to say that a mean difference or a correlation coefficient differs "significantly" from zero. Instead, we want to be moderately confident that our statements about the potential behavior of persons scoring at different levels on a test are accurate. We have emphasized the overlap coefficient and expectancy tables because they automatically portray the *practical importance* of a relationship between measures. As a somewhat arbitrary but meaningful choice, we have recommended that relationships showing O's above 80 per cent (corresponding to a difference between means of half a standard deviation) are not sufficiently strong to be of practical consequence. In other words, statements based on such weak relationships cannot be sufficiently accurate to add useful meaning to the test being validated.

Unfortunately, many psychologists appear content to build their theoretical castles on the quicksand of merely rejecting the null hypothesis, apparently gaining satisfaction from reporting statistically "significant" relationships. When large numbers of subjects are used, nearly all comparisons of means yield "significant" differences and nearly all correlations are "significantly" different from zero. The following table shows the magnitudes of mean differences in standard deviation units "significantly" different for different numbers of subjects in two groups.

NUMBER OF SUBJECTS IN EACH OF TWO SAMPLES BEING COMPARED	NECESSARY DIFFERENCE BETWEEN MEANS IN STANDARD DEVIATION UNITS FOR "SIGNIFICANCE" AT THE 5% LEVEL	CORRESPONDING OVERLAP O	r_{pb}
10	.89	66%	.41
25	.57	78	.27
50	.40	84	.20
75	.32	87	.16
100	.28	89	.14
150	.23	91	.11
200	.20	92	.10
500	.13	95	.06
1,000	.09	96	.04

Our purpose in selection research is to discover relationships large enough to be *both* practically important *and* statistically significant. As implied by the table above, it is possible to include just the right number of persons in a sample so that a statistically significant result will also be sufficiently large to be important. The sample should be *large* enough to assure that sizable relationships, if present, will be detected; yet the sample should be *small* enough to assure that trivial associations will be excluded from significance. Hays (49, pp. 323–335) has presented a number of equations for determining optimum sample size for different statistical decisions. We have said that a difference between means of one-half to two-thirds of a standard deviation (corresponding to $r \cong .35$ or $O \cong 75\%$) is usually large enough to be of practical consequence. Hays' equations show that samples of fifty to sixty subjects (that is, two samples of twenty-five to thirty subjects each) are large enough to assure high likelihood of showing statistical significance for such differences while disregarding as nonsignificant the differences as small as one-third of a standard deviation (corresponding to $r \cong .15$ or $O \cong 90\%$). Thus, sample sizes of fifty to sixty are about right for conducting initial validation studies. If results on such samples attain statistical significance, the results are probably also of practical importance. The results would still need to be cross-validated on other samples in order to provide empirical verification of the stability of the relationships obtained, but we can place more faith in the outcomes of two studies (validation and cross-validation) each utilizing fifty subjects than we can in a single study utilizing 100 subjects.

To sum up then, we propose that statistics with magnitudes independent of sample size (such as O, r, r_{pb}, and η) be used in addition to significance testing in order to denote the practical usefulness of test validation and selection research studies. In every instance, cross-validation should be conducted in order to confirm the stability of the relationships discovered.

What Makes a Test Good

Hundreds of psychological tests of all types have been published and are currently available for use in selection and placement programs. Many are carefully developed, validated, and standardized; they can prove extremely useful in personnel decisions; others, however, may be entirely useless for pinpointing human traits or for predicting behavioral tendencies. How can a potentially useful test be recognized? What makes a test good? [See APA's *Test standards for psychological and educational tests* (3).]

The Test Manual

The primary basis for judging a test should be the amount and kind of evidence that the author *and* the publisher can present for deciding what the test measures and how its scores may be interpreted. *All* good tests are supported by a manual outlining exactly what the test is presumed to measure and as much research evidence as is necessary to support these presumptions. Thus, a test is judged *not* by its cover, *not* by its title, and most certainly *not* by the advertising brochures or other persuasive tidbits designed to sell it. A test *is* judged most appropriately by the content of its manual. At the very least, a test manual should include the following information:

PURPOSE

There should be a statement of why the test was developed. What did the author have in mind? What kind of human behavior was he interested in when he set out to build a new test? For what types of persons is the test intended and in what kinds of situations should it be used?

STEPS TAKEN IN THE TEST'S DEVELOPMENT

This must include a careful accounting of how test items were written and the empirical or other analytic procedures used for selecting items to be retained in the final form of the test.

EVIDENCE OF PRECISION AND STABILITY OF MEASUREMENT

It is insufficient merely to present a single estimate of the so-called reliability of a test. Instead, the manual should present several different measures of the test's precision along with estimates of the stability of the trait being measured. Moreover, careful descriptions of the subjects used in these studies and the conditions under which the studies were conducted are a necessary part of every manual. As we said in Chapter 2, the concept of "test reliability" is not a unitary concept; it is being replaced by broader recognition that the different estimates do not duplicate one another in the information they convey about test precision and trait stability. Thus, only by performing and reporting in the manual *several* studies related to measurement precision can a test author properly and adequately portray the psychometric characteristics of his test.

VALIDATIONAL EVIDENCE

In the same vein, many lines of evidence must be brought to bear in describing the "validity" of a test. We have already discussed in this chapter the different strategies for learning what a test is measuring. Obviously, such research evidence should form the central focus of any test manual. The manual should include a comprehensive accounting of as much validational evidence as is necessary to support any and all claims made for the test. The evidence should inform and educate the potential user about both appropriate and inappropriate uses of the test. If no validational evidence is included in the manual, the test should be frankly labeled as experimental, and any potential user should be forewarned that he will be expected to undertake his own research for providing validational information about the test.

NORMS AND CASE HISTORIES

Normative information should be provided, showing how different groups of persons score on the test. Norms should be provided for the kinds of persons and the types of situations for which the test's use is recommended. Case histories of the test's use with specific individuals should be provided in order to illustrate how the test has actually been used for making personnel decisions and what happened to the individuals for whom these personnel decisions were made.

GUIDES FOR INTERPRETING THE TEST

As a summary section, the manual should present the various lines of evidence available on the test in the form of recommendations or guidelines for interpreting the test and for using it in personnel selection and placement or in selection research studies.

PRECISE DIRECTIONS FOR ADMINISTRATION AND SCORING

Finally, the exact conditions and methods for administering the test in a standardized way should be outlined. Scoring of the test should also be described. In particular, if the scoring depends heavily on the judgment of the scorer (for example, projective tests such as the Rorschach or the Thematic Apperception Test), the rules for assigning scoring weights to examinees' responses must be described in detail and evidence should be presented of the degree of agreement typically obtained by different scorers.

Danger Signals

Providing the above kinds of information should be the responsibility of the test author and publisher. Many publishers do not typically provide such information; in fact, it is not uncommon to learn that no manual even exists for a test. The potential user of tests should be wary indeed of sales pitches proclaiming that a test will solve all sorts of selection problems, that it will tell the user exactly what to do in making personnel decisions, or that it is based on some great "theory" of human behavior. Tests having no more than such claims behind them have little to recommend them, and they should be avoided. Applying the above standards for choosing tests for selection studies will quickly reduce the number of potential tests from hundreds to just a few. These few will provide a much greater chance of improved accuracy in personnel decisions.

Decision Making
in Personnel
Selection
and Placement

The Nature of Personnel Decisions

Categorical Prediction

The time has come to pull together what we have said in previous chapters and to show more specifically how our model for selection research (outlined in Chapter 6) may be used to gather and to co-ordinate the information necessary for making decisions about people. The implications of the model for studying relatively homogeneous subgroups of people, job behaviors, and job outcomes have already been outlined, but these take on added importance when we consider the essentially categorical nature of personnel decision making. In marked contrast with the precise, quantitative designations made in the physical sciences, personnel decisions nearly always involve categorical judgments. Predictions of such personal outcomes as successful completion of college, occupational choice, achieving "success" in one's occupation or marriage, or even living "happily ever after" are common in psychology. Selection and placement decisions in industry are also usually categorical, seeking to "pigeon hole" persons according to expected behaviors, to discern how they may impress others, or to predict what they may do or how they might react under a variety of job circumstances. We have emphasized the danger of defining behavioral categories so broadly that the people in them do not really belong together. The classic approach to selection research has failed often to take proper note of job differences, of changes in man-job interactions, or of the differing behavioral avenues leading to the same broad "success" or "failure" outcomes. Since one of our major aims is to make the most accurate personnel decisions possible, we will usually reject the traditionally broad categories in favor of more narrowly defined and behaviorally oriented ones. At the same time, we must avoid defining behavioral categories so narrowly that they lose their relevance or importance for making personnel decisions. For example, even though using sugar and cream in one's coffee might be highly predictable, it is irrelevant to any meaningful job behavior and would not merit attention in selection decisions.

Utility of Decisions

In other words, we must be concerned not only with the *accuracy* but also with the *importance* of the decisions being made. Accuracy and importance can be included under the single rubric *utility*. Utility has to do with the over-all usefulness of personnel selection and placement procedures—the importance of wrong and of right decisions and of the different kinds of errors that may be made. This chapter is devoted both to a further explication of the decision methods suggested by our selection research model and to how the concept of utility affects judgments about selection procedures.

The Classic Psychometric Approach

Recognizing that most judgments in personnel selection and placement are essentially categorical contrasts sharply with classic psychometric approaches in test development and test validation. Much of the classic psychometric theory was developed early in this century by Charles Spearman, who sought to adapt the measurement concepts of the physical sciences to the measurement of human characteristics. The physical sciences deal with the quantification of continuous variables such as length, weight, and temperature; emphasis is given to precise measurement and to accuracy of *point* (rather than category) estimates. Spearman was greatly concerned about errors of measurement in psychology, and he elaborated the theory and methods for estimating the magnitude of such errors.[1] What have been the major effects of these contributions on psychological measurement and on procedures of personnel decision making?

[1] See Gulliksen (43) for a comprehensive presentation of classic psychometric theory.

Effects of Classic Psychometric Theory

First, Spearman's emphasis on precision of measurement helped to reduce the amount of subjectivity in behavior observation and measurement, led to standardized procedures, and aided the development of the methods for estimating test precision and trait stability outlined in Chapter 2.

Second, in the search for errors and their estimation, emphasis was placed exclusively on the instrument rather than on the person being measured. Measurement errors were assumed to be random; the possibility of interactive effects between persons and instruments was not recognized. On the basis of such assumptions, it was concluded that the amount of error differed only from instrument to instrument but that *all* persons assessed with any given instrument would be measured with the same precision.

Third, errors were treated as essentially equivalent, no matter where they occurred along the measuring scale. No distinction was made between different types of error such as the contrast between false positives and false negatives discussed in Chapter 1. Two errors of the same magnitude were viewed as equivalent even though one might simply transpose two persons within the same behavior category while another might erroneously transpose two persons between different behavior categories. Thus, classic psychometric theory gave little or no attention to the likelihood that errors may differ in kind as well as in magnitude. Also, the relative costs of making different types of wrong decisions were not considered.

Implications of the New Model

For personnel decision making, the first of the above effects was a salutary and a needed one. Unfortunately, it was accompanied by the other two effects, and these resulted in a too ready acceptance of an oversimplified model for selection research—a model which, as we have seen, did not really cope with the complexities of personnel decision making. In contrast, our model and the strategies and statistics presented in the last chapter emphasize:

1. Categorical judgments as opposed to quantitative estimates.

2. Accuracy of specific decisions as opposed to over-all precision of measurement.

3. The relative cost of different types of error as opposed to a minimization of all errors.

4. Individualized prediction strategies as opposed to global or "across-the-board" strategies.

5. Estimates of the utility of the over-all personnel decision procedure as opposed to "just" calculating validity coefficients.

Of the above, we have already discussed our reasons for emphasizing categorical predictions instead of quantitative estimates; category judgments fit the real world of human discourse more closely, and they comprise the kinds of selection and placement decisions typically made in industry, the armed forces, and government.

Estimates of decision accuracy were highlighted by the statistics in the last chapter. For example, expectancy charts are peculiarly well fitted for deriving probability statements. Moreover, by emphasizing cross-validation and practical importance, we have said in effect that a difference—to be a difference—must *make* a difference.

The relative costs of different types of decision errors (see Chapter 1, pages 7–8) have been discussed only briefly. This is given more attention in our discussion of utility later in this chapter.

In presenting the paradigm for selection research in Chapter 6, we illustrated how individualized selection strategies can be developed by discovering differentially predictable subgroups of persons. At the time we promised a more complete accounting of the methods for subgrouping jobs, persons, tests, etc., and of methods for developing individualized selection strategies. To these matters we now turn.

Individualizing the Personnel Decision

Moderator Variables

First, as we consider individualized strategies, we must ask whether classic psychometric theory is right or wrong in ignoring possible interactive effects between persons and measurements, and in assuming that all persons are measured with the same degree of precision by any given test. Ghiselli (33) has done a substantial amount of research on this question and has concluded that persons do show stable individual differences in the precision of their scores on any given test. In one study, he administered two forms of a complex reactions test to 775 semiskilled workers. For all workmen, the correlation between scores on the two forms of the test was .92. Working with tests for two-thirds of the men, he found that those with almost identical scores on the two forms were older and more highly educated than those with sharply different scores on the two forms. Using age and education, he developed a simple scoring key and applied it to persons in the remainder of the sample, thereby cross-validating his results. In the second sample, persons scoring highest on this crude scoring key obtained very nearly identical scores on the two forms of the complex reactions test ($r = .97$), and persons scoring lowest on the scoring key obtained differing scores on the two forms ($r = .82$). This means that it was possible to identify a subgroup of persons for whom the test measured with greater precision. More important, the actual qualities (age and education) related to the greater precision of measurement were specified. Thus, all persons in the original group were *not* measured with equal precision—a fact with obvious implications for differential predictability and for individualized selection strategies.

The characteristics or measures (age and education in the above example) that identify separate subgroups have been given many different labels, but the term *moderator variable* is coming to be the most widely used. Moderator effects occur in a large number of ways. Let us consider some of them and then speculate on how such effects may aid in developing individualized selection strategies.

Dunnette and Kirchner (17) have studied the different patterns of concurrent validities obtained when careful techniques of job analysis are used to discover groupings of jobs relatively homogeneous in responsibilities. Different validities were obtained for engineers grouped according to functional similarities (research, development, production, and sales), salesmen (industrial and retail), and clerical employees (stenographers and clerk typists). These studies highlight the feasibility of studying job differences and the differential predictability of effectiveness in various homogeneous job clusters.

Synthetic Validity

As suggested by these studies, differences in the duties required by different jobs will ordinarily result in predictors showing substantially different relationships with global ratings of proficiency from job to job. It is likely, of course, that much greater consistency would be observed in relationships between test scores and ratings of proficiency for carrying out the actual tasks or elemental behaviors that cut across many different jobs. This is the essential assumption of *synthetic validity*. The approach involves assembling a set of tests to predict proficiency in a job on the basis of the tests' predetermined relationships with the specific behavioral elements or components of the job. For example, most jobs can be rated according to the amount of detail work they require, and tests (particularly those designed to measure perceptual speed and accuracy and/or compulsivity) can be "validated" against ratings of proficiency in handling detail work. Similarly, test scores can be compared with ratings on such diverse job elements as doing arithmetic, spelling words properly, gladhanding customers' representatives, typing, being forceful and assertive, etc. Presumably, any job can be analyzed into its major elements and a battery of tests tailor-made to sort out applicants who may be expected to show high proficiency in each of the behaviors comprising the major elements of the job. Thus, according to Balma (5) synthetic validity is "the inferring of validity in a specific situation from a logical analysis of jobs into their elements, a determination of test validities for these elements, and a combination of elemental validities into a whole" (page 395). It should be apparent that the synthetic validity approach fits perfectly into our model for selection research, particularly at the point calling for the discovery and the separate validation of predictors against specific job behaviors. An example of a selection study using the synthetic validity concept (42) is given in the next chapter.

Differentially Predictable People

Many studies have shown different validities for different subgroups of individuals. For example, Seashore (65) summarized a large number of scholastic success studies showing almost uniformly that the grades of women (in both high school and college) are significantly more predictable than those of men. It is also well established that differing patterns of validity are typically obtained for subgroups differing in amounts of education and/or years of job experience. It may seem obvious that such factors as sex, education, and experience provide useful moderating variables in validation research. However, researchers also have identified variables that are much less obvious but which *do* make substantial differences in the patterns and magnitudes of validities obtained. For example, Grooms and Endler (37) showed that the grades of anxious college students were more easily predicted ($r = .63$) with aptitude and achievement measures than were the grades of nonanxious students ($r = .19$); and Frederiksen, Melville, and Gilbert (27, 28) have shown that interest in engineering (as measured by the Strong test) has a higher validity for predicting grades for non-compulsive students than for compulsive ones. Berdie (6) showed that the grades of engineering students with relatively consistent scores on an algebra test were more predictable from the total test score than were the grades of students with less consistent scores.

Configural Scoring and Actuarial Pattern Analysis

Since it is abundantly clear that subgroups of differentially predictable persons can be identified, it seems likely that predictors might be used in combination—not in the multiple regression sense, but in a *configural* sense—to identify groups of persons who will also show differing patterns of behavior on the job. What is meant by *configural*? Consider an example: A group of male applicants could be classified as either married or single. They could also be classified according to amount of education, college degree versus high school only. These two biographical characteristics could then be tried out singly as potential predictors of some job outcome (for example, job tenure); or they might be taken together configurally by determining the job outcomes separately for each of the four possible groups (married college graduates, single college graduates, married high school graduates, and single high school graduates). Thus, any set of predictors can be grouped meaningfully to create relatively homogeneous subgroups, and separate predictions can be made based on the patterns of job behavior shown by each group.

Lykken and Rose (60) applied this approach, which they call *actuarial pattern analysis,* to various combinations of scales on the Minnesota Multiphasic Personality Inventory (MMPI). By using just two scales configurally (with scores on each scale trichotomized), they were able to make more accurate diagnostic classifications than were made with a complex multiple regression combination of eleven of the MMPI scales. In an industrial application, Sorenson (67) used configural subgrouping of biographical information in an effort to predict "success" (defined as total income) for stock and bond salesmen. He achieved more accurate predictions in the cross-validation group for sets of characteristics taken four at a time configurally than for any combination of factors taken singly.

Developing Moderator Tests

It is possible also to "create" moderator tests by item analysis procedures. Again, Ghiselli (30, 31) has been at the forefront in developing procedures for doing so. There are two basic approaches:

1. When both the predictor and the behavior to be predicted are measured on continuous distributions, the first step is to express each in standard scores. Next, the difference between the two standard scores is determined for eacl person. Small differences occur for persons who are very accurately predicted—that is, their relative status on the behavior to be predicted is nearly the same as their standing on the predictor measurement. In contrast, large differences occur for persons who are poorly predicted—that is, their relative status on the behavior to be predicted differs substantially from their standing on the predictor measurement. It is possible then to compare the accurately predicted persons with the poorly predicted persons in their responses to other tests and inventories and to discover, through item analysis, a set of responses (comprising a moderator test) that accurately differentiates the two groups. The final step is to cross-validate the results on either a "hold-out" group or an independently selected group.

2. The second approach can be called a quadrant analysis and is typically used when the data are expressed in categories; or if both distributions are continuous, categories can be formed by splitting both distributions at their medians. Consider the following diagram:

JOB BEHAVIOR RATING

		Does Not Show Behavior	Does Show Behavior
PREDICTION BY	*Will Show Behavior*	"Over Predicted" II	"High Hits" I
PREDICTOR TEST	*Will Not Show Behavior*	"Low Hits" III	"Under Predicted" IV

Persons in quadrant I were predicted to show a certain behavior and they did; they are termed "high hits." In contrast, persons in quadrant II were also predicted to show this behavior, but they did not show it; they were "over predicted." Item analyses may be undertaken to discover a set of responses (moderator test) that will successfully differentiate between the "high hits" and the "over predicted" persons. In like manner, a second moderator test may be developed to differentiate between the "low hits" and the "under predicted persons."

After moderator tests have been developed by either of the above methods, they may be used for prescreening. Applicants can be specified as either "predictable" (selection would be made on the basis of their scores on remaining tests in the battery) or "unpredictable" (other bases would be used for selection).

Differentially Valid Tests

The most desirable other basis for deriving selection decisions for the so-called unpredictable persons would be to discover other predictors which are valid for them. In other words, moderator tests would serve as initial screening tests for designating the particular tests to be used later for each applicant. Ghiselli (32) compared scores from two or more predictors with each individual's standing on the job behavior measure. For each person, one of the predictors was more accurate than the others; thus, the total group of subjects was subgrouped according to the predictor or predictors that most accurately designated their standing on the job behavior measure. Item analyses were then carried out to discover one or more moderator tests for identifying the particular predictor set to be used for each individual applicant. Ghiselli has shown that this procedure successfully increases the accuracy of selection decisions over that obtained when using just a single predictor for all persons. In one study, two tests used singly correlated only .17 and .51, respectively, with another measure of behavior. After developing and using a moderator test to assign each subject to the test most predictive for him, the over-all correlation was raised to .73.

Individualized Selection Strategy

These methods mark the beginnings of efforts to account for complexities ignored by the oversimplified selection research of the past and by classic psychometric theory. Moderator tests to identify groupings of tests, people, and job behaviors should provide a more thorough understanding of what is going on in selection and placement studies. Figure 8–1 presents a hypothetical example of how methods of the kind we have been discussing can be used to develop individualized selection programs. Admittedly, this is an elaborate and highly idealized version of such a program, but it does illustrate a number of important characteristics for more accurate selection and placement than might be realized if just one procedure were applied to all applicants.

1. The diagram shows the potential advantages of sequential strategies in arriving at personnel decisions. After each procedure, the decision maker is directed either to hire, reject, or collect more information. In no instance is any applicant exposed to all procedures; he proceeds only to the point where a maximally accurate hire or reject decision may be made *for him*. The sequential strategy usually results in economies in the selection process because each procedure is used *only* at the point where it has been shown to be optimal.

2. The diagram also shows the tactics to be employed by the personnel decision maker with sufficient research information to know the relative accuracy of different tests for different individuals under particular circumstances and for specific jobs. He can operate much more flexibly as he accumulates information on a job applicant, and he can apply at each stage the tests and procedures optimally predictive of desired job behavior.

3. Finally, the diagram accurately portrays the true complexity of decisions about people. At first, the complexity might be viewed as a disadvantage, but this should only be true for those personnel decision makers who wish to hide their heads in the sand. It is true that the extensive amount of research data necessary for implementing the individualized, multistage strategy shown in Figure 8–1 will rarely be entirely available. Still, the pattern of personnel decision making shown there represents the idealized end result toward which we may strive through a series of approximations, coming closer and closer to the goal as we learn more and more about the relatively unique patterns of predictor–job behavior relationships for various groups. Many firms today are using elaborate sequences of screening procedures—interviews, testing, reference checking, more

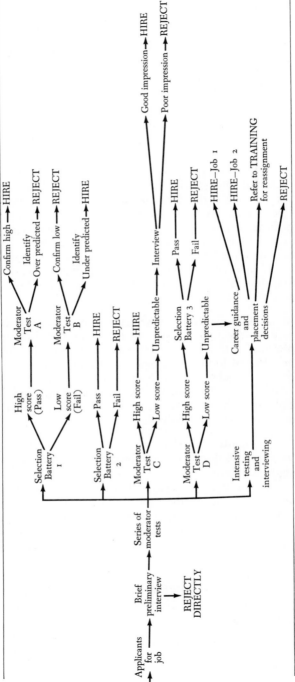

FIGURE 8-1. *Flow chart of hypothetical selection program emphasizing individualized, multistage sequential selection decisions.*

interviews, multiple assessments, etc.—which very closely approach our diagram in complexity. However, these procedures typically are based on tradition, hunch, or fiat rather than careful research evidence. Our idealized diagram should force personnel decision makers to attend more carefully to what is needed for making more informed judgments about people and stimulate them to begin gathering the evidence from which their selection strategies may be optimized.

Clinical Assessment and Selection Strategies

The Clinical Approach

People are complicated, and predicting their behavior is exceedingly difficult. The burden of working through the full array of selection research studies suggested by the schema in Figure 8–1 has frustrated many psychologists, and some have adopted a completely individualized prediction system without first establishing the nature of the complex linkages depicted by our selection research model or by the multistage procedure shown in Figure 8–1. It is common for psychologists, when working with individual cases, to adopt a *clinical approach*.

Instead of combining predictors according to some systematic procedure determined by prior research studies, the clinical approach is highly subjective; an individual's test scores and other predictor information are interpreted by the clinician on the basis of his own experience with similar cases, his inferences about job requirements, and any theories he may have about how the various predictor patterns indicate behavioral predispositions. Clinical prediction requires much greater skill than prediction based on the statistical combination of predictor variables. The skilled clinician must know all about the predictors, the special circumstances, if any, for which they are being used, and all the aspects of human behavior for which they may be relevant. This is no small order; it is little wonder, that studies comparing clinical and statistical prediction almost invariably[2] have shown

---

[2] A very recent study by Lindzey (58) does show that a clinical analysis of TAT protocols was much more successful in identifying homosexuals than a statistical scoring scheme developed from the same TAT materials. This is the only instance from among over fifty published studies in which the clinical method of prediction proved superior, and predicting such behavior as homosexuality has only limited relevance to industrial selection.

statistical prediction to be at least as accurate as or better than clinical prediction.

When Must Clinical Prediction Be Employed?

There are at least two strong logical arguments for using clinical methods:

1. Often no other basis for prediction exists. Hundreds of firms throughout the country employ only small numbers of persons—far too few for a carefully conducted selection research or test validation study. In most such instances, the only recourse is to combine predictor information clinically, taking account of the accumulated validity information available for the predictors and inferring their meaning for the specific situation. The psychologist who makes such clinical predictions should still remain alert to opportunities to validate his judgments; and, in time, he should be able to accumulate evidence showing how accurate his selection recommendations have been. Outstanding industrial examples of such follow-up studies of clinical judgment have been those by Dicken and Black (15) and by Albrecht, Glaser, and Marks (1). The latter study is presented and discussed in the next chapter.

2. Some writers, notably Cronbach and Gleser (13), argue that clinical methods are capable of providing many elements of information or of answering many questions about an applicant, whereas a statistical combination of predictors can make only narrow predictions related to those specific behaviors against which the combination has already been validated and cross-validated. There is a good deal of merit to this argument. For example, a clinical procedure such as a personal interview yields a wealth of information; to be sure, much of it is of limited dependability and only remotely relevant to selection decisions, but this breadth of information represents a rich source of hypotheses to be confirmed or refuted by further selection procedures. In this context, clinical methods fit perfectly into the sequential scheme shown in Figure 8–1. The methods would presumably be used to develop leads and to suggest hypotheses or things to look for, and more objective procedures might then confirm or disconfirm these hunches. But it is all too easy when using clinical procedures to develop hypotheses that become self-fulfilling—that is, later observations may be

unconsciously distorted to conform with and confirm earlier inferences. In Webster's research (79) interviewers formed fairly firm judgments of the interviewee during the first five minutes, and they interpreted all subsequent information to confirm these first impressions.

Whence Clinical Prediction?

Over-all, the best conclusion is to use clinical prediction with great caution, assessing the accuracy of judgments whenever possible. The best bet for predicting specifically defined domains of job behavior is still a statistical combination of predictors developed from a prior research study. However, clinical combinations and judgments can yield many hypotheses and can often be the first step toward developing more objectively based and more systematically applied prediction strategies. The clinical approach obviously is the most individualized prediction strategy possible; as such, some might argue that it should represent our ultimate aim. However, *accurate* decisions usually demand careful validation studies and selection research. As we gain more and more information, accurate individualized decisions should approach the idealized multistage pattern in Figure 8–1.

Individual versus Institutional Decisions

In Chapter 1, we contrasted and discussed institutional and individual decisions. In institutional decisions, a major goal is to maximize the net personnel effectiveness over a series of similar decisions (for example, hiring many secretaries in a firm); individual decisions are relatively unique and often nonrecurring, such as an individual's choice of a career, a marriage partner, or a horse to bet on in a particular race. Individual decisions are essentially clinical; each person's own value system determines the kinds of variables and over-all considerations to be taken into account as he evaluates different possible courses of action. Since each decision is relatively unique, no prior development of a statistical weighting scheme for the variables is possible; each individual decision maker must combine the variables clinically to fit the total set of circumstances as he sees them. To be sure, knowledge based on statistical studies of how other people have fared after undertaking different actions can help in individual decision making. For example, data are nearly always available to show the proportions of students in different intervals on a scholastic aptitude test who ultimately complete college successfully. Still, an individual's decision about his future is proved over time to be either right or wrong, wise or unwise. Testing may give an individual information to help increase his certainty about choosing from among different actions, but he can derive only modest comfort from population statistics or "odds" when faced with the necessity of choosing from among actions affecting his own future. Such "odds" cannot incorporate the special values, the unique desires, or the particular criteria against which he will, over time, evaluate his own past decisions. Thus, individual decisions are essentially clinical, and can only be evaluated in terms of each person's expectations and their relative importance *for him*.

Utility in Personnel Decisions

We mentioned utility briefly toward the first of this chapter. Now we consider it in more detail. Utility refers to the over-all usefulness of a personnel selection or placement procedure. As such, the concept encompasses both the accuracy and the importance of personnel decisions. Moreover, utility implies a concern with costs—costs related to setting up and implementing personnel selection procedures and costs associated with errors in the decisions made.

Costs in Personnel Decisions

Listing the kinds of costs involved is not difficult, but their estimation is. First, the different types of costs may be grouped into *actual* and *potential* costs.

1. *Actual costs* (costs actually incurred in hiring an applicant).
   a. *Recruiting and assessment costs*—salaries of personnel staff, advertising expenses, travel expenses, and testing personnel evaluation costs.
   b. *Induction and orientation costs*—administrative costs of adding the employee to the payroll, and salaries of the new employee and others responsible for orienting him to his new job.
   c. *Training costs*—salaries of training and development staff, salary of the new employee during training, and costs of any special materials, instruments, or facilities for training.
2. *Potential costs* (costs that might be incurred if a wrong selection decision is made).

a. *Costs associated with hiring a person who subsequently fails*—record-keeping costs, termination costs, costs of undesirable job behavior such as materials or equipment damaged; loss of customers, clients, or patients; loss of good will, etc.; and costs incurred in replacing failing employee.

b. *Costs associated with rejecting a person who would have been successful on the job*—competitive disadvantage if he is hired by another firm (for example, loss of a top sports star to a competing team), and costs of recruiting and assessing an additional applicant to replace the rejectee.

In evaluating the above costs, one needs also to estimate the potential return to the firm of hiring a successful employee—one who contributes significantly to the attainment of organizational goals. Actual hiring costs and costs due to wrong decisions need to be minimized while the potential return from hiring "good" employees is maximized. Estimating the *utility* of a selection procedure therefore requires cost estimates.

Estimating and Measuring Utility

Cronbach and Gleser (13) state that this is the Achilles' heel of utility in personnel decision making. Estimating costs may be straightforward for factors such as travel expenses, salaries, and advertising and recruiting costs, but it becomes subjective and rather arbitrary for factors such as the effects of undesirable job behaviors, possible losses in competitive advantage, and the psychological or attitudinal losses that would often accompany job failures and discharges. Yet, as Cronbach and Gleser also note, the necessity for such subjective judgments is by no means unique to utility estimates. *Any* approach designed to judge the "goodness" of selection procedures demands equally subjective and usually arbitrary judgments. Taking utility into account forces us to enumerate the various possible consequences of a personnel decision and to give careful thought to the possible costs associated with different outcomes. A few examples should illustrate how utility considerations can be helpful in deciding how to use a selection procedure.

EXAMPLE I

Meehl and Rosen (62) have discussed an inventory developed by Danielson and Clark (14) designed to reject men from Army induction who would encounter psychiatric disabilities during basic training. The inventory was relatively short, and the cost of its administration would probably not exceed $5 per man. A good, probably conservative estimate of other costs for recruiting and examining Army personnel would be $200 per man. Let us assume that the total cost of basic training, including induction, amounts to $5,000 per man. The cost of a psychiatric breakdown is impossible to estimate, but it obviously would be very great in terms both of human suffering and of dollars. The patient would need treatment in Army hospitals; and, upon discharge, he would receive a pension if his disability were shown to be service-connected. Quite aside from the human anguish involved, the cost (including loss of training and recruiting costs) might be $20,000 per man. Using an optimum cutting score,[3] Danielson and Clark stated that their inventory would identify 55 per cent of persons with psychiatric disabilities while mis-identifying as disturbed only 19 per cent of the well-adjusted inductees. Now, let us assume that we want a monthly output of 10,000 psychiatrically healthy men from basic training. What would be the total cost if the Danielson and Clark inventory were *not* used?

In order to estimate the cost, we need one further statistic: the base rate for psychiatric disability for all inductees. We shall accept the estimate given by Meehl and Rosen that 95 per cent make a good adjustment and that 5 per cent suffer psychiatric disability. Then, in order to obtain an output of 10,000 healthy soldiers, the input would be:

$$\text{INPUT} = \frac{10,000}{.95} = 10,526$$

And the total cost would be:

Recruitment and examination cost	$(10,526)(200) = \$\ 2,105,200$
Induction and training costs	$(10,000)(5,000) = \ 50,000,000$
Cost of psychiatric disabilities (including lost training costs)	$(526)(20,000) = \ 10,520,000$
Total	$\$62,625,200$

[3] Danielson and Clark unfortunately failed to cross-validate their cutting score; thus, the inventory would probably do less well in an independently selected group of subjects. For purposes of illustration, we may still use their figures, however.

TABLE 8–1. *Cumulative per cent distributions for short-term, long-term, and intermediate-term office employees.*

	PER CENT SCORING HIGHER			
Score	Long-term (18 Months or Longer)	Intermediate* (9–18 Months)	Short-term (9 Months or Less)	Difference (Long – Short)
26	4	2	0	4
25	11	5	0	11
24	16	8	0	16
23	20	11	3	17
22	24	15	3	21
21	31	15	3	28
20	38	20	5	33
19	47	25	5	42
18	53	30	8	45
17	58	37	15	43
16	64	42	22	42
15	71	50	30	41
14	75	55	35	40
13	84	65	43	41
12	84	70	53	31
11	91	80	68	23
10	98	90	83	15
9	98	90	83	15
8	100	96	93	7
7		96	93	7
6		97	95	5
5		99	98	2
4		100	100	0

* These data were not actually obtained in the study, but it seems reasonable to assume, for purposes of illustration, that their percentile falls half way between those for long-term and short-term employees.

What would be the cost if the Danielson and Clark inventory were used? Here the computation of the input is slightly more complicated because the cutting score rejects 19 per cent of the potentially well-adjusted men, and these rejectees need to be replaced by additional recruits. Thus:

$$[.95 \ (\text{INPUT})] \times .81 = 10,000$$
$$\text{INPUT} = 12,995$$

Of these, 650 [(12,995) (.05)] would be potential psychiatric failures, of whom 358 [(650) (.55)] would be rejected. The remaining 12,345 would be potentially well-adjusted soldiers, but 2,345 [(12,345)(.19)] would be rejected. Hence, the total costs, using the inventory, would be:

Recruitment and examination costs	(12,995)(200) =	$ 2,599,000
Administration of inventory	(12,995)(5) =	64,975
Induction and training costs	(10,000)(5,000) =	50,000,000
Costs of psychiatric disabilities (including lost training costs)	(20,000)(292) =	5,840,000
Total		$58,503,975

Thus, to the extent that our crude cost estimates are accurate, the total monthly saving from using the inventory is $4,121,225—over $400 per man successfully trained. The utility of such a selection device would therefore be very high, in spite of the fact that many (2,345) potentially good men would be rejected during the selection procedure. The cost of errors of false positives (labeling a potentially healthy recruit as psychiatrically unfit) are practically inconsequential in comparison with the cost or seriousness of false negatives (identifying as psychiatrically fit a recruit who later suffers a psychiatric breakdown). In our illustration, the *number* of errors of the former type was very large in comparison with those of the latter type; yet the inventory still had high utility because of the great difference in the relative seriousness and cost of the two kinds of error.

EXAMPLE 2

In the last chapter, we described a study in which biographical factors were scored and these scores were related to turnover among female clerical workers. The data from this study can be used to show how utility considerations can aid in determining the best cutting score for the biographical scores. Table 8–1 shows the percentile distributions in the cross-validation group for girls who were short-term (averaging four months with the firm) and long-term (staying eighteen months and longer). Also shown is a distribution of scores for girls staying with the firm between nine and eighteen months.

A number of possible costs can be estimated from Table 8–1. Assume that the cost of recruiting girls rises as more and more need to be screened—for example, that the first 200 can be recruited, interviewed, tested, etc., at an average cost of only $25 per girl, that the next 100 averages $30 per girl, and so on until the average for any number of girls over 500 is $100. This assumption is realistic because it takes account of the increasing difficulty of contacting and bringing into the firm more and more applicants. Next, assume that the cost of hiring a new clerical employee, paying her, and orienting her to the job is $500 per girl. This certainly is a conservative estimate, assuming that only about one month will be required for a girl to become productive and useful. We shall also assume that there is no real cost associated with losing or rejecting a potential long-term employee other than the additional recruiting costs incurred in order to meet a given employment quota.

In order to calculate total costs, it is necessary to know base rates. Before using the biographical scores, about half the girls hired stayed eighteen months or longer, 30 per cent less than nine months, and 20 per cent in the range nine-to-eighteen months. The total cost, the cost per productive employee, and the numbers of applicants screened and hired are shown in Table 8–2 for ten different scores on the biographical inventory.[4] The relationship between cost per productive employee and different cutting scores on the biographical questionnaire is depicted graphically in Figure 8–2. It can be seen from both Table 8–2 and Figure 8–2 that the maximum utility of the biographical questionnaire occurs at a cutting score of 18; below 18, too many

---

[4] The data in Table 8–2 were computed by assuming a need for at least 100 long-term employees. The computations shown below, for the score of 18, illustrate the methods used.

For Score 18: From Table 8–1, 53% long-term score 18 and above.
    30% intermediate score 18 and above.
    8% short-term score 18 and above.

Number recruited and screened $= \dfrac{100}{(.50)(.53)} = 378$

Number of potential intermediate girls $= (378)(.20) = 76$, of whom 23 $[(76)(.30)]$ would be hired.

Number of potential short-term girls $= (378)(.30) = 113$, of whom only 9 $[(113)(.08)]$ would be hired.

Hence, total hired $= 100 + 23 + 9 = 132$

Estimated costs:

Recruiting and screening:	first 200 $= (200)(25)$	$=$	\$ 5,000
	next 100 $= (100)(30)$	$=$	3,000
	next 78 $= (78)(50)$	$=$	3,900
	Total		\$11,900
Induction, salaries, orientation	$= (132)(500) =$		66,000
Cost of recruiting replacements for short-term girls	$= (9)(50)$	$=$	450
	Total cost		\$78,350

Cost per productive employee $=$ 636
(assuming that short-term girls are not "productive" employees but that intermediate-term girls are)

TABLE 8-2. *Number of applicants screened and hired and related costs for various cutting scores on the biographical questionnaire.*

SCORE	NUMBER SCREENED	NUMBER HIRED	SELECTION RATIO	NUMBER SHORT-TERM	RECRUITING COST	TRAINING COST	REPLACEMENT COST	TOTAL COST	PER PRODUCTIVE EMPLOYEE
0 (No selection)	200	200	1.00	60	5,000	100,000	1,800	106,800	763
8	200	194	.97	56	5,000	97,000	1,680	103,680	751
12	238	171	.72	38	6,140	85,500	1,140	92,780	698
15	282	153	.54	25	7,460	76,500	890	84,850	663
17	345	142	.41	16	10,250	71,000	800	82,050	651
18	378	132	.35	9	11,900	66,000	450	78,350	636
19	426	127	.30	6	14,950	63,500	450	78,900	652
20	526	129	.25	8	23,100	64,500	800	88,400	731
23	1,000	131	.13	9	70,500	65,500	900	136,900	1,122
25	1,818	118	.065	0	152,300	59,000	0	211,300	1,791

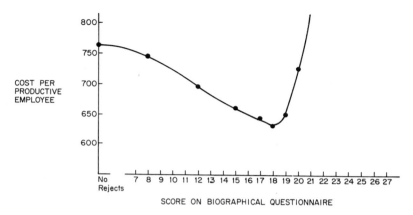

FIGURE 8–2. *Relationship between cost per productive employee and various cutting scores on biographical questionnaire.*

potentially short-term girls are accepted and the cost of training them results in a relatively high net cost per productive employee; above 18, the cost of recruiting additional applicants becomes rapidly prohibitive. Thus, from the crude cost estimates we have made, we would conclude that the biographical scoring procedure possesses maximum usefulness when all applicants scoring below 18 are rejected and those scoring 18 or above are hired; this corresponds to a selection ratio of about one in three (.35).

This example has evaluated the utility of adding a scored biographical questionnaire to the existing recruiting and selection procedures for female office applicants. The questionnaire would not be used to replace existing procedures; it would merely be added as a final hurdle for girls who already had proved acceptable on the basis of other employment procedures. Presumably, if it were added, the potential savings could amount to about $125 per productive employee hired.

Utility: A Way of Thinking

The above examples merely illustrate the emphasis and possible results when utility is taken into account in evaluating a selection procedure. But the cost estimates were extremely crude and quite arbitrary. In actual practice, careful cost-accounting procedures would be employed where feasible, but some costs cannot be reduced to dollars and cents—such as the human suffering, pain, and anguish in a psychiatric breakdown. Thus, "utility" should be viewed more as a way of thinking about personnel decisions and selection procedures than as a set of formal rules or prescriptions for attaching numbers or cost figures to evaluations of different outcomes. Our examples fail to consider the many intangibles among possible outcomes. As Cronbach and Gleser (13) point out:

> Personnel decisions require a balancing of seemingly non-comparable outcomes. The personnel manager may let a humanitarian outcome such as the self-respect of an aging worker offset tangible losses in production. A school may select students on the basis of factors (e.g., religion, social class) that have no relation to probable academic achievement; in so doing, the policy maker is allowing outcomes other than achievement to compensate him for the fact that he is not securing the best possible students (pp. 121–122).

Thus, utility does *not* imply the necessity or even the desirability of reducing all outcomes to a dollar scale, or even necessarily to a common scale, but it *does* imply a careful identification and listing of all possible outcomes—accompanied by a judgmental weighing of the values (both dollar and human) associated with each.

Most of all, the concept of utility forces an awareness of the relative importance of different outcomes and of different kinds of selection errors. This is in sharp contrast with the classic psychometric emphasis on errors as essentially equivalent.

In our first example, a false positive error was much less serious than a false negative one. There are many instances in industry where the same situation may prevail. For example, the competition in industry for top-notch executives is intense. Costly selection procedures and low selection ratios for executive applicants may be unwarranted if they result in large numbers of false negatives—the rejection of applicants who actually could fulfill the behavioral requirements of the job. Careful study *might* show that it would be less costly and more efficient to hire such applicants for probationary periods rather than to continue to use elaborate and costly screening procedures.

Also, any existing possibilities within a firm for career counseling, training, and job transfer should be taken into account in utility of personnel decisions. Thus, even if a person turns out to be a "dud" on the job for which he was hired, a transfer or specialized training might save the firm's investment in him. Naturally, such personnel actions would also cost something, but these costs can also be estimated, prorated, and weighed when considering the over-all utility of the selection or placement decision.

In practically all instances, personnel decision makers operate with little or no knowledge of the relative accuracy of their decisions; and even when they have sought to determine accuracy, they have been content with computing simple indices (such as correlation coefficients or mean differences) grounded in classic psychometric theory and yielding undifferentiated estimates of the magnitude of personnel decision errors. Hopefully, utility considerations will take precedence over these procedures in the years ahead, and personnel decision makers will accordingly become more aware of the importance of "hits" and "misses" in their decisions.

Personnel Classification and Job Placement

Measuring and Utilizing Human Individuality

We said in Chapter 1 that an idealized industrial society would place all persons on jobs best suited to them, an aim assuming not only that each person should use his own abilities in the best possible way but that society should also apportion its manpower resources optimally among available career assignments. We have also stated that a pure selection strategy is inherently wasteful because large numbers of applicants are simply rejected and not considered for other possible jobs. Human attributes vary along many relatively independent ability, interest, personality, and biographical dimensions; obviously, any individual's status on such measures is apt to vary considerably from measure to measure. In fact, a person's individuality is best characterized by his unique configuration or profile of scores on a variety of individual differences measures. The broad aim of personnel decision making is to estimate or measure as accurately as possible each person's individuality and to place him in an assignment for which his pattern of predicted job behavior is appropriate both to his own long-term goals and to the goals of his employer. Thus, personnel classification and job placement seek the optimal matching of men and jobs within the constraints dictated by available manpower and available jobs. When only a few jobs and many men are available, personnel classification and job placement give way to strategies of pure selection. When many jobs are available (as with most large industrial firms, government agencies, and the armed services), procedures directed toward optimal classification and placement may be realistically undertaken. The opportunity to use a classification strategy as opposed to pure selection is primarily a function of the size of the institution for which personnel decisions are being made and the diversity of jobs available for personnel assignment.

Advantages of Differential Job Placement

When carefully validated programs of differential placement are implemented, the net gain *both* to the institution and to the individual applicants is great. For example:

1. Applicants will be considered for several jobs rather than for only one. Thus, instead of being rejected outright if he lacks the qualifications for a particular job, an individual will normally be considered for other jobs and will very likely be offered employment in one. This practice will nearly always work to the advantage of the individual applicants for employment with a firm.

2. The institution will usually save in recruiting costs because many applicants who might otherwise be rejected (when using a pure selection strategy) are instead placed on other jobs in the firm.

3. By utilizing an optimal classification strategy, the institution is also assured that the average net outcome resulting from man-job assignments will be maximum. Available manpower will be utilized most efficiently. Naturally, the development and implementation of an optimal classification strategy is mathematically complex, but many fairly simple methods (such as the one presented later in this section) are available for closely approximating optimality. Moreover, the ready availability of large-scale electronic computers renders even the most complex mathematical procedures computationally feasible.

4. By including utility considerations in the actual statements of predicted outcomes, attention can be given both to individual and to institutional goals. For example, distress and costs associated with a psychiatric breakdown, possible job dissatisfaction related to poor job placement, or pain and anguish associated with job failure—all outcomes related to *both* individual and institutional goals—can be weighted subjectively according to their importance and in-

corporated into the payoff matrix from which the classification strategy is developed.

5. The last but most important advantage accruing from a personnel classification strategy has to do with a possible over-all increase in job effectiveness. As we saw in Chapter 7, the accuracy of a test battery for identifying a given pattern of job behavior can be estimated by computing r, R, r_{pb}, O, or η, but the actual usefulness of the test for making personnel decisions is strongly influenced by the selection ratio—the proportion of applicants hired.

Brogden (8) has shown how differential placement, by allowing one to maintain more advantageous selection ratios, can materially increase the efficiency of a selection or placement program. Table 8–3 compares results obtained when

TABLE 8–3. *Mean job effectiveness scores* for persons placed on two, three, or four jobs by pure selection or by differential placement strategies when the predictors are uncorrelated. (From Brogden, 8, with permission.)*

	SELECTION RATIO FOR EACH JOB	PURE SELECTION (ONE PREDICTOR)	DIFFERENTIAL PLACEMENT (SEPARATE PREDICTOR FOR EACH JOB)
Two jobs	10%	.70	.87
	15	.58	.76
	20	.50	.68
	25	.40	.61
Three jobs	10%	.58	.87
	15	.36	.75
	20	.34	.66
	25	.21	.57
Four jobs	10%	.49	.86
	15	.33	.73
	20	.21	.63
	25	.00	.50

* The Mean Effectiveness Score is the Mean Standard Score on some over-all job performance index, assuming that the mean would be zero for an unselected group of applicants, and that the correlation between predictors and the job performance index is +.50.

TABLE 8–4.   *Mean job effectiveness scores* for persons placed on two jobs by pure selection or by differential placement strategies for different selection ratios and different amounts of correlation between two predictors.* (From Brogden, 8, with permission.)

SELECTION RATIO FOR EACH JOB	PURE SELECTION	DIFFERENTIAL PLACEMENT Correlations between Predictors				
		0	.2	.4	.6	.8
5%	.88	1.03	1.02	1.01	1.00	.96
10	.70	.87	.86	.84	.82	.79
20	.48	.68	.67	.65	.62	.59
30	.32	.55	.53	.50	.46	.43
40	.18	.42	.41	.37	.34	.29
50	.00	.31	.28	.25	.22	.17

* The Mean Effectiveness Score is the mean standard score on some over-all job performance index, assuming that the mean would be zero for an unselected group of applicants and that the correlation between predictors and the job performance index is +.50.

a set of predictors are used in an undifferentiated way to hire persons for all jobs (pure selection) and results obtained when the predictors are separately validated against desired behavior on each of the jobs (differential placement), assuming that the separately validated predictors yield uncorrelated prediction scores. To see how more advantageous selection ratios may be utilized in differential placement, suppose that a firm has openings for ten clerical employees in each of four jobs—Numerical File Clerk, General Clerk, Alphabetical File Clerk, and Junior Calculating Clerk—and 100 applicants have applied for employment. If pure selection were used with a single battery of tests validated against job performance on all four jobs taken together, it would be necessary to use a selection ratio of 40 per cent (40 persons hired from 100 applicants). Table 8–3 (see portion in box) shows the gain in mean job effectiveness (from .49 to .86) that would be realized by separately validating the tests for each job and applying differential placement with four separate selection ratios of 10 per cent each. Note particularly that the gain is substantial (from .00 to .50), even when *all* applicants are hired (four separate selection ratios of 25 per cent) for the four jobs.

It is obviously unrealistic, however, to assume that the separate predictors in differential placement would ever be correlated zero. Table 8–4 shows the effects of different amounts of correlation between two predictors used for differential placement. The gain in predictive efficiency is still substantial even when the predictors are correlated very highly. For example, the table shows (see portion in box) that even when *all* applicants are hired and placed on two jobs, a moderate gain in job effectiveness may be realized by using differential placement even when the two predictors are correlated as highly as .80.

Relation of Differential Placement to Individualized Prediction

The above considerations take on added relevance when viewed against the multistage individualized personnel decision strategies we recommended earlier in this chapter. Differential or individualized strategies for selection and placement offer potential gains to the employing organization, not only because the validity estimates are "tailormade" (and, therefore, probably higher) for the subgroup on whom they are developed but also because the differential strategies permit more advantageous selection ratios. Thus, efforts toward identifying differentially predictable groupings of people, jobs, and job behaviors should yield substantial payoffs in increased employee effectiveness *and* in improved matching of individuals with suitable jobs.

The advantages of a differential placement strategy are clearcut, but how is such a strategy implemented? What type of information is necessary for developing such a strategy? How are optimal cutting scores for different predictors established? Finally, how do we evaluate the effectiveness of a differential placement strategy? Before we consider possible answers to these questions, let us restate what personnel classification and differential job placement entail.

The Classification and Placement Strategies Restated

According to Thorndike (74), "The pure classification situation is most nearly approached in the military establishment, where a large flow of untrained youths continually pours into the organization and must be channelled into dozens of different types of specialized training and work, and where everyone . . . must be used in some capacity"

(p. 216). The major purpose in pure classification is to assign all individuals to duties (jobs, training schools, etc.) according to quotas established by need and available facilities so that the average "success"[5] of all individuals is a maximum. In other words, we seek to maximize the utility of the personnel classification process. Of course, the *pure* classification situation is rare, even in the armed services. The more usual situation is probably best characterized by the day-to-day manpower needs of the typical large industrial firm. The total number of applicants usually exceeds the number of jobs available so that nearly always *some* individuals will be rejected. Differential placement sizes up each applicant according to how he might do on each of the jobs available and then either places him on one of them or rejects him. Differential placement is really a special case of classification that also uses a "reject" category along with the other decision categories established by the firm's job quotas.

Many constraints are present in any placement decision, such as the stated job preferences of the applicants, special skills (for example, typing ability), experience, or educational requirements (for example, an engineering degree) and the long-term estimates of manpower needs. Such constraints usually automatically determine the broad occupational group—sales, clerical, engineering, production, etc.—for which an applicant will be considered. The differential placement strategy is reserved for placing applicants on different jobs *within* these broad groupings.

The first step in using a differential placement strategy is to determine the jobs or task clusters for which it is appropriate. For example, all female applicants requesting clerical work might be considered as candidates for any one of eight to ten different clusters of clerical tasks, ranging from routine filing work to receptionist duties or from strictly typing to serving as an executive secretary. Similarly, all applicants seeking engineering employment might be considered as candidates for different types of engineering task clusters, ranging from pure research activities to production and trouble-shooting duties or to technical service and industrial selling pursuits. Once the task and duty clusters to which applicants are to be assigned have been identified, it is necessary to develop separate equations expressing the relationship between predictors and outcomes for each of the jobs. To maximize

---

[5] As should be apparent, our use of the term "success" is very broad, including both institutional and individual goals and focusing on desired elements of job behavior rather than on global or "ultimate" measures of job success.

"success," it is necessary to estimate an expected utility for each individual for each job, and to use the individual-job utility matrix (often called a payoff matrix) to accomplish the best possible pattern of differential job placement.

An Example of Optimal Personnel Classification

Personnel classification by differential placement is illustrated in the following hypothetical example.[6]

THE JOB PLACEMENT PROBLEM

Suppose the fifteen girls described in Chapter 2 are joined by one more, Peggy Jo, and that they apply together to a large Las Vegas gambling house for jobs. Suppose further that this particular gambling house has openings for girls in all four of its major jobs, including Blackjack Dealers, Showgirls, Waitresses, and Cashiers. The management of the casino, desiring to utilize womanpower to the fullest degree, decides to undertake a carefully developed program of differential job placement. Let us assume that a battery of selection instruments (tests, physical measurements, biographical questionnaires) has been carefully validated against desired behaviors and outcomes on each of the jobs and that these can be scored and summarized in a single index estimating the expected utility for placing each girl on each job.

ESTIMATING UTILITY SCORES

Let us examine some of the objective and subjective elements that might enter into the development of the utility index. First, of course, we would need validity information—estimates of how well each predictor actually predicts desired job behavior for each of the jobs. Letting our imagination run rampant, we suggest that the data in Table 8–5 are illustrative of the kinds of validities that would be obtained for the predictors against the job behaviors indicated. In calculating the utility index, the validities would, of course, be expressed as expectancy charts and estimates made of the probability that various behaviors would be shown by girls obtaining various scores on the predictors. Subjective judgments would have to be made about the

[6] Since differential placement is merely a special case of pure classification, we have chosen a classification situation for illustrative purposes. In an actual placement situation, the number of applicants would exceed the number of job openings, and a reject category would be utilized for those "left over" after the quotas had been satisfied.

TABLE 8-5. *Chart showing desired job behaviors, predictor measures, and hypothetical validity coefficients* for various predictor–job behavior relationships.*

	SHOWGIRL	BLACKJACK DEALER	WAITRESS	CASHIER
DESIRED JOB BEHAVIOR OUTCOMES	Applause and whistles from audience after performance	Deals at least 40 hands per hour	Remembers orders of each diner	Makes wrong change an average of less than once per working day
	Dances gracefully and artistically	Averages less than one misdeal per hour	Is pleasant, friendly, and courteous	Handles customers rapidly; line at register never exceeds 4 or 5 even at peak hours
	Sings on key	Maintains distance ("stony silence") from players	"Kids" with jocular customers	Pleasant, friendly, and courteous
	Projects self to audience	Knows when to call guard for help with troublesome or irate players	Doesn't flirt with men who are accompanied by ladies	
	Audience quiets down during her performance and gives her undivided attention		Does flirt with men who are not accompanied by ladies	
			Adds up check correctly	

PREDICTOR
MEASURES

PREDICTOR MEASURES				
Abstract Reasoning Test	.05	.30	.35	.40
Vocabulary Test	.00	.40	.30	.20
Arithmetic Test	.00	.40	.40	.50
Finger Dexterity Test	.10	.50	.15	.20
Perceptual Speed and Accuracy Test	.00	.40	.10	.25
Index of Curvaceousness (Average of bust and hip minus waist)	.65	.05	.30	.00
Pulchritude rating by interviewer	.70	.15	.35	.05
Measure of assertiveness	.40	.50	.15	.00
Measure of heterosexual interests	.50	.00	.30	.00
Measure of deference	.10	−.40	.40	.15
Measure of affiliative tendencies	.25	−.50	30	.30

* Validity Coefficients in the above chart are point biserial correlations against dichotomous behavior observations (Does show behavior versus Does not show behavior).

relative importance of each job to the over-all goal of the organization—making money. For example, the jobs of Showgirl and Blackjack Dealer are undoubtedly the most important, and a "showstopping" performance is the most important behavior for showgirls.

In addition, the relative cost of wrong personnel decisions must be considered. Hiring an unattractive girl for the job of Showgirl could lead to an immediate loss of customers to the casino, but hiring an inefficient Cashier would probably merely be vexing. All these factors, as well as validities and the probabilities of desired behavior outcomes would have to be incorporated into the single index of expected utility for placing each girl on each job. A common approach to the task is simply to weight the more important job behaviors more heavily by giving greater emphasis to the predictors that are most valid for them; with the more important jobs, the probability estimates can be multiplied by a constant in order to increase the differentiation between high and low scores on those jobs.

THE PAYOFF MATRIX

Table 8–6 presents the payoff matrix for our sixteen young ladies; the figures in the table are based on an arbitrary scale of utility, the higher numbers denoting high predicted "payoff" for the particular job placement and lower numbers denoting low predicted "payoffs." Note also that the number of openings available for each job is shown—5 for Blackjack Dealer, 3 for Waitress, 6 for Showgirl, and 2 for Cashier. It is now necessary to decide how to assign the girls to the various job openings.

ASSIGNMENT BY PURE SELECTION

One approach would be to place on each job the girls with the highest estimated utilities for that job. If this could be done, the highest possible average utility (7.75) would result. However, this approach will lead only to confusion. For example, which three of the four girls—Amber, Heather, Joanie, or Sheila—should be chosen for the three openings in the Waitress job? How shall we decide where to place Deborah, Elizabeth, Heather, and Sheila—all of whom are among the highest scorers on two or more jobs? And what is to become of poor Hedy and Melody, both of whom score below the cutting point on all the jobs? Obviously, some other approach must be taken if optimum use is to be made of the skills of all these young ladies.

TABLE 8–6. *Payoff matrix showing expected utilities* for placing applicants on each of four different jobs and number of openings in each job.*

	BLACKJACK DEALER	WAITRESS	SHOWGIRL	CASHIER
1. Amber	6	9	4	3
2. Bridgit	5	6	8	2
3. Cleopatra	7	4	5	8
4. Deborah	8	5	9	6
5. Elizabeth	8	6	6	7
6. Ella	7	5	5	7
7. Heather	9	9	7	3
8. Hedy	4	8	5	4
9. Jean	6	6	3	8
10. Joanie	5	9	5	6
11. Marilyn	7	7	4	5
12. Melody	5	6	4	5
13. Millicent	7	5	6	4
14. Peggy Jo	3	7	5	3
15. Rita	5	8	5	6
16. Sheila	8	9	3	5
Number of job openings	5	3	6	2

* The utility scale is an arbitrary one incorporating predictor validities (in the form of probabilities) and judgments about the relative importance of different jobs, different job behaviors, and different kinds of personnel decision errors. High numbers denote high predicted payoff from the job placement; low numbers denote low predicted payoff from the job placement.

AN APPROXIMATE SOLUTION TO THE PROBLEM

Brogden (7) and Thorndike (74) have proposed somewhat different approximate solutions to the problem. We have incorporated elements of both their approaches into the single solution shown in Table 8–7. The steps involved in this approach are outlined below:

1. First, the jobs are arranged across the top of the page in order of importance. Showgirl is most important, Cashier least important.

2. Frequency distributions of the utility scores for each job are plotted; instead of tally marks, the identification number for each job applicant is placed in the appropriate

row for each of the distributions. If several applicants have the same utility score for any given job, their order in the row is determined by the difference between their score for that job and their highest score for any other job. For example, six girls have utility scores of 5 for the job of Showgirl. The differences between 5 and their highest scores in other jobs are shown below:

NUMBER	NAME	DIFFERENCE	NUMBER	NAME	DIFFERENCE
3	Cleopatra	−3	10	Joanie	−4
6	Ella	−2	14	Peggy Jo	−2
8	Hedy	−3	15	Rita	−3

Hence the order in the row is 14 and 6 first (either 14 or 6 could have been first) followed by 3, 8, 15, and finally 10.

Arranging the scores in this way accomplishes three important purposes. First, ordering the utility values within *jobs* assures that first consideration will be given to securing persons with high utility scores in each job. Second, ordering persons with the same utilities in any given job according to their difference scores increases the chances that applicants will be placed on the job for which they have obtained the highest utility index. Third, when it becomes necessary to place a person on a job for which his utility score is not the highest, the selection will be made from among persons whose scores are relatively similar for all jobs rather than from among persons whose scores are sharply different from job to job.

3. Tentative cutting scores are then set for each job so that the number of applicants above each score is exactly equal to the number of job openings. Where the required number of applicants is obtained after including some but not all of the persons within a given utility score category, a vertical line is drawn to separate the candidates included from those not included.

The reason for ordering the candidates within each utility score category should now be more apparent. The first applicants chosen from each category will be those who "fit" the job to which they are assigned at least as well as or better than any of the other persons in that same category. The tentative cutting scores are indicated for each job by drawing a light horizontal line underneath the ap-

TABLE 8–7. *Sample worksheet showing steps involved in approximate solution for placing applicants on jobs according to established quotas.*

	SHOWGIRL Job I	BLACKJACK DEALER Job II	WAITRESS Job III	CASHIER Job IV
UTILITY INDEX				
9	(4)'	7'	1 (1,10,16)' 7	
8	(2)	5',4',16'	2 (8)15	1,2
7	(7)'	1 13',6,(11),3	14,11	(9)(3)'
6	(3)',5'	9,1	12,5,2,9	6,5
5	1,2 (4),6,8,3,15,10	2 (12),(15)2,10	6,13,4	15,10,4
4	12,11,1	8	3	12,11,16
3	9,16	14		13,8
2				14,7,1
				2
Number of Openings (Quota)	6	5	3	2
Assignment	2,14,4,7,13,5	16,6,11,12,15	1,10,8	9,3

DIFFERENCES BETWEEN CUTTING SCORES

	First Cutting Scores				*Second Cutting Scores*		
	II	III	IV		II	III	IV
I	2	4	3	I	0	3	3
II		2	1	II		3	3
III			−1	III			0

JOB ASSIGNMENTS

	Showgirl	*Blackjack Dealer*	*Waitress*	*Cashier*	
	Bridgit	Ella	Amber	Cleopatra	
	Deborah	Marilyn	Hedy	Jean	
	Elizabeth	Melody	Joanie		
	Heather	Rita			
	Millicent	Sheila			
	Peggy Jo				Over-all
Mean Utility Index	6.83	6.40	8.67	8.00	Mean 7.19

propriate score and labeling it 1 (to indicate the first tentative set of scores).

4. Next, it is necessary to identify the candidates above the cutting score on more than one job. This is done by examining the various distributions and placing primes (′)

on those numbers above the cutting point on more than one of them. In our example, candidate 4 (Deborah) is above the cutting scores on both the Showgirl and the Blackjack Dealer distributions; candidate 16 (Sheila) is above the cutting scores on both the Blackjack Dealer and Waitress distributions; and so on. Because of this overlapping of candidates on several jobs, a rule is necessary for deciding where to place them (see 5).

5. We assume that it is desirable to place a candidate on that job for which his deviation from the cutting score is greatest. This may seem arbitrary, but it means that we will place each candidate on that job for which his relative superiority in comparison with other high-scoring candidates is the greatest. If a candidate deviates from the cutting scores by equal amounts in two jobs, he will be placed on the job regarded as more important.[7]

In order to accomplish the actual assignment of applicants, therefore, we first develop a small matrix showing the differences between the cutting scores. The matrix for the first set of cutting scores is shown immediately below the worksheet.

We are now ready to make job assignments. First, consider candidate 4 (Deborah), who is above the cutting scores on both the Showgirl and Blackjack Dealer distributions. The difference in her scores for the two jobs is -1 $(8 - 9)$. This difference is less than the difference of 2 (see small matrix) between the cutting scores for the two jobs; hence, she is placed on the Showgirl job, and her number is crossed off in the distribution of scores for the Blackjack Dealer job. Candidate 7 (Heather) is also placed as a Showgirl because the difference of 2 $(9 - 7)$ between her two scores is exactly the same as the cutting score difference; she is, therefore, placed on the more important of the two jobs. In the same way, all other comparisons are made and candidates assigned accordingly. In our example, candidates 2, 4, 5, 7, 13, and 14 are thereby assigned to the Showgirl job, thus filling the quota; candidate 16 is the only one assigned as a Blackjack Dealer; candidates 1 and 10 are

---

[7] Of course, the ranking of the jobs in "importance" may change from time to time. For example, if *all* the waitresses in our problem were suddenly to walk off the job, it would become critically important to obtain waitresses and the job would be temporarily advanced in the rankings.

assigned as Waitresses and 9 and 3 as Cashiers. These placements are indicated on the worksheet by circling the appropriate numbers.

6. The next step is to set new cutting scores in order to replace candidates deleted from some of the job distributions. For the job Blackjack Dealer, it is necessary to reduce the cutting score until four additional candidates have been identified. Candidates 3, 9, and 1 have already been placed on other jobs; thus, the new cutting score must be reduced to 5. In similar fashion, one additional candidate is necessary on the Waitress job, and the cutting score is reduced to 8 (note that candidate 7 has already been placed as a Showgirl). A second matrix based on this second set of cutting scores is developed to be used in placing candidates who are now above these new cutting scores on more than one distribution. However, examination of the worksheet reveals no further conflicts, and candidates 6, 11, 12, and 15 are, therefore, placed as Blackjack Dealers—completing the quota for that job—and candidate 8 is placed as a Waitress. Had all the candidates not been placed in this second iteration, new trials would have been carried out until all jobs had been filled and all candidates assigned.

Note that the six girls with highest utility scores for the most important job, Showgirl, actually are placed in that job, yielding a mean predicted utility of 6.83. The Blackjack Dealer job suffers somewhat because precedence has been given to the Showgirl job; even so, the mean predicted utility of girls placed on it is 6.40 and all the girls placed there have scores of at least 5 or higher. Over-all, the mean utility score is 7.19, a value not substantially lower than the maximum possible of 7.75 that could not be obtained because of the practical requirement of placing each candidate on just one job.

Another advantage of this method should be noted. If an organization's manpower needs can be anticipated sufficiently far ahead of time, quotas for each job can be expressed as relative proportions of persons to be placed on each job. These quotas can then be used to determine appropriate cutting scores for a preliminary group of applicants. Assuming that the scores for the preliminary group are representative of those to be expected from subsequent job candidates, these cutting scores and the corresponding decision rules could be applied day to day for making job assignments. Such an approach has been suggested and utilized by Cardinet (10).

Application in a Real Employment Setting

In actual application, our proposed method of differential classification would probably not be used mechanically, although it could be computerized. But many constraints would be operating, not the least of which would be the job preferences of applicants. For example, it is possible that Amber has her heart set on being a Showgirl, and that she would not accept an offer of a Waitress job—the job shown to be the optimal assignment for her by our classification procedure.

More typically, the decision rules established by a program of differential validation and differential job placement would be used solely as a guide for determining the job placement most likely to be optimal for any given applicant. The preferences of the applicant, the immediate needs of the organization, and other practical matters would have to be considered before a final decision could be made. In most employment settings, therefore, the personnel decision maker, armed with as much information as possible about where a given candidate should be placed, would then set out either to make the appropriate job placement or to determine why it might not be feasible to do so. However, in that one great stronghold of pure personnel classification—the armed services—highly efficient computerized methods have recently been adopted for classifying men into jobs or training schools most appropriately—maximizing the over-all predicted average effectiveness commensurate with the many constraints operating. A description of the manpower assignment methods utilized by the Marine Corps is given in the next chapter.

The Goal of This Chapter

In this chapter, we have tried to cope with most of the issues and questions raised by our introductory discussion of selection and placement in Chapter 1. The reader should now possess a fairly clear view of how measures of individual differences may be incorporated with the study of jobs and observations of job behavior to develop strategies for making administrative decisions about people. Clearly, we believe the calculation of a so-called validity coefficient for a predictor–job behavior relationship to be merely a first step in personnel decision making. For such coefficients to prove useful in personnel decisions, they *must* be translated into the best estimates possible of behavior outcomes and associated utilities in any personnel employment or classification situation. In this chapter we have suggested the kinds of evidence used to carry out personnel decisions; we have also discussed guidelines for gathering such evidence.

part three

Selection and
Placement Programs

chapter nine

Examples of Selection and Placement Studies and Research Results

So far, we have depended rather heavily on hypothetical examples to illustrate many of the principles and procedures in personnel selection and job placement research. We did this in order to simplify and clarify our presentation. In this chapter, we will describe several examples of excellent selection and placement studies. This should show that good selection research can and has been done; and, more importantly, this will summarize tangibly most of the major principles and procedures presented in previous chapters.

Identifying Management Potential

The Employee Relations Research Department of the Standard Oil Company of New Jersey recently completed a study designed to shed light on two questions: (1) how may "success" in management be measured, and (2) how may employees possessing the potential for becoming successful managers be identified early in their employment careers? The investigation designed to answer these questions has been described by Laurent (56, 57).

A total of 443 managers working for Standard Oil Company (N.J.) and five of its affiliate companies comprised the persons studied. The sample included managers in many functions ranging across marketing, research, production, and accounting. Since all these functions were present in the sample, it was decided not to consider separately the job responsibilities and job behaviors in each of the functional groupings; it was necessary, therefore, to be satisfied with a general or global definition of managerial success rather than doing a careful analysis of the actual behaviors leading to job success or job failure. Thus, "success" was defined more or less in layman's terms—that is, according to the visible outcomes of successful managerial job behavior such as the amount of salary earned and the organizational level attained. The measures chosen for estimating over-all "success" included:

1. *Position level.* This was the relative level in the organizational hierarchy attained by a manager.

2. *Salary history.* Each man's salary history was studied. Adjustments were made for the effects of inflation, age, and rate of salary progress so that the final index could be reasonably regarded as indicating actual differences among the various managers in over-all merit.

3. *Effectiveness ranking.* Managers at similar levels in the organization were grouped together and ranked by higher officials for "overall managerial effectiveness."

These measures were combined into an Over-all Success Index, and statistical precautions were taken to assure that the index was independent of both age and length of job experience. This step is particularly important because a success measure highly correlated with age or experience would suggest that "success" was simply a matter of staying in the firm long enough, and the primary aim of the study was the *early* identification of management potential. Thus, even though the study utilized a concurrent design, precautions were taken to increase the likelihood that the results would also be predictive.

Each manager took a lengthy battery of tests and completed a background survey covering home and family background, education, vocational planning, finances, hobbies and leisure time activities, health history, and social relations. The tests included measures of verbal ability, inductive reasoning, management judgment (the ability to size up and choose an effective action in different human relations situations), an inventory of managerial attitudes, and personality measures similar to those described in our discussion of typical behavior inventories. The scores on these tests were correlated with the standings of the managers on the Overall Success Index. In addition, each of the items in the background survey was examined to discover the elements of biographical information related to the success measure.

Since many items and even more responses were examined, it was imperative that the stability of relationships be checked by cross-validation. In this study, a technique called Double Cross-Validation was used. The total of 443 managers was divided randomly into two subsamples of 222 and 221. Then, only responses showing the same relationship with the Overall Success Index in *both* subsamples were retained and scored in the background survey. One further precaution was taken to assure independence between predictors and age and experience: no item from the background survey was scored if it showed a significant relationship with either age or experience.

Finally, the tests and biographical responses showing the highest and most stable correlations with the Overall Success Index were combined by multiple regression methods to yield a single score on the tests and questionnaire materials. Figure 9–1 is an expectancy chart showing the accuracy of this combined score as an indicator of over-all managerial success. The chart gives the odds of being in the top half on the success measure for managers scoring at five different levels on the combined test score. The value of R for the relationship shown in Table 9–1 is .70 and the value of O is 53 per cent. The more successful managers show higher inductive and verbal reasoning abilities, and they show better judgment of effective actions in interpersonal situations as measured by the management judgment test. In addition, their responses on the background survey indicate a history of independence, maturity, sociability, and social responsibility.

DISCUSSION

This study is an example of a large-scale successful effort to validate tests and biographical information directly against job behavior measures. In particular, it illustrates the usefulness of biographical information for indicating job behavior and suggests that such information should nearly always be included in selection research studies. Moreover, the investigation points up the appropriate use of a cross-validation design. By splitting the sample in half, Laurent was able to test the stability of relationships empirically as well as by statistical inference; thus, added confidence in the statistical stability of the predictor-success relationships was obtained. Finally, the study shows that a global measure of "success" can prove useful even though more finely specified observations and measures of job behavior should

TABLE 9–1. *Expectancy chart showing chances of being in the top half on the over-all success index for Standard Oil managers with different composite test scores.*

	NUMBER OF PERSONS	CHANCES IN 100 OF BEING IN TOP HALF ON OVER-ALL SUCCESS INDEX	ODDS
Highest 20 per cent on tests	88		9 in 10
Next 20 per cent on tests	89		7 in 10
Middle 20 per cent on tests	89		5 in 10
Next 20 per cent on tests	89		3 in 10
Lowest 20 per cent on tests	88		1 in 10

O = 53%   R = .70

usually be expected to yield higher and more diagnostic relationships between predictors and behavior measures.

The study also highlights a major point related to the relative usefulness of concurrent and predictive designs in test validation and selection research. The test and inventory responses of the managers in this study were not obtained early in their careers; they were obtained after each man had been in the company many years and had attained a definite level of "success." The test and inventory responses of these men probably differed from what they would have been at the beginning of the men's careers. In fact, many of the answers obtained might have been, in part, *due to* experiences during their careers (types of jobs, kinds of bosses, degree of success attained); and it may be inappropriate to infer that the valid *concurrent* responses are also valid *predictive* responses.

At first, this problem may not seem to apply to the biographical inventory. However, the items of a background questionnaire differ greatly in their degree of objectivity. To be sure, information involving dates, places, physical descriptions, and events are not likely to suffer distortion when one is asked to describe his early background. On the other hand, if he is asked to provide information on which subjects he liked best in college, what his goals were early in his career, or how hard he worked in college, a manager might very well perceive things differently today than he did earlier. Thus, a most important step in studies of this type is to demonstrate that the valid responses in the concurrent study are also predictive.

A Study of Moderator Variables

Even though the multiple regression equation developed in the Standard Oil study did yield a high level of predictive accuracy ($R = .70$), Hobert (52) showed that accuracy could be increased by developing moderator variables to identify subgroups of more- and less-predictable managers. Hobert used the quadrant analysis method described in Chapter 8. First, he depicted the relationship between the combined test score and the Overall Success Index in a scatter diagram. He divided the test scores and the success index scores at their respective medians, thereby defining four subgroups—*Low Hits* and *High Hits,* for whom the combined test scores accurately designated success status; *Under Predicted* managers, for whom test scores were erroneously below the median; and *Over Predicted* managers, for whom test scores were erroneously above the median. Using one-half the sample and setting the remainder aside for cross-validation, Hobert examined the test scores and biographical responses of persons in each quadrant. He discovered that sixteen scales (out of thirty-five) successfully differentiated (by at least 20 per cent) between Low Hits and Under Predicted persons, and that twelve scales (out of thirty-five) successfully differentiated (by at least 20 per cent) between High Hits and Over Predicted persons. The "Low Hit" set of sixteen scales, when combined, formed a moderator variable (designated the "Low Hit Moderator") with scores ranging from 0 to 16 (higher scores identifying Under Predicted persons). On this moderator variable, 79 per cent of the Low Hit group scored below 10, but only 23 per cent of the Under Predicted persons scored below 10. The set of twelve predictor scales, when combined, formed a second moderator variable (designated the "High Hit Moderator") with scores ranging from 0 to 12 (higher scores identifying Over Predicted persons). On this second moderator variable, 82 per cent of the High Hit group scored below 8, but only 21 per cent of the Over Predicted persons scored below 8. Using the above cutting scores, Hobert applied the two moderator variables to the scores of managers in the cross-validation group. Figure 9–1 shows how this was done. The data in Table 9–2 show clearly that use of these two moderator variables resulted in a substantial increase in the accuracy of designating a manager as either above or below the median

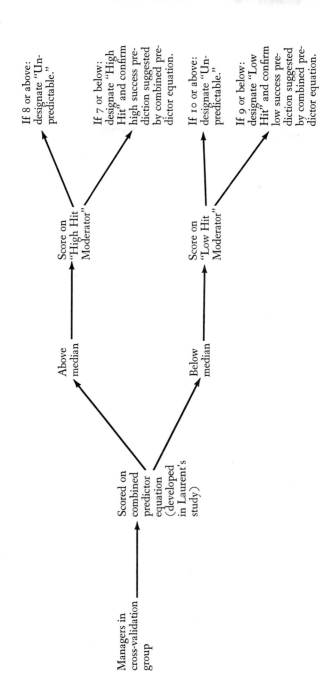

FIGURE 9–1. *Strategy for multistage, sequential personnel decisions applied to managers in the cross-validation group.*

TABLE 9–2. *Mean over-all success index scores, point biserial correlations, and overlap coefficients for managers in cross-validation group for whom prediction equation is used with and without moderator variables.*

PREDICTED STATUS ON OVER-ALL SUCCESS INDEX	USING COMBINED PREDICTION EQUATION ONLY				USING COMBINED PREDICTION EQUATION PLUS MODERATOR VARIABLES			
	N	Mean Over-all Success Index	Point Biserial Correlation r_{pb}	Overlap Coefficient O	N	Mean Over-all Success Index	Point Biserial Correlation r_{pb}	Overlap Coefficient O
Above median	99	6.30	.66	38%	79	6.54	.73	28%
Below median	121	3.76			86	3.49		

on the Overall Success Index. The managers assigned above the success median by the moderator variable had a higher mean success index than those assigned without the moderator. In similar fashion, the managers assigned below the success median by the moderator variable had a lower mean success index than those assigned without the moderator. The increase in the point biserial correlation coefficient from .66 to .73 and the decrease in overlap from 38 to 28 per cent are both substantial.

DISCUSSION

This study illustrates the potential usefulness of moderator variables for identifying more- and less-predictable subgroups. The example is primarily methodological, outlining the steps in the quadrant analysis approach. It also illustrates with actual data the feasibility of carrying out an individualized, multistage, sequential strategy in personnel decision making. When implemented, the moderator variables developed by Hobert would be used in exactly the way depicted in Figure 9–1. Of course, the increase in decision accuracy for persons assigned by the moderators to the High Hit and Low Hit groups is accompanied by one distinct disadvantage—decisions cannot be made for those fifty-five persons designated by the moderators as unpredictable. Further studies would ordinarily be conducted to discover additional valid predictors for use with these persons. Until such measures had been validated, other bases would need to be used for making decisions about them, but these decisions would need to be accompanied by an awareness that accuracy would be lower than for those assigned to the High Hit and Low Hit groups.

A Demonstration of Synthetic Validation

In the last chapter, we discussed the possibility of analyzing dissimilar jobs according to common major elements and validating tests against performance on the separate job elements. When tests have been validated in this way, a potentially valid test battery can be *synthesized* for any job containing the elements studied. Guion (42) recently performed a study designed primarily to demonstrate the procedures involved in this process of *synthetic validation*. The study was done among the forty-six employees of a small electrical goods company in which no more than three persons were doing any one kind of job. Guion soon determined, however, that the various jobs could be described in terms of varying amounts of seven elements: Salesmanship, Creative Business Judgment, Customer Relations, Routine Judgment, Leadership, Handling Detail Work, and Organizing Duties. The president and vice-president of the firm, after deciding which jobs contained each of the elements, spent many hours independently ranking employees according to their relative proficiency in performing each of the job elements. Finally, the two men also ranked all employees according to their "overall worth to the organization." The two men agreed closely in their rankings of employees' proficiency (r's ranged from .82 to .95).

The scores obtained by employees on a variety of tests (including both ability measures and typical behavior inventories) were compared with their rated levels of proficiency on each job element. Several of the tests showed very strong relationships with different aspects of proficiency. For example, proficiency in Creative Judgment was highly related to scores on a design judgment test; Leadership ratings were strongly associated with verbal ability scores; proficiency in Salesmanship was most closely related to sociability test scores, etc. Guion then developed two-variable expectancy charts for each of the job elements.[1] His approach was essentially the same as the actuarial pattern analysis described by Lykken and Rose (60)—that is, Guion simply examined the proficiency ratings for employees with different patterns on a given pair of tests and calculated an expected proficiency rating. For example, 80 per cent of employees scoring in the highest categories on the design judgment and adaptability tests were given "superior" ratings on Creative Business Judgment; but only 25 per cent of employees scoring in the lowest categories on both tests were rated "superior." Guion used these expectancy charts to develop scoring patterns to reflect the proficiency ratings for each job element.

To sum up, seven elements were found to be sufficient for describing forty-six jobs in a small firm and for evaluating the proficiency of employees doing these jobs. Test scores differentiated proficiency in performing the various job elements, and these data were used to form

---

[1] No expectancy chart was developed for the job element of Routine Judgment because validities were too low to be of practical importance. Thus, it was dropped from subsequent analyses.

expectancy charts so that each test score could be interpreted as an estimate of proficiency in one or more of the job elements.

The next step in the study was to try the results out on a cross-validation group, thirteen employees hired since the first study had been undertaken. First, their jobs were studied to decide which job elements each encompassed. Second, the expectancy charts and scoring systems developed from the previous data were used to estimate the relative job proficiency of the thirteen. Third, the president and vice-president ranked the thirteen according to proficiency in performing various job elements and in terms of "over-all worth." Finally, the estimates based on test scores were compared with the top executives' rankings. The results obtained are shown in Table 9–3. The test patterns developed in this demonstration of synthetic validation "hold up" effectively in the cross-validation group; of thirteen classifications, ten (77 per cent) are correct.

TABLE 9–3. *Degree of agreement between job proficiency estimates based on test scores and actual job proficiency ratings for thirteen employees in cross-validation sample.*

		JOB PROFICIENCY OBSERVED AND RATED BY TOP EXECUTIVES	
		Among Lower Half	Among Top Half
JOB PROFICIENCY ESTIMATED FROM TEST SCORES	Among Top Half	2	5
	Among Lower Half	5	1

In a second phase of this study, Guion ignored possible job differences and developed an expectancy chart describing the relationship between the two best tests and the ratings of over-all worth for all forty-six employees. However, when these results were applied to the cross-validation sample, only a chance number (6, or 46 per cent) of correct classifications was made. Apparently, "overall worth" is too global for describing and assessing proficiency in these many different jobs. The results of Guion's study testify to the usefulness of defining job proficiency explicitly in terms of job elements rather than relying on a global rating.

DISCUSSION

Guion's synthetic validation illustrates a number of important principles. Most important, it shows the feasibility and usefulness of the rather tedious analyses in synthetic validation; it shows how such analyses can provide generalizations about relationships between test responses and job behaviors. When enough such generalizations are accumulated, there will be less need for specific validation studies in each new situation; careful analysis of the components of a job and synthesis of an appropriate test battery will be sufficient.

Moreover, the study shows (1) that rather small N's can yield both statistically and practically useful results; (2) that a global estimate of job effectiveness such as the "overall worth" rating in this study may often not be behaviorally rich enough to yield stable results on cross-validation (especially when several different jobs are involved in the study, and "overall" proficiency in each may depend on varying patterns of proficiency in underlying elements); and (3) that expectancy charts and actuarial pattern analysis can be useful even when N's are small (cross-validation as used by Guion is the key safeguard, a step that needs to be applied for all selection and validation).

Finally, Guion's methods of job analysis and of proficiency rating deserve special comment. The choice of the job elements to be studied came only after reading many job descriptions and preparing lists of actual job duties based on them. Great care was taken in grouping the duties into broader job elements, and this was done in close consultation with top executives and job incumbents. Thus, the method used by Guion, in broad outline, is similar to the methods of job analysis we discussed and advocated in Chapter 4. The pains taken for obtaining good observations of the subjects' job behaviors were equally impressive. The executives who carried out the rankings were involved at each stage; they helped develop the definitions of the various job elements, focusing as closely as possible on specific examples of observable behavior to be used in making the ratings. Moreover, the rankings were obtained independently from two equally well-qualified observers, and the independent rankings were correlated, thereby yielding a "check" on the semantic clarity of the job element definitions as well as on the relative precision with which the behavior could be observed and recorded for different employees.

Guion's study constitutes a solid example of successful test validation carried out in a complex situation of many different jobs and a limited number of subjects.

A Follow-up of Clinical Assessment Procedures

In Chapter 8, we discussed clinical prediction. Clinical procedures are frequently used when the number of subjects appears too small or the diversity of jobs so great as to preclude a full-fledged statistical validation. Clinical procedures are often believed to yield a broader range of behavioral predictions than may be possible with tests validated against the narrower types of job behavior often employed in statistical prediction studies.

Two studies relevant to these arguments have been reported recently by Albrecht, Glaser, and Marks (1) and by Dicken and Black (15). The methods employed in both were similar and the results and conclusions essentially equivalent; hence, we shall discuss only the one by Albrecht et al.

The subjects were thirty-one district marketing managers, each assessed by clinical procedures (a personal history form, an extensive interview, and brief intelligence and critical thinking tests) shortly after being promoted to their managerial jobs. The psychologists conducting the assessments ranked the subjects according to predicted job effectiveness in four broad areas: (1) Forecasting and Budgeting Effectiveness, (2) Sales Performance, (3) Interpersonal Relationships, and (4) Overall Performance. After a year on the job, the men were ranked on each of these job skills by two managers above them and by their peers; the three sets of rankings were combined to form a composite index for each subject in each job area. The psychologists' clinical predictions were correlated with the composite success scores, and scores on the two tests were also correlated with the composite rankings. The correlations obtained are shown in Table 9–4.

In their conclusions, the authors emphasize that the correlation coefficients for clinical predictions are moderately high and that they exceed the values obtained with the two tests. Dicken and Black (15) obtained correlations of similar magnitude based on clinical interpretations of many more tests, including not only ability tests but also vocational interest and personality inventories. They, too, found that clinical judgments yielded correlations higher in magnitude than most of those based on individual test scores.

DISCUSSION

These studies are solid investigations designed to determine the efficacy of clinical judgments. They mark a direction that should be followed by other psychologists who make clinical interpretations of test and interview information. Such persons should remain alert to opportunities for validating their judgments so that evidence may be accumulated on the accuracy of selection recommendations based on such judgments. Each of the above studies is a true predictive study; assessment information was obtained prior to the gathering of behavior observations and job behavior measurement. Therefore, the results can more readily be generalized to other predictive situations than is the case for studies utilizing concurrent validation designs.

TABLE 9–4. *Correlation coefficients between clinical predictions, test scores, and composite rankings of effectiveness in four job areas for thirty-one marketing managers.*

JOB AREA	CLINICAL PREDICTION	INTELLIGENCE TEST	CRITICAL THINKING TEST
Forecasting	.49	.41	.30
Sales	.58	−.07	.12
Interpersonal	.43	.18	.18
Over-all	.46	.23	.24

Another property of many clinical validation studies is also illustrated by the two discussed above. Clinical judgments in employment settings are nearly always put into written reports to company officials responsible for making personnel decisions about job candidates. These reports typically discuss the applicants' qualifications in terms of the same personal characteristics or job behaviors that may form the basis for later supervisory ratings. Such reports can seriously color or "contaminate" the results of later job behavior observations. In many follow-up studies of clinical judgments, it is difficult to know how seriously contaminated the job behavior observations may be by knowledge gained from the earlier clinical reports. Thus, clinical follow-ups must take special precautions against the possibility of such contaminating knowledge. Both Albrecht et al., and Dicken and Black took such precautions.

One final property of most clinical studies (also illustrated by the two above) deserves special comment. The results from such studies do not typically specify exactly the rules or procedures for obtaining valid clinical judgments. In this sense, a clinical study possesses less potential for generality of results than does a carefully conducted statistical validation. Clinical studies do not usually yield expectancy tables or precise statements about the odds of certain behaviors being associated with certain test scores. For example, even though the study by Albrecht et al., did show correlations of respectable magnitudes, there is nothing in their research report to indicate the mechanisms used by the psychologists for deriving their valid clinical judgments. Thus, other investigators and other psychologists probably gain less from such a report than they would from a similar report of a validation of a statistical combination of predictor measures. Guion's report, discussed previously, shows that synthetic validation can probably be applied to most situations usually regarded as exclusively within the domain of clinical prediction. Synthetic validation *does* yield expectancy tables, probability estimates, and statements defining the mechanisms for making potentially valid behavioral prediction, and in these respects yields more information than is yielded by most clinical follow-up studies.

Predicting Primary Negligence and Settlement Cost in Auto Accidents

Since 1959, Haner (44, 45, 46) has conducted an extensive series of studies designed to validate biographical factors and attitude inventory responses for predicting primary negligence in auto accidents involving males under 25 years of age. His research has been conducted with such care that it constitutes an excellent illustration of many important principles in selection research. In 1959, all males under age 25 then insured with Farmers Mutual Reinsurance Company were divided, on the basis of their driving records, into those with good records, poor records, and intermediate records; insureds who had driven less than two years or less than 5,000 miles per year were designated as "unclassifiable." All classified persons were then asked to report to their home office representatives to complete a personal history form and an attitude inventory containing statements designed to measure such behavioral tendencies as responsibility, impulsiveness, detachment, acceptance of regulation, aggressiveness, and frustration tolerance. A group of 2,000 respondents was divided into validation and cross-validation groups and scoring keys established to differentiate between persons with different kinds of driving records. The questionnaires were then introduced into the underwriting program (in September, 1959) and their usefulness for predicting outcomes such as primary negligence and size of settlement costs (medical and property) have since been determined annually. Each time a claim is made, it is classed as involving (1) primary negligence by the insured, (2) partial or contributory negligence on his part, (3) no legal negligence, or (4) damage due to vandalism or natural causes (windstorm, hail, etc.). The primary negligence classification is the only one considered by Haner in validating his inventories. The judgment is highly reliable; of several hundred claims, Haner and the claims manager disagreed on the classification of only four. Over the years, Haner has continually shortened and improved his questionnaires. Today, for example, the attitude inventory contains several "check" scales to detect tendencies toward falsification, fence straddling, lack of comprehension, or low consistency in responding. The data in Table 9–5 show the relationship between scores[2] on the biographical and attitude inventories and both accident frequency and accident cost. The cost ratio in the table is an index showng the relative average settlement costs for the claims incurred. Thus, the cost per insured per year for persons in Inventory Category IV with Personal History score o (cell No. 16) is 6.56 times as high as for persons in Category I with PH scores of 9 or higher (cell No. 1). This means that the premium for the latter persons could be only 15 per cent of that for the former persons and the same loss ratio would still be achieved.

DISCUSSION

Even though Haner's studies do not involve selection in an employment setting, they are illustrative of many of the selection research principles presented in this book. For example:

1. The concept of utility undergirds his whole research program; the study is a clear example of how predictor

[2] Scores on the personal history form range from o upward; scores on the inventory are expressed in four categories: I, II, III, and IV. Category I is the lowest risk group; category IV, the highest.

TABLE 9-5. *Accidents per hundred car-years and cost ratios for insureds with various combinations of scores on the personal history form and attitude inventory.*

		PERSONAL HISTORY FORM			
INVENTORY SCORE GROUP		0	1–4	5–8	8 and Higher
I. Accident claims per 100 car-years		Insufficient Data	14.2	8.4	3.8
Cost ratio		4	$2.56 — 3	$2.36 — 2	$1.00 — 1
II. Accident claims per 100 car-years		8.6	13.8	12.3	8.7
Cost ratio		$5.54 — 8	$5.15 — 7	$2.43 — 6	$1.86 — 5
III. Accident claims per 100 car-years		13.8	13.2	14.7	10.5
Cost ratio		$4.47 — 12	$4.80 — 11	$3.74 — 10	$5.11 — 9
IV. Accident claims per 100 car-years		15.7	14.8	Insufficient Data	
Cost ratio		$6.56 — 16	$3.80 — 15	14	13

validities can in many instances be expressed directly in dollars-and-cents.

2. Haner's observation and measurement of "job behavior" (that is, being responsible for accidents) shows great care in analyzing, classifying, and specifying the exact behaviors which are under control of the examinee and which should, therefore, be predictable.

3. The emphasis in Haner's research is on establishing actual predictive relationships rather than "merely" concurrent ones. As already noted, this is a commendable practice, but it seems even more important in this research as a way of assuring that the personal history and inventory responses actually are *predictive* of later accident behavior rather than possibly being the *result of* involvement in accidents.

4. The several detection scales for identifying falsification, lack of comprehension, etc., reduce imprecision in measurement due to chance response tendencies and other distorting response dispositions. By dropping persons who distort their responses from his analyses, Haner assures a higher level of test and measurement precision than would be possible if they were retained.

5. The pattern of results in Table 9–4 illustrates the multiple action of two measures for predicting behavior and the usefulness of considering their joint interaction instead of combining them in a single linear regression equation. For example, the relationship between Personal History Score and both frequency and cost of accidents is distinctly curvilinear for the data in cells 9, 10, 11, and 12. A similar curvilinear relation exists between Inventory Score and both behavior measures for data in cells 3, 7, 11, and 15. Thus, the multiple regression model is inappropriate for the data, and Haner has wisely employed actuarial pattern analysis to depict the relationships between the two predictors and the two behavior measures.

A Computer-Based Manpower Classification System

The United States armed services take in thousands of men per month who must be placed among an extremely broad range of duty assignments, training programs, and schools. Each man inducted must be utilized somewhere in the system. The problem closely approaches pure classification, and it becomes desirable—for both the armed services and for the men involved—to assure that assignment procedures successfully achieve a close match between human skills and job requirements. Until recently, manpower assignments in the armed services were made monthly by large teams of classification technicians who sorted through cards containing recruit information (personal data, test scores, etc.) and used their best judgment as the main basis for filling the various duty assignment and training school quotas. This manual procedure too often yielded assignments like the mathematician—potato peeler example we discussed in Chapter 1—*not* because of any ineffectiveness or ignorance of the classification technicians, but rather because of the great degree of complexity involved in attempting to make optimal job assignments for thousands of men into thousands of jobs.

In recent years, the availability of highly efficient large-scale electronic computing systems has made possible the development of computer-based methods of manpower assignment in the United States armed services. One of the most advanced of these has been developed and implemented by Hatch (48) for the United States Marine Corps. The broad outlines of his system and the results obtained are described below.

First, any large institution, such as one of the armed services, must operate within an amazing array of constraints dictated by existing rules and regulations, previous practices, and assumptions about the "types" of persons required for different job assignments. The relative validity of such rules, practices, and assumptions is not really subject to argument, for these constraints simply define "the way things are." One of the major problems faced by Hatch, therefore, was to discover and to incorporate all such constraints into his new procedures and to show that a computer-based system actually could adhere to them more closely and more efficiently than the judgmental approach utilizing manual procedures. Even more important, it was necessary to utilize fully all existing knowledge about the validity of various tests for predicting success in the different duty assignments. Fortunately, the Marine Corps, in cooperation with Army personnel research groups, had already developed equations for weighting each recruit's test scores to predict "success" in each of the many different duty assignments and training schools in the Marine Corps.

The basic information input for making monthly manpower assignments throughout the Marine Corps includes the following:

1. A matrix showing all the recruits' weighted test scores (Area Aptitude Scores) for each of the assignments needing men that month.

2. Other personal data on the recruits, including citizenship status, special skills and proficiencies (for example, ability to type, run a calculator), educational background, length of enlistment, stated job preference, etc.

3. Current month's quotas (that is, number of recruits needed) for each of the duty areas in the Marine Corps.

4. A listing of *mandatory* and *desirable* manpower requirements[3] associated with each of the duty areas.

5. The relative priorities (that is, estimates of the relative importance) of the various duty assignments and training schools.

The major purpose to be served by a computer-based assignment system thus becomes one of satisfying *all* mandatory requirements and as many of the desirable requirements as possible commensurate with maximizing the over-all mean Area Aptitude Score for all assignments made. The classification problem faced by the Marine Corps is essentially the same as illustrated by our Las Vegas Gambling Casino example in Chapter 8. The Marine Corps problem involves much greater complexity, however, because of the much larger number of assignments required, the many job areas involved, and the constraints imposed by mandatory and desirable requirements. Even so, Hatch and his associates have developed and successfully implemented a highly efficient computer program for making manpower assignments in the U.S. Marine Corps.

Of course, all the manpower quotas can only rarely be met by *either* the computer system or the manual assignment system. This is

---

[3] *Mandatory* requirements define absolute essentials for any particular assignment. Examples of mandatory requirements include: citizenship status for entry into electronics training; a stipulation that no assignee may have an Area Aptitude Score below a certain minimum cutoff; a stipulation that the mean Area Aptitude Score for all assignees in an area must be at or above a certain level. *Desirable* requirements are those urgently sought for a particular assignment; these may be relaxed, if necessary, in order to meet quotas or to assure satisfying other more crucial restrictions. Examples include: ability to type fifteen words per minute for entry into clerical assignments; a four-year enlistment term for assignment to the longer or more costly training schools; physical stature characteristics for certain assignments; recruit's stated assignment or job area preference.

TABLE 9–6. *Comparative data for manual and computer solutions for USMC duty assignments for months of May–November 1964.*

MONTH	TOTAL OF ALL QUOTAS	TOTAL RECRUITS ASSIGNED	MANUAL ASSIGNMENTS			COMPUTER ASSIGNMENTS		
			Per Cent Failing to Meet Requirements	Per Cent of Job Areas with Assignees Failing to Meet Requirements	Mean Area Aptitude Score for Persons Assigned	Per Cent Failing to Meet Requirements	Per Cent of Job Areas with Assignees Failing to Meet Requirements	Mean Area Aptitude Score for Persons Assigned
May	1,382	926	51.4	69	110.7	19.4	30	113.5
June	1,140	1,098	12.2	18	108.9	10.6	12	112.5
July	850	679	24.7	56	112.2	12.7	12	117.3
August	1,116	697	40.6	65	112.9	20.7	10	117.6
September	2,450	1,587	17.6	44	112.0	0.0	0	117.3
October	1,420	711	21.4	90	113.7	0.0	0	116.7
November	1,447	971	41.2	64	113.1	8.8	4	118.8

because the mandatory requirements for most months are overly restrictive for manpower talent in the recruit pool, and a feasible solution is not available. However, by means of computer programs designated FEASFIND and QUOTFIND, the computer-based solution accomplishes the following:

1. Determines whether or not the mandatory requirements can be met.

2. Assigns men meeting the desirable requirements to the maximum extent possible.

3. Assigns men failing to meet desirable requirements to as few different assignment categories as possible.

4. Systematically reduces area quotas to accomplish a feasible solution, reducing the quotas unevenly among duty areas of different priority (that is, by reducing quotas less among high priority assignments than among lower priority assignments, thereby maintaining quotas for the more important assignments and relaxing them for the less important ones).

Table 9–6 shows comparisons between the computer-based and manual assignments for the months May–November, 1964. Clearly, the computer solutions achieve the primary purpose of an increased Overall Mean Area Aptitude Score, and this is accompanied by a greatly improved "batting average" for satisfying all desirable requirements specified for the various assignment categories. Moreover, the computer solution is accomplished in a few minutes per month rather than in week-long efforts of a large crew of classification technicians.

DISCUSSION

Our major reason for presenting this example is to illustrate the feasibility of using computers as aids in personnel classification. The USMC study provides empirical evidence, derived from the "real world," confirming the applicability of the basic procedures described and illustrated with the hypothetical Las Vegas Casino data. As these procedures become more widely known and computer systems more readily available, we shall see more and more carefully derived, systematic solutions to difficult problems of personnel classification.

chapter ten

A Final Word

Our major theme in this book has been that wise personnel decisions demand evidence about the individuality of people, the special requirements of jobs, and interactions between the two. Systematic procedures for gathering evidence about people, jobs, job behaviors, and for estimating their interrelationships have been described. It is our firm belief that these methods can be, are being, and should continue to be used for making informed and wise decisions about individuals in our society—a step toward assuring that the *right* people move into the *right* jobs at the *right* times and under the *right* circumstances.

Yet, in recent years, systematic procedures for making personnel decisions—particularly those involving the use of psychological tests— have been the target of widespread criticism. Most such critics seem to believe that the users of psychological tests and other systematic personnel procedures uniformly and invariably assume that people and jobs are static entities, and that their proper linkage through selection and placement is only accomplished by a coldly mechanistic process, giving little heed to human values, preferences, or aspirations.

It should be abundantly clear to the reader that we hold no such simple view of men, jobs, or their interrelations. We have tried to convey our strong belief that personnel decision making is never ending, encompassing not only individual diagnosis and job analysis but also the related approaches of job design, career guidance, and personnel development and training. At any point in time people differ greatly from one another, but this fact carries no necessary implications about the static or dynamic nature of human abilities, needs, motives, and behavioral tendencies. In fact, the pervasiveness of both inter- and intra-individual differences and of temporal changes in human qualities are precisely why psychologists must take such special care in individual diagnosis as a basis for making sound personnel decisions. Scientific evidence about the individuality of people should supplant the hunches, arbitrary judgments, nonvalid rules of thumb, and methods of trial and error that unfortunately have characterized so many programs of personnel selection and job placement in the past.

Learning about people systematically and scientifically is the best avenue toward wise and effective utilization of our human resources. A functioning society demands and utilizes a vast range and diversity of talent, and programs of personnel selection and placement are merely systematic efforts to make sense of society's needs in relation to the diversity of talent available. Forehand (26) calls personnel selection a gigantic casting process—a process in which auditions occur and in which human behavior is assessed, wisely or unwisely, validly or invalidly. Obviously, the fairness of such auditions and their relevance to performance is the central concern of the personnel decision maker. Our purpose in this book has been to outline procedures which we believe will more often than not result in valid auditions.

In doing so, we have tried diligently to avoid any implication that the task of personnel selection is in any sense completed after a candidate has been "tested" or diagnosed. Ideally, personnel decision making extends much further to include possibilities for job redesign, counseling and guidance, the removal of organizational constraints, and the design of specialized training or development programs. Individual diagnosis, to be sure, is merely the first step, but it is the *crucial* first step—undergirding and directing decisions in each of the other areas listed above. Thus, mapping the individuality of persons is necessary not only for personnel selection and placement, but for all other personnel programs as well.

In essence, we believe, quite simply, that it makes unusually good sense to utilize knowledge growing out of the science of human behavior as fully as possible when making decisions about the expected behavior of human beings. We hope that we have convinced the reader that this simple but fundamental point of view has merit.

references

1. Albrecht, P. A., Glaser, E. M., and Marks, J. Validation of a multiple-assessment procedure for managerial personnel. *J. appl. Psychol.*, 1964, *48*, 351–360.

2. Albright, L. E., Glennon, J. R., and Smith, W. J. *The use of psychological tests in industry*. Cleveland: Howard Allen, 1963.

3. American Psychological Association. *Standards for psychological and educational tests*. Washington, 1966.

4. Anastasi, Anne. *Psychological testing*. New York: Macmillan, 1961. 2nd Ed.

5. Balma, M. J. The concept of synthetic validity. *Personnel Psychol.*, 1959, *12*, 395–396.

6. Berdie, R. F. Intra-individual variability and predictability. *Educ. psychol. Measmt.*, 1961, *21*, 663–676.

7. Brogden, H. E. An approach to the problem of differential prediction. *Psychometrika*, 1946, *11*, 139–154.

8. Brogden, H. E. Increased efficiency of selection resulting from replacement of a single predictor with several differential predictors. *Educ. psychol. Measmt.*, 1951, *11*, 173–196.

9. Buros, O. K. (Ed.). *Sixth mental measurements yearbook*. New Brunswick, N.J.: Gryphon Press, 1965.

10. Cardinet, J. The use of profiles for differential classification. *Educ. psychol. Measmt.*, 1959, *19*, 191–205.

11. Chauncey, H., and Dobbin, J. E. *Testing: Its place in education today*. New York: Harper & Row, 1963.

12. Cronbach, L. J. *Essentials of psychological testing*. New York: Harper & Row, 1960. 2nd Ed.

13. Cronbach, L. J., and Gleser, Goldine. *Psychological tests and personnel decisions*. Urbana: Univ. of Illinois Press, 1965.

14. Danielson, J. R., and Clark, J. H. A personality inventory for induction screening. *J. clin. Psychol.*, 1954, *10*, 137–143.

15. Dicken, C. F., and Black, J. D. Predictive validity of psychometric evaluations of supervisors. *J. appl. Psychol.*, 1965, *49*, 34–47.

16. Dunnette, M. D. A modified model for test validation and selection research. *J. appl. Psychol.*, 1963, 47, 317–323.

17. Dunnette, M. D., and Kirchner, W. K. Validation of psychological tests in industry. *Pers. Adm.*, 1958, 21, 20–27.

18. Dunnette, M. D., and Kirchner, W. K. Psychological test differences between industrial salesmen and retail salesmen. *J. appl. Psychol.*, 1960, 44, 121–125.

19. England, G. W. *Development and use of weighted application blanks.* Dubuque, Iowa: Wm. C. Brown Co., 1961.

20. Fine, S. A. Matching job requirements and worker qualifications. *Personnel*, 1958, 34, 52–58.

21. Fine, S. A., and Heinz, C. A. The estimates of worker trait requirements for 4000 jobs. *Pers. guid. J.*, 1957, 36, 168–174.

22. Flanagan, J. C. The critical incident technique. *Psychol. Bull.*, 1954, 51, 327–358.

23. Fleishman, E. A. The description and prediction of perceptual-motor skill learning. In Glaser, R. (Ed.), *Training research and education.* Pittsburgh: Univ. of Pittsburgh Press, 1962.

24. Fleishman, E. A., and Fruchter, B. Factor structure and predictability of successive stages of learning Morse Code. *J. appl. Psychol.*, 1960, 44, 97–101.

25. Fleishman, E. A., and Harris, E. F. Patterns of leadership behavior related to employee grievances and turnover. *Personnel Psychol.*, 1962, 15, 43–56.

26. Forehand, G. A. Comments on comments on testing. *Educ. psychol. Measmt.*, 1964, 24, 853–859.

27. Frederiksen, N., and Gilbert, A. C. Replication of a study of differential predictability. *Educ. psychol. Measmt.*, 1960, 20, 759–767.

28. Frederiksen, N., and Melville, S. D. Differential predictability in the use of test scores. *Educ. psychol. Measmt.*, 1954, 14, 647–656.

29. Freeman, F. S. *Theory and practice of psychological testing.* New York: Holt, Rinehart & Winston, 1962. 3rd Ed.

30. Ghiselli, E. E. Differentiation of individuals in terms of their predictability. *J. appl. Psychol.*, 1956, 40, 374–377.

31. Ghiselli, E. E. The prediction of predictability. *Educ. psychol. Measmt.*, 1960, 20, 3–8.

32. Ghiselli, E. E.   Differentiation of tests in terms of the accuracy with which they predict for a given individual. *Educ. psychol. Measmt.*, 1960, *20*, 675–684.

33. Ghiselli, E. E.   Moderating effects and differential reliability and validity. *J. appl. Psychol.*, 1963, *47*, 81–86.

34. Ghiselli, E. E.   *Theory of psychological measurement.* New York: McGraw-Hill, 1964.

35. Ghiselli, E. E., and Haire, M.   The validation of selection tests in the light of the dynamic character of criteria. *Personnel Psychol.*, 1960, *13*, 225–231.

36. Gough, Harrison.   *California personality inventory manual.* Stanford: Consulting Psychologists Press, 1957.

37. Grooms, R. R., and Endler, N. S.   The effect of anxiety on academic achievement. *J. ed. Psychol.*, 1960, *51*, 229–304.

38. Guilford, J. P.   The structure of intellect. *Psychol. Bull.*, 1956, *53*, 267–293.

39. Guilford, J. P.   Three faces of intellect. *Amer. Psychologist*, 1959, *14*, 469–479.

40. Guilford, J. P.   *Fundamental statistics in psychology and education.* New York: McGraw-Hill, 1965. 4th Ed.

41. Guion, R. M.   *Personnel testing.* New York: McGraw-Hill, 1965.

42. Guion, R. M.   Synthetic validity in a small company: A demonstration. *Personnel Psychol.*, 1965, *18*, 49–65.

43. Gulliksen, H.   *Theory of mental tests.* New York: Wiley, 1950.

44. Haner, C. F.   Use of psychological inventory in writing insurance for youthful male drivers. *Traffic Safety*, 1963 (March), 5–9.

45. Haner, C. F.   Use of personal history data in an underwriting setting. *Traffic Safety*, 1963 (Sept.), 19–22.

46. Haner, C. F.   Underwriting via psychological measurement—Five years later, *The National Underwriter*, 1965 (May 14, No. 20).

47. Harris, E. F., and Fleishman, E. A.   Human relations training and the stability of leadership patterns. *J. appl. Psychol.*, 1955, *39*, 20–25.

48. Hatch, R. S.   *Development of a computer-based solution to Marine Corps classification and assignments requirements.* Technical Progress Reports, 1–4, submitted to Headquarters, USMC by Decisions Systems, Inc., 1964–65.

49. Hays, W. L. *Statistics for psychologists*. New York: Holt, Rinehart & Winston, 1963.

50. Helmstadter, G. C. *Principles of psychological measurement*. New York: Appleton-Century-Crofts, 1964.

51. Hemphill, J. K. *Dimensions of executive positions: A study of the basic characteristics of the positions of ninety-three business executives*. Bureau of Business Research Monograph No. 98. Columbus: Ohio State Univ., 1960.

52. Hobert, R. D. Moderating effects in the prediction of managerial success from psychological test scores and biographical factors. Unpub. Ph.D. dissertation; Minneapolis: Univ. of Minn., 1965.

53. Kahneman, D., and Ghiselli, E. E. Validity and non-linear heteroscedastic models. *Personnel Psychol.*, 1962, *15*, 1–11.

54. Kirchner, W. K., and Dunnette, M. D. Identifying the critical factors in successful salesmanship. *Personnel*, 1957, *34*, 54–59.

55. Knauft, E. B. Construction and use of weighted checklist rating scales for two industrial situations. *J. appl. Psychol.*, 1948, *32*, 63–70.

56. Laurent, H. *Early identification of management potential*. Social Science Research Report. New York: Standard Oil Co. (N.J.), 1961.

57. Laurent, H. *The identification of management potential*. Paper delivered at American Psychological Association Annual Convention, St. Louis, Mo., 1962.

58. Lindzey, G. Seer versus sign. *J. exp. res. Pers.*, 1965, *1*, 17–26.

59. Locke, E. A. What's in a name? *Amer. Psychologist*, 1961, *16*, 607.

60. Lykken, D. T., and Rose, R. Psychological prediction from actuarial tables. *J. clin. Psychol.*, 1963, *19*, 139–151.

61. McNemar, Quinn. *Psychological statistics*. New York: Wiley, 1962. 3rd Ed.

62. Meehl, P. E., and Rosen, A. Antecedent probability and the efficiency of psychometric signs, patterns, or cutting scores. *Psychol. Bull.*, 1955, *52*, 194–216.

63. Rimland, B. Multidimensional scatterplotting: A graphic approach to profile analysis. *J. appl. Psychol.*, 1960, *44*, 404–406.

64. Rogers, B. F. The current status of the United States Air Force officer effectiveness report. Unpub. M.A., thesis; Tallahassee: Florida State Univ., 1960.

65. Seashore, H. G. *Women are more predictable than men.* Presidential address, Division 17, American Psychological Association Annual Convention, New York, Sept., 1961.

66. Smith, Patricia, and Kendall, L. M. Retranslation of expectations: An approach to the construction of unambiguous anchors for rating scales. *J. appl. Psychol.,* 1963, 47, 149–155.

67. Sorenson, W. W. Configural scoring of biographical items for predicting sales success. Unpub. Ph.D. dissertation; Minneapolis: Univ. of Minn., 1964.

68. Spearman, C. *The abilities of man.* London: Macmillan, Ltd., 1927.

69. Sprecher, T. B. Clarifying anchored rating scales based on performance incidents. *J. appl. Psychol.* (in press).

70. Stone, C. H., and Kendall, W. E. *Effective personnel selection procedures.* Englewood Cliffs: Prentice-Hall, 1956.

71. Strong, E. K., Jr. *Vocational interests of men and women.* Stanford: Stanford Univ. Press, 1943.

72. Strong, E. K., Jr. *Vocational interests 18 years after college.* Minneapolis: Univ. of Minn. Press, 1955.

73. Super, D. C., and Crites, J. O. *Appraising vocational fitness.* New York: Harper & Row, 1962.

74. Thorndike, R. L. The problem of classification of personnel. *Psychometrika,* 1950, 15, 215–235.

75. Tilton, J. W. The measurement of overlapping. *J. educ. Psychol.,* 1937, 28, 656–662.

76. Tupes, E. C., and Christal, R. E. *Recurrent personality factors based on trait ratings.* Technical Report ASD-TR-61-97. Personnel Laboratory, United States Air Force, Lackland Air Force Base, 1961.

77. U.S. Employment Service, Department of Labor. *Dictionary of occupational titles, entry occupational classification.* Part IV Washington: U.S. Government Printing Office, 1944.

78. U.S. Employment Service, Department of Labor. *Dictionary of occupational titles,* Vols. I and II. Washington: U.S. Government Printing Office, 1949.

79. Webster, E. C. *Decision making in the employment interview.* Montreal: The Eagle Publishing Co., 1964.

appendix

TABLE A. *Conversion from standard scores to percentile equivalents in a normal distribution.*

STANDARD SCORE $\left(\dfrac{X-M}{SD}\right)$	APPROXIMATE PER CENT OF PERSONS EARNING LOWER SCORES	STANDARD SCORE $\left(\dfrac{X-M}{SD}\right)$	APPROXIMATE PER CENT OF PERSONS EARNING LOWER SCORES
−3.00	0.1	−1.05	14.7
−2.95		−1.00	15.9
−2.90	0.2	−0.95	17.1
−2.85		−0.90	18.4
−2.80	0.3	−0.85	19.8
−2.75		−0.80	21.2
−2.70	0.4	−0.75	22.7
−2.65	0.4	−0.70	24.2
−2.60	0.5	−0.65	25.8
−2.55	0.5	−0.60	27.4
−2.50	0.6	−0.55	29.1
−2.45	0.7	−0.50	30.8
−2.40	0.8	−0.45	32.6
−2.35	0.9	−0.40	34.5
−2.30	1.1	−0.35	36.3
−2.25	1.2	−0.30	38.2
−2.20	1.4	−0.25	40.1
−2.15	1.6	−0.20	42.1
−2.10	1.8	−0.15	44.0
−2.05	2.1	−0.10	46.0
−2.00	2.3	−0.05	48.0
−1.95	2.6	+ and −0.00	50.0
−1.90	2.9	+0.05	52.0
−1.85	3.2	+0.10	54.0
−1.80	3.6	+0.15	56.0
−1.75	4.0	+0.20	57.9
−1.70	4.5	+0.25	59.9
−1.65	5.0	+0.30	61.8
−1.60	5.5	+0.35	63.7
−1.55	6.1	+0.40	65.5
−1.50	6.7	+0.45	67.4
−1.45	7.4	+0.50	69.2
−1.40	8.1	+0.55	70.9
−1.35	8.9	+0.60	72.6
−1.30	9.7	+0.65	74.2
−1.25	10.6	+0.70	75.8
−1.20	11.5	+0.75	77.3
−1.15	12.5	+0.80	78.8
−1.10	13.6	+0.85	80.2

TABLE A. (cont.).

STANDARD SCORE $\left(\dfrac{X-M}{SD}\right)$	APPROXIMATE PER CENT OF PERSONS EARNING LOWER SCORES	STANDARD SCORE $\left(\dfrac{X-M}{SD}\right)$	APPROXIMATE PER CENT OF PERSONS EARNING LOWER SCORES
+0.90	81.6	+2.00	97.7
+0.95	82.9	+2.05	98.0
+1.00	84.1	+2.10	98.2
+1.05	85.3	+2.15	98.4
+1.10	86.4	+2.20	98.6
+1.15	87.5	+2.25	98.8
+1.20	88.5	+2.30	98.9
+1.25	89.4	+2.35	99.1
+1.30	90.3	+2.40	99.2
+1.35	91.2	+2.45	99.3
+1.40	91.9	+2.50	99.4
+1.45	92.7	+2.55	99.5
+1.50	93.3	+2.60	99.5
+1.55	93.9	+2.65	99.6
+1.60	94.5	+2.70	99.7
+1.65	95.1	+2.75	
+1.70	95.5	+2.80	99.7
+1.75	96.0	+2.85	
+1.80	96.1	+2.90	99.8
+1.85	96.8	+2.95	
+1.90	97.1	+3.00	99.9
+1.95	97.4		

TABLE B. *Conversion from percentile standing to standard score equivalents in a normal distribution.*

PERCENTILE SCORE	STANDARD SCORE	PERCENTILE SCORE	STANDARD SCORE
0.1	−3.09	3.5	−1.81
0.5	−2.58	4.0	−1.75
1.0	−2.29	4.5	−1.70
1.5	−2.17	5.0	−1.64
2.0	−2.05	5.5	−1.60
2.5	−1.96	6.0	−1.55
3.0	−1.88	6.5	−1.51

TABLE B. (cont.).

PERCENTILE SCORE	STANDARD SCORE	PERCENTILE SCORE	STANDARD SCORE
7.0	−1.48	30.5	−0.51
7.5	−1.44	31.0	−0.49
8.0	−1.41	31.5	−0.48
8.5	−1.37	32.0	−0.47
9.0	−1.34	32.5	−0.45
9.5	−1.31	33.0	−0.44
10.0	−1.28	33.5	−0.43
10.5	−1.25	34.0	−0.41
11.0	−1.22	34.5	−0.40
11.5	−1.20	35.0	−0.39
12.0	−1.18	35.5	−0.37
12.5	−1.15	36.0	−0.36
13.0	−1.13	36.5	−0.35
13.5	−1.10	37.0	−0.33
14.0	−1.08	37.5	−0.32
14.5	−1.06	38.0	−0.31
15.0	−1.04	38.5	−0.29
15.5	−1.01	39.0	−0.28
16.0	−0.99	39.5	−0.27
16.5	−0.97	40.0	−0.25
17.0	−0.95	40.5	−0.24
17.5	−0.93	41.0	−0.23
18.0	−0.91	41.5	−0.21
18.5	−0.90	42.0	−0.20
19.0	−0.88	42.5	−0.19
19.5	−0.86	43.0	−0.18
20.0	−0.84	43.5	−0.16
20.5	−0.82	44.0	−0.15
21.0	−0.80	44.5	−0.14
21.5	−0.79	45.0	−0.12
22.0	−0.77	45.5	−0.11
22.5	−0.76	46.0	−0.10
23.0	−0.74	46.5	−0.09
23.5	−0.72	47.0	−0.07
24.0	−0.71	47.5	−0.06
24.5	−0.69	48.0	−0.05
25.0	−0.67	48.5	−0.04
25.5	−0.66	49.0	−0.03
26.0	−0.64	49.5	−0.01
26.5	−0.63	50.0	0.00
27.0	−0.61	50.5	0.01
27.5	−0.59	51.0	0.03
28.0	−0.58	51.5	0.04
28.5	−0.57	52.0	0.05
29.0	−0.55	52.5	0.06
29.5	−0.54	53.0	0.07
30.0	−0.52	53.5	0.09

TABLE B (cont.).

PERCENTILE SCORE	STANDARD SCORE	PERCENTILE SCORE	STANDARD SCORE
54.0	0.10	77.5	0.76
54.5	0.11	78.0	0.77
55.0	0.12	78.5	0.79
55.5	0.14	79.0	0.80
56.0	0.15	79.5	0.82
56.5	0.16	80.0	0.84
57.0	0.18	80.5	0.86
57.5	0.19	81.0	0.88
58.0	0.20	81.5	0.90
58.5	0.21	82.0	0.91
59.0	0.23	82.5	0.93
59.5	0.24	83.0	0.95
60.0	0.25	83.5	0.97
60.5	0.27	84.0	0.99
61.0	0.28	84.5	1.01
61.5	0.29	85.0	1.04
62.0	0.31	85.5	1.06
62.5	0.32	86.0	1.08
63.0	0.33	86.5	1.10
63.5	0.35	87.0	1.13
64.0	0.36	87.5	1.15
64.5	0.37	88.0	1.18
65.0	0.39	88.5	1.20
65.5	0.40	89.0	1.22
66.0	0.41	89.5	1.25
66.5	0.43	90.0	1.28
67.0	0.44	90.5	1.31
67.5	0.45	91.0	1.34
68.0	0.47	91.5	1.37
68.5	0.48	92.0	1.41
69.0	0.49	92.5	1.44
69.5	0.51	93.0	1.48
70.0	0.52	93.5	1.51
70.5	0.54	94.0	1.55
71.0	0.55	94.5	1.60
71.5	0.57	95.0	1.64
72.0	0.58	95.5	1.70
72.5	0.60	96.0	1.75
73.0	0.61	96.5	1.81
73.5	0.63	97.0	1.88
74.0	0.64	97.5	1.96
74.5	0.66	98.0	2.05
75.0	0.67	98.5	2.17
75.5	0.69	99.0	2.33
76.0	0.71	99.5	2.58
76.5	0.72	99.9	3.09
77.0	0.74		

index